Martin Jarvis was born in Cheltenham and raised outside London in South Norwood. He was educated at Whitgift School, Croydon, and London's Royal Academy of Dramatic Art. His leading roles in West End and Royal National Theatre productions include plays by Ayckbourn, Frayn, Nichols, Pinter, Shakespeare, Shaw and Wilde. He first came to prominence on television in *The Forsyte Saga*, and he has appeared in countless TV films and series, including *David Copperfield, Rings on Their Fingers, Inspector Morse, Scarlet & Black* and *Sex 'n' Death* in Britain, and *Murder, She Wrote* and *Space Above and Beyond* in America. His films include *Buster, Absence of War, Titanic* and *The X-Ray Kid*. An award-winning performer and audio producer, his BBC Worldwide recordings of *Just William* and *A Night to Remember* are bestsellers.

He has two sons, Toby and Oliver, and is married to actress Rosalind Ayres. He divides his working life between London and Los Angeles. In 2000 he was awarded the OBE.

ACTING STRANGELY

A *funny kind of life*

Martin Jarvis

Methuen

Published by Methuen 2000

3 5 7 9 10 8 6 4 2

First published in the United Kingdom by
Methuen Publishing Limited
215 Vauxhall Bridge Road
London SW·1V 1EJ

Copyright © 2000 Martin Jarvis

The right of Martin Jarvis to be identified as the
author of this work has been asserted by him in accordance
with the Copyright, Designs and Patents Act, 1988.

Photographs © BBC Picture Archive, Zoe Dominic Photography, John Haynes,
Rosalind Ayres, Cristofer Gross, *Croydon Times*, David Sim, Crispian Woodgate,
Arthur Hamer, Lewis Morley, Frazer Ashford and Hill's Welsh Press

Methuen Publishing Limited Reg. No. 3543167

A CIP catalogue record for this book
is available from the British Library

ISBN 0 413 745503

Typeset in Goudy by MATS, Southend-on-Sea, Essex

Printed and bound in Great Britain by
Cox & Wyman Ltd, Reading, Berkshire

For Margot, Denys and Angela

Forewarned

This book is not strictly an autobiography. My mother and father, who so sportingly allowed me to skip homework in the interests of the school play, only figure briefly. Likewise my sons Toby and Oliver who, after a few student days as theatrical dressers, decided on careers in music and the Bar. What you will find here are some of the funny – sometimes peculiar – acting adventures that I have had, both in Britain and America.

After the publication of the hardback edition of *Acting Strangely* in 1999, I was reproved by several friends and colleagues for not including what they insisted were their own favourite tales of my professional mishaps or misjudgements. 'The reader should be told!' they cried. Such requests being endorsed by my publishers, I had no choice but to introduce what has turned out to be an additional nine thousand words or so into this paperback. Mostly comedy, though I have taken the opportunity to write further about the serious business of working on Ayckbourn's plays. There's more about the Royal Academy of Dramatic Art in the sixties and (for screenwriter David Freeman) a couple of extra guest appearances from the manic American manager, Travis. I have provided actor and voice expert John Baddeley with the Dickensian finger-on-a-stick story he enjoys so much. Former BBC producer Ralph Wilton will now be able to read the account of our shared debut as Covent Garden toreadors. Writer Kathy Eldon demanded I tell of my shaming entrapment on the emergency staircase of a high Los Angeles building while on my way to meet Mr Big of Hollywood. I have duly disclosed. And political analyst Sherry Bebitch Jeffe was adamant that I confess to having been arrested in Mexico during the filming of *Titanic*. All is now revealed.

Happily, this expanded edition allows me even greater scope in characterising many of the extraordinary people I have encountered, worked with, learned from. Nearly all of them have made me laugh, occasionally with disastrous results. But eccentric as some of them may seem, none, in these pages, acts quite so strangely as me.

Acknowledgements

I thank the following for their generosity while I was writing this book. In Britain: Tricia and Norrie Giles, Mary Kalemkerian, Carol Heaton, Antony Topping, Larry and Davina Belling, Pete Atkin, Nigel Rees, Ian and Victoria Hislop, Christopher Matthew, Angela and Greg Hart, William Johnson, Nick Harrad, Gyles and Michèle Brandreth, Gillian Rhind, Clive Stanhope, Johnny and Jan Wright. In America: Christine Conrad, Andrea King, Jeralyn Badgley, Erin Connor, Gordon King, Jeff Danis, Bruce Mehdiani, Jeff Hixon, Sherry and Doug Jeffe, Ken Danziger and Tina Scott. Even more grateful thanks to my publishers, Michael Earley and Eleanor Knight, and most of all, always, to Rosalind Ayres.

Martin Jarvis
London
August 2000

February 1999

Los Angeles

Crouched behind the wheel, anxious, sweating slightly, despite my elderly Acura's air-cooling system, I am hammering along a California freeway.

It's all David Hare's fault.

He told me, a few years ago, he wished I would act more in the theatre. I had just finished working with him on his film *Absence of War*, so I wasn't quite sure what he was driving at. But when the offer came from one of America's premier West Coast theatres to play the energetic Tom Sergeant in David's virtual two-hander, *Skylight*, I jumped at it.

Only one problem. The theatre is not actually in Los Angeles, where my wife Rosalind Ayres and I have a house. The South Coast Repertory, a democratic jewel set in the Republican stronghold of Costa Mesa, Orange County, is fifty miles down the freeway towards San Diego. The drive, as I had already discovered, can take more than two hours. Tonight's rush hour out of LA is no exception.

The sun burns low to my right over the Pacific as I race, crawl, and race again down the six-lane highway. Infinitis, Buicks, BMWs, Chryslers, the occasional dark-windowed stretch-limo – we all jostle for pole position. At Long Beach, with twenty miles still to go, I am suddenly at a standstill, hemmed in by Big Rigs and sports utility vehicles of every kind. Trapped.

It's now seven o'clock. The play begins at eight.

Music blares from open-roofed cars. My own voice blasts from the Acura's tape-deck in the character of Shaw's knife-happy Cutler Walpole in *The Doctor's Dilemma*. The silky tones of Ian McDiarmid, as Sir Colenso Ridgeon, curl on the air. A Mexican in a battered Toyota van catches some of this, looks across from the next lane and smiles curiously. I am using the drive-time to monitor the final edit of Shaw's satire on the medical profession. This is the radio version of Michael Grandage's Almeida Theatre production, in which Ian, myself and others had appeared the previous summer. During the post-London tour, I had, as an independent producer, taken the entire *Doctor's Dilemma* cast into a sound studio where we recorded the play as a major drama for BBC Radio 3. For once, the actor in control. The actor as employer.

As we begin to creep forward again and the language of Shaw competes with rap music from a Ford Bronco (GBS almost winning) I'm the actor as victim. The hired hand. This afternoon I have been in Hollywood, dubbing lines for my role as villainous Mr X in the film *The X-Ray Kid*. Victim of studio schedules and the unpredictability of the LA rush hour, I seriously wonder if I am going to make it to the theatre in time. I have no understudy. The show cannot go on. As usual I have crammed too much into one afternoon.

Suddenly the procession fast-forwards. By the time I'm passing Bellflower Boulevard we're all speeding again. Nearly half past seven. Might just do it. Another ten minutes and I am sashaying, lane by lane, to an inside position, then racing up the ramp to make a cool exit into Costa Mesa.

It's the only cool exit I shall be making tonight.

Minutes more, and I am parked, free of the car and hurtling towards the stage door. It has been a beautiful day, temperatures in the mid-seventies, and now the evening is filled with the scent of jasmine. Floodlit fountains play in the theatre forecourt. The audience is already gathering in the warm dusk, mostly in shirt-sleeves or cotton dresses.

Five minutes to eight.

I sprint backstage. Sorry everybody.

Cindy Katz, the brilliant American actress who plays my lover, Kyra, hugs me in some relief. She disappears, ready for her first short scene with young Lars Carlson as my teenage son. I'm not on until Scene 2. Luckily. From which time I don't stop talking for two hours.

Into costume. Smart shirt and tie, woollen Armani business suit, heavy overcoat. Just what I need on a balmy Californian night. Even this is David Hare's fault: he sets *Skylight* in a freezing North London flat where Tom deliberately keeps his coat on throughout the first act. What is he trying to do to me?

Also, the production is presented 'in-the-round'. This means that Tom never stops moving, to be sure of sharing his restless energies evenly with the whole audience. Round and round the stage I go, like a caged lion, each night. It's a sweat bath, with a little vertigo on the side.

I'm in the wings now. Breathless, perspiring already in my weighty outfit, I wonder for a moment what on earth I am doing here. I tell myself I could be back in London.

'Are you sure you want to do this?' my long-suffering agent Jean Diamond had said, as I prepared to fly to Los Angeles on Christmas Day. She proffered an eleventh-hour carrot: 'There are two West End plays and a lot television around. And what about all your radio stuff?'

I thought of advice Albert Finney had once given me: 'It's all about the part. If you like it, do it.'

I still believed that.

'Bit of a challenge,' I told her.

It was. Cancelling Christmas. Doing that drive every day. Learning those lines. Walking those miles round the stage.

And yet.

What a play. What a part. Maybe sometimes you should go the distance. Even when you don't have to. There's something liberating, too, about working in-the-round. Keep moving and they can't touch you for it.

I had begun my acting life in a similar theatre, just before I went to Rada. Is this part of the appeal? Does this theatrical venue, in the well-heeled California southland, remind me of the

Pembroke Theatre-in-the-Round in suburban Croydon all those years ago?

My cue's coming up.

Still off-stage, I start running on the spot, thumping my feet noisily on the floor. Why act so strangely? To suggest the sound of my coming upstairs to the shabby flat, of course. I never mind doing my own sound effects. Or even, like now, actually *being* one.

As I land heftily on the last imaginary stair and push my way, sweating, through the door and into the blaze of light, I think, suddenly, that's another thing that reminds me of Croydon.

Look, Move, Speak

December 1953

Croydon

I was twelve, at school. Mr Evans, producer of the Junior School Christmas concert, had awarded me the part of an off-stage yodeller.

I was a sound effect.

On stage, three Brylcreemed juniors swaggered in front of a Swiss alpine backcloth. They were reciting a witty piece, written by Mr Evans, concerning our school life. The climax was a satirical verse in which they referred to a school hero who was known, famously, to yodel in the rugby changing-rooms after victory on the playing fields. He was called Inverarity and, as his weird name was uttered by our blazered smiling trio, my part was to yodel – in perfect rhyming symmetry – 'Yodel-ar-i-tee!'

God knows why I was given this task. I hadn't understood the subtlety of rhyming my yodel with the sound of this boy's ludicrous name. There had been a rehearsal the day before, but somehow we hadn't got to that bit.

Now, as my cue came up, I was struck dumb. My mouth was dry, my throat drier. The yodel could not be summoned up. There was a pause. Three over-made-up faces, awaiting their alpine pay-off, turned and glared into the wings. I opened my mouth. Still nothing. They beseeched me with sweating looks. I opened my mouth again.

'Yodel-ar-i-tee,' I murmured quietly. The on-stage trio looked panicked. What to do? They couldn't continue without this great burst of sound. But I was frozen. I just couldn't do it. 'Yodel-ar-i-tee', I whispered again. Suddenly from behind me in the darkness of the wings I heard an echoing blast, a big-dippering booming note that jolted me with its sonic force. It was our director who, possibly unsure whether I was equal to the complexities of the part, had lurked near, ready to perform on my behalf.

'Yodel-ar-i-tee . . . !' he resounded, and then repeated it. All round the stage and around the school hall itself, with its captive audience of boys and parents, Mr Evans' alpine rescue call rang out. The on-stage trio smirked, completed their incomprehensible recitation and the curtain fell to stupendous applause.

Mr Evans disappeared to usher on the next item and I sloped off backstage to wait, wretchedly, until the end of the show before meeting up with my mother, as arranged. She had made the twenty-five-minute trip on the 68 bus from South Norwood to see, more accurately to hear, my debut. As the crowd jostled out into the nippy air and proud performers were greeted by beaming parents, my mother smiled at me uncertainly. 'Was that really you making all that noise?'

I couldn't lie. 'No,' I said, 'it was Mr Evans. I dried up.'

I sat silently as the bus took us under the Christmas lights of Croydon High Street, along Whitehorse Lane past the Crystal Palace football ground and up South Norwood Hill. The sodium lamps turned our faces orange and our gloves purple as we started the five-minute walk down Cypress Road to Sunset Gardens and home. I felt foolish. I couldn't get that non-yodel out of my mind. Aged twelve and already a never-was. And it wasn't the first time I had had my chance and missed it. At my junior school, aged eight, I'd had a great opportunity. Somehow I had landed the part of the Forest Woodman in Form 2B's play. Rehearsals had been a nightmare. There were textual arguments with Miss Fisher, the Titian-haired beauty who was both our form-mistress and director. My difficulty was that I couldn't sort out which parts of the script were stage directions and which were my actual lines of dialogue. So when I banged my hand on my desk three times and called 'Who visits me in my little hut so late into the night?' Miss Fisher looked up sharply and said, 'No, Jarvis, tap, tap, tap.'

I looked at her blankly and told her that I *was* tapping.

'I *know*,' she replied tersely, 'but you *shouldn't* be.'

I looked down at the script, then up at her. 'Yes, I should,' I said helpfully. 'I have to tap. It says so here.' If I'd known the term I would have told her it was meant to be a sound effect. There it was on the page: 'Tap, tap, tap', and then 'Who visits me?' and so on. I held up my copy of *Ten Plays for Small People* in much the same way as, many years later, I observed the great Alan Badel shove a copy of Shaw's *Man and Superman* under the nose of a director who just wouldn't see the point.

Miss Fisher snatched the script from my hand and screamed, 'Jarvis, you don't tap – you *say* "Tap". Do you *understand*?' I looked round at the rest of 2B. They looked away. No one met my gaze. Even my best friend, Stoneham, who had a brand-new school blazer every year (his father owned a gent's outfitters in Herne Hill) raised an eyebrow and looked out of the window.

I understood, but I had reservations. As Miss Fisher briskly reassigned my role to another boy and demoted me to a Forest Creature, I still worried over the weird combination of speech and motive in the complex character of the Forest Woodman. What kind of a man would *say* 'Tap, tap, tap' sitting in a hut in the forest in the middle of the night?

A year later, true to the best traditions of British theatre, Miss Fisher gave me another chance. Perhaps she felt that my argument had some merit after all. More likely, she was merely providing the same kind of opportunity that, thirty years on, Harold Pinter offered when, after I had not been spectacularly impressive as Hector in his National Theatre production of *The Trojan War Will Not Take Place*, he invited me to appear in his small gem of a film *Precisely*. I was as thrilled to be directed by him again as I was to work, once more, under the firm directorial hand of my flame-haired ex-form-mistress. I was now in 3B, where she was conducting reading-aloud classes, and, I imagine to her great surprise, I was turning out to be quite good. Though the first time I stood up to read she stopped me at once and ordered me to slow down. I had only got out a few words.

My own sense that I was achieving something came when we

had a visitor to the classroom – an austere young man with a long wodge of dark hair falling over one eye. I somehow got it into my head that he was Miss Fisher's boyfriend. I don't know why I should have thought that; it seems rather surprising that a young schoolmistress's boyfriend should visit her in her classroom in the middle of a lesson – even so lissome a beauty as Miss F.

The thought occurs to me now that the young man might have been a school inspector. Or a student-teacher. At any rate he listened carefully, hands in pockets, to various piping renditions of passages from *Puck of Pook's Hill*. He leant casually close to Miss Fisher's desk, sometimes gazing into the middle distance, sometimes looking up at the ceiling like someone savouring a young wine and trying to decide if it was worth recommending. Every so often he turned his eyes directly on to Miss F., who sat, legs enwrapped in a long blue skirt that flowed around the base of her high stool. 'Now,' she said suddenly to her guest, 'listen to this.' Flashing a quick glance in my direction, she ordered me to read. I stood up and began to read aloud – to the class, to Miss Fisher, to our mysterious visitor, not too fast I hoped, trying to deliver it in the way I'd been told: experience the firm colours of Kipling's prose; communicate something of what the story means (so far as I understood it); be *inside* those words. And try not to sniff before each line.

When I had finished and sat down, she turned to the young man and I heard her say, in a low tone, 'You see. You see.'

He nodded, glanced at me expressionlessly, looked back at her and said, 'Mm.'

Their comments could have meant anything. It's all a matter of inflection. At the time I had a sense that I had done something quite well – but later I wondered whether all she was implying was 'This boy can eat up the words faster than lightning,' or 'This is the idiot I told you about who wouldn't say, "Tap, tap, tap".'

And now, four years on, I couldn't produce a yodel. I sat on the lounge floor and tucked my feet under the legs of the embroidered footstool that formed a mini-table from which to eat my cheese-on-toast.

'How was the concert?' asked my father, looking up from reams of paper. He was in 'insurance', preparing life-expectancy risk figures for the office brochure, making little alterations in the margin like 'aged 65 and over' and 'sum payable on life of assured'. I sometimes helped by reading these annotated pages back to him while he scribbled further notes on yet more closely typed sheets.

'It was a very good show,' said my mother. Turning tactfully to me she added, 'I'm sure you'll have more to do next year.' My ten-year-old sister Angela, watching 'How Do You View', starring Terry-Thomas, on our still-new Pye nine-inch (bought for the Coronation) echoed Mum's assessment in a suave imitation of Terry-Thomas himself: 'Jolly good show, chaps. Jolly good show.' Dad handed me a sheaf of stuff and said, 'Well done, boy. Want to read these out while I check? Turn that down a bit, Angela.' I moved to lean against the end of the settee so that the full light from the standard lamp fell on the papers. I read out: 'Sum payable at 48 and over – with profits. Sum payable at 55 and over – with profits. Sum payable at 65 and over.' Loud and clear. Not too fast. 'Sum guaranteed on death –' Didn't dry up once. Well, it was easy at home. And I was motivated, comfortable. I knew what I was doing: reading insurance risks aloud to Dad for him to check their accuracy. Quite dramatic – all these risks, who might die? who was going to live? Yodel-ar-i-tee!

Despite my mother's optimism it was two years before I got a proper part. Mr Etherington, the ebullient head of the English department and therefore an acknowledged expert on drama, decided it was time, after various musical extravaganzas, for the school to perform Shakespeare. *Romeo and Juliet.* A notice went up one day outside Big School. (Whitgift, a minor public school, Croydon's pride, aped the terms of a bygone scholastic era. Big Side, Little Side, the Quad – these romantic evocations of Tom Brown and Billy Bunter seemed slightly at odds with Whitgift's position at the end of South Croydon High Street and a stone's throw from the bus garage.) But now here was Mr Etherington, a fan of Stratford-upon-Avon and the early days of the Old Vic, advertising for actors.

I auditioned for the part of Juliet. My voice was breaking and even I could tell, as I clomped about the school stage, croaking out 'Gallop apace you fiery footed steeds', that the mystery, sexuality, and tonal subtleties of that spirited young Italian girl still belonged outright to Croydon's most famous actress, Peggy Ashcroft, who had played the part twenty-five years before. M. Jarvis, despite the increased confidence that two years of Dramatic Society play-readings and rugby for the Under 15s had provided, was not remotely going to teach the torches to burn bright as the nubile young Capulet. That role was neatly captured by J. Halliday, whose piping treble and androgynous charm ensured him a personal success in the part. Unluckily for the theatrical profession, after leaving school and enjoying a triumphant three years at Cambridge, Halliday eschewed the acting career he could have pursued and opted for the equally unpredictable world of politics. When I last heard of him, he was something immeasurably powerful in the Home Office.

I was happy to find that I had at least secured the part of Lady Capulet, Juliet's mum. This was a fully fledged production, with wigs and costumes from Nathan's, London's foremost costumiers, and assistance from a professional make-up artist, Mr Ernie Gibb.

I read the play. I studied the part. I began to see great possibilities in it. There was definite character to Lady C. She was tough. She bawled out the male members of her family for brawling in the streets of Verona. If I had ever heard the phrase, I would have put her down as the original Italian momma. And what a challenge. Her first words as she tries to prevent her husband from joining in the fray: 'A crutch, a crutch, why call you for a sword?' Not easy.

Mr Etherington's direction owed much to his admiration for the great Shakespeareans of a previous generation. Flamboyant speech and grand gesture were what he required. And pace. He loved pace. The faster we spoke, the better he liked it. He would surely have disapproved of Miss Fisher's methods. He took up a position halfway down the hall, in the central aisle between the rows of wooden seats (Big School held eight hundred), and, pipe in mouth, text in hand, would actually conduct us: 'Come on, pace, pace, pace.' Those fiery footed steeds Halliday was so keen to speed up would probably have fallen, steaming, at the outskirts of Verona, and never made it to the finish. Strangely, he conducted with his back to the stage, and sometimes, pipe and book dancing madly, wouldn't turn to look at us for minutes on end. He was concerned, primarily, with the words. At the time we thought it funny and often, while continuing to exceed the verse-speaking speed limits, would leap about the stage in grotesque attitudes, making rude faces and crude gestures, engaging in mock fights, never letting up with the iambics, until finally he turned round – a little startled at the way his initial blocking of a scene had developed, but pleased at the new stage-pictures now created: 'Good, Jarvis, climbing up the wall works well. Extraordinarily powerful. After all, she's very disturbed.'

I wasn't sure, though, that my physicality as Juliet's mum was quite right. I was determined to be creative. I had recently seen that great cockney comedian and pantomime dame Tommy Trinder at Croydon's Grand Theatre. I decided, as rehearsals grew more intense, to base my performance on my memory of his tough, controlling Widow Twankey in *Aladdin*. Firstly, his habit of clasping his hands in front of his ample bosom suited my own bossy approach to Lady C. Then his nippy strut as he beseeched the audience (and Wishee Washee) as to the whereabouts of his son Aladdin, matched perfectly my own interpretation of the scene in my daughter's bedroom a few days before her wedding. And his voice. Trinder's cockney gravel became, suddenly, a refined falsetto, before swooping again to the lower register of his much-loved catchphrase ''Ere, you lucky people!' This twinned appropriately with the vocal surging of my breaking alto.

A few days before the dress rehearsal, Mr Etherington beckoned me with his pipe to join him for a chat. 'Look,' he said, 'you're playing a woman and you're doing it jolly well too, but –' My heart galloped apace – oh lord, is he going to fire me? Is it the Forest Woodman scenario all over again? But there's been no tap-tap-tap problems, and surely I've taken direction well? 'But,' he went on, 'we've got to make you *look* like a lady too.' He then told me the costumes had arrived from Nathan's, that they had been specially made for Stratford's last production of *Romeo* and that mine was a magnificent blue and pink number adorned with a hundred sparkling jewels. Apparently Lady Redgrave (Rachel Kempson) had looked magnificent in it. 'Now,' said Mr Etherington, 'contours. Got to give you a bit of a body-line. Thing to do,' he took his pipe from his mouth and cleared his throat, 'thing to do is borrow a bra from your mother or your girlfriend, stuff it with your rugby socks and er – Bob's your auntie. All right, Jarvis, run along.'

'Thank you, sir.'

The part was still mine but this was a problem I hadn't foreseen. Borrow a bra from my mother? I knew I would never be able to raise such a topic. Or my girlfriend? What? Except for vague yearnings after Beryl Ballard, whom I used to see on the 68 bus, school beret pinned precariously to the back of her Marilyn Monroe locks, I never went near girls. And certainly it would be impossible to obtain a girlfriend in time for the dress-rehearsal. Imagine sloping up to Beryl on the top-deck: 'Excuse me, Beryl, would you like to see *Kiss Me Kate* at the Essoldo on Saturday? Oh, and by the way, can I borrow your bra?' Imagine the cackling laughter of Beryl and her cronies, Barbara, Janet and Maureen. To say nothing of the conductor: ''Ere, I 'eard that – get back downstairs or I'll turn you off the bus.'

In the end I concocted something from my gym-shoe bag. Stuffing it with rugby socks, shorts and shirt to fill it out, I put my arms through the two looped drawstrings and, if I didn't bend too far forward, it worked pretty well. I had considered leaving the gym shoes in there too, but Lady Redgrave's stylish slip-ons didn't fit me, so I wore my own instead. They were black, and not dissimilar to the neat little boots that had peeped from beneath Tommy Trinder's skirts.

I had a modest success as Lady Capulet. My best moment was when, sweeping off-stage with a Twankeyish toss of head and swoop of voice, clasped hands resting on my bosom, I spoke the lines, 'Talk not to me, for I'll not speak a word./Do as thou wilt, for I have done with thee.'

At the final performance I heard a peculiar and, for a moment, unidentifiable sound exploding behind me. It took me a moment to realise, as I skidded to a halt in the wings, that it was not a fart, but the sharp cupping sound of people putting their hands together in approval. An exit round.

Whitgift School was surprising in its catholicity of taste. It left you to get on with what you wanted to do (in my case English and acting) and didn't bother you unduly with things you didn't like (maths, physics and chemistry). My growing obsession with plays (Shakespeare in particular) meant that I enjoyed the English classes most and wrote intense essays on 'The Role of the Fool in *King Lear*', and 'Was Henry the Fifth Really a Boy Scout?' History and French claimed a little of my attention, no doubt because of the theatrical connections of one and the tooth-cracking vocal challenges of the other. But it was drama, actors and acting that filled my head. My friend David Nordemann (known as Nordy) was equally obsessed. We were determined to make our mark.

It began when I was asked by mild-mannered Mr Kelly, who took us for Literature Appreciation once a week, to give a talk on Shakespeare. By this time I was in the lower-sixth. Influenced partly by a new television programme called 'Candid Camera', Nordy and I concocted a daring scheme. It contained all the drama of Shakespeare, coupled with the tension of the prisoner-of-war films that kept us on the edge of our seats at the Odeon. How to pull the wool over the eyes of the goons? Would we be discovered? Could I really imitate the voices of our favourite actors? Would the Commandant penetrate my disguise? More exciting than double maths.

We set to work. First we spent several evenings listening to records of Laurence Olivier's speeches from his films of *Henry V* and *Richard III*; then John Gielgud's radio recordings of *Richard II* and *Hamlet*. Next we evolved a system of dubbing music on to my newly acquired Grundig tape-recorder. For hours we sat in my bedroom listening to the mellifluous trumpet of Gielgud and the witty articulation of Olivier.

Then we began to put our plan into practice, with my

imitation of our heroes. 'Now is the winter of our discontent,' I rasped into the Grundig. 'To be or not to be-ee-eeeeee . . .' I keened into the mike from the back of my throat, bruising my tonsils and collapsing in a fit of coughing, only alleviated by swigs from the bottle of Bulmer's cider which Nordy had smuggled up the stairs while Mum, Dad and Angela were in the lounge watching 'Inventors' Club'. The cider seemed to buff up my vocal cords into a fruity resonance. We were tipsy with the spirit of John and Larry. Soon we had compiled a twenty-minute 'cover-version' of their greatest hits. It was heady fun, and, with chunks of William Walton's music as backing, we were ready to go over the top.

'Well Jarvis,' beamed Mr Kelly expectantly, 'you're going to talk to us about – ah – Shakespeare?'

'Yes sir.'

The Grundig was already set up at the front of the class with Nordy as technical operator. Absurdly, the subject of my talk was how our two greatest Shakespearean actors approached their roles. Illustrated by some supposedly genuine soundbites. Of course it was all fantasy – I had no idea how Olivier had studied his great parts, what depths of research, interpretation and craft went into his acclaimed performances. Nor what sensitivity, grace and supreme understanding of the verse had brought Gielgud his outstanding successes. All I had to go on was the thrill of having seen both these gods in *Richard III* at the Classic cinema, South Croydon, and listened to their records over and over again. I knew every line by heart.

I looked round at the class, sniffed and began: 'Shakespeare had no scenery in his theatre' (I'd got that from one of Sir John's records) 'so,' I went on, 'the *words* had to convey the whole picture. Here is, er, Sir John Gielgud in a speech from *Richard II*.' Nordy pressed the play button and we both held our breath as my clotted tones burst from the tape-recorder, backed by some scratchy Tchaikovsky:

> Down, down I come – like glistering phaeton
> wanting the manage of unruly jades.

The words, Shakespeare's words, echoed round the room. Nordy and I glanced at each other: it didn't sound too bad. Bit nasal. Sort of Gielgud. The class listened – fidgeted uneasily. Mr Kelly sat back at his desk.

Here cousin, see-ee-ee-eeize the Crown –

As Nordy pressed the stop button, and with one eye on Mr Kelly who looked encouraging, I said, 'Now – erm – another aspect of, er, kingship is brilliantly conveyed by Sir Laurence Olivier as the wronged Prince of Denmark.' Nordy pressed play, and the romantic staccato of Olivier's silver notes (as near as cider, catarrh and hero-worship could get me to them) emerged from the speaker:

To bi – or not – to bi . . .

It seems absurd now: that an adenoidal rendering of these great speeches by a spotty theatre-mad seventeen-year-old should have been enough to persuade a class of equally spotty Croydon boys that what they were hearing was authentic. Yet they seemed to fall for it. Mainly, I'm sure, because most of them had never heard of Gielgud, thought Olivier was a brand of cigarettes, and that while I was boring on about old Shakespeare they might as well finish their chemistry homework.

After the class had been subjected to the last chunk of the Jarvis/Olivier version of 'We few, we happy few, we band of brothers,' onto which Nordy had added rousing cheers from the Olivier record plus a great upsurge of Walton's music, Mr Kelly rose from his desk and said cordially, 'Well, well. Thank you Jarvis. You too, Nordemann. And, ah, interesting to note, everyone,' he turned to the class, who were packing their completed homework away, 'how, ah, youthful these actors sound in their great roles. Good.' He nodded, smiled, said 'Well done', and off he went, leaving us to unplug and pack up.

Nordy and I exchanged glances. Had we fooled the goons and

made it under the wire? It seemed to have worked. We didn't know whether to be gratified or disappointed.

I think, though, Mr Kelly knew the score.

I had been hanging around Croydon's old Grand Theatre for a year or so. It had seen grander days and now, in 1958, there were rumours that Croydon Council, who owned the site, was consigning it to history in the interests of providing a supermarket. In its last days, the Grand had played host to a professional repertory company who put on a different play each week. This was staggering to me, since at school we rehearsed our yearly Shakespeare for three months. Passing the theatre one day, I saw a poster for a touring production of Look Back in Anger. I had read about this play and how its young author, John Osborne, had turned British theatre upside down with his red-hot domestic diatribe against the establishment.

When I got home I told my father that I would be going to see it. 'You are not,' he replied immediately. He too had heard about it and was convinced it was not suitable. I was deeply disappointed and debated whether to slip in to the Saturday matinée while pretending I had to stay at school for extra rugby practice. But things change, goal-posts shift, nothing remains unaltered. I don't know whether Dad had investigated further about Osborne's ground-breaking play. Perhaps he had read W. A. Darlington in the Daily Telegraph. Darlington was a fine critic who loved the theatre. Could it be that, in his weekly column, though mourning what seemed to be the demise of the well-made play, the structural expertise of Rattigan and the elegant facility of Coward, Darlington had recognised that Osborne was an important new writer? At any rate, a day or two later Dad suddenly announced that I could go after all, and he would be accompanying me. He probably knew I would find a way of seeing it anyway and, if I was going to be corrupted by the new kitchen-sink drama, then he, as a dedicated insurance man, had better be there to limit any damage.

There was an undeniable sense of occasion about the Grand that Saturday afternoon as we sank into our plush stalls seats.

This was no rep production. I had seen the resident company in
a number of light comedies: Gwen Watford as a charming
Clarissa in an Agatha Christie thriller, *Spider's Web*; and
somebody called Frank Finlay playing an elderly school teacher
in *A Touch of the Sun* by N. C. Hunter. I had been fascinated by
the play and was amazed that such an old man could remember
all those lines. When I saw Finlay emerge from the stage door
(one of my favourite lurking areas) I was stupified to see he was
only about the same age as our young teacher Mr Branston, newly
arrived from Oxford to take charge of French, Spanish and
cricket. Clearly Mr Finlay was equally versatile. And now here
was a play from the famous Royal Court Theatre itself and,
judging from the exciting biographies in the programme, some of
the actors (Alan Dobie, Mary Ure, John Welsh) had been in the
original production.

Look Back in Anger, as it turned out, was fine. The setting, an
ordinary sitting room, seemed almost familiar; the weary Alison
at the ironing board reminded me of a younger version of my
hard-working mother preparing my father's shirts for the office
and all the school stuff for Angela and me. Even the speeches
from Jimmy Porter himself seemed natural – and funny. It wasn't
the brisk elegance of *Plaintiff in a Pretty Hat* or the sophisticated
wit of *Hay Fever* that I had seen the local company perform only
weeks ago. Nor was it the raucous comedy of Tommy Trinder.
Though there was something about the way Jimmy Porter
harangued his absent mother-in-law and pretended she might be
hiding in the water-cistern – 'Can you hear me, mother?' – that
was startlingly reminiscent of Trinder motoring about the stage,
shouting, 'Can you 'ear me at the back?' We didn't know it, but
Osborne was already in the process of creating a Trinderesque
character: Archie Rice in *The Entertainer*.

Dad was much relieved, when we trooped out into the street,
that the play had seemed so familiar, so accessible – so hilarious.
'Well, boy, very good, I thought,' he said. 'Can't see what all the
fuss was about.'

The visit of the Royal Court company more or less marked the end of the Grand Theatre. In the ensuing weeks the local rep put on a couple more comedies and another pantomime. I even attempted to get into the panto myself. I was hanging around the Circle Bar after school as usual, in case some of the actors came in for a coffee and I could listen to their theatrical chat or hear them order an espresso in their chocolate voices.

Actually the actors rarely seemed to use the coffee bar, and most of the gossip I overheard was from the elderly females in black cardigans who sold programmes, took coats and umbrellas and served in the bar. One late afternoon I sat in a corner, pretending to learn my lines for *Hamlet* in which, thanks to Mr Etherington's continued confidence in me, I had recently landed the title role. I was hoping that someone would ask me what I was studying, when I spied a battered black book on one of the rickety tables. It had 'Auditions' written on the front. I took a quick look round. The owner of this intriguing volume must have been here earlier and forgotten it. I leant forward, edged it casually towards me, flicked it open. Not much of interest. A few lists of names, none of which I recognised. Some telephone numbers and addresses. I turned a page, and there at the top was written, 'Whittington Auditions'. Then some more names. *Dick Whittington* was the pantomime that the company was putting on in a few weeks' time. I had read in the *Croydon Advertiser* that it would be very much a local show, with most of the cast taken from the rep actors and the local dancing school. Even the small pony that gave rides in Kennard's Arcade (Croydon's premier department store) during the Christmas holidays would be making a guest appearance. There would be no Tommy Trinder this year to keep things going – and after the pantomime the theatre would finally be closing.

I got out my pen and under the names on the Whittington page I wrote my own name and telephone number – then 'actor and conjuror'. I don't know what made me add 'conjuror'. Perhaps it was a memory of last year, when Abanazar had abandoned the plot for ten minutes to perform various illusions, including the Chinese Rice Bowls, and filled the stage with paper flowers. My own conjuring skills were minimal, though I had made a trip to Ellisdon's of Holborn and invested in a few 'effects' from their magic department. I could make a coin disappear from under a glass. I could tear and restore a piece of tissue-paper and produce an egg from a small black bag. Not quite Abanazar standard but, as I knew from my much-thumbed Arden edition of *Hamlet*, 'the readiness is all'.

It seems extraordinary to me now that, in wanting so much to be involved in things theatrical, I should behave so ludicrously. Suppose a few days later my mother answered the phone and called up the stairs to tell me it was the director of the pantomime asking me to come and demonstrate my magic act. What magic act? Even more horrific, in retrospect, would have been the offer of a part. What part? A villager? Dick? The cat? And yet, in my fantasy, I half expected this to happen. Naturally it never did. The panto went ahead and in its final week the manager (so we read in the *Advertiser*) absconded with the box-office takings. The Grand Theatre closed for good, remained empty for a year, and then the town planners moved in and bashed it to the ground.

By 1960 a new theatre had sprung up in Croydon, half a mile from the site of the old one. I had never heard of Stephen Joseph and the Theatre-in-the-Round he had created in the town library of Scarborough just a few years before. But Clement Scott Gilbert, a wealthy American theatre-lover and businessman, clearly had that remarkable space in mind when he built its replica, the Pembroke Theatre-in-the-Round, within the shell of a disused church hall behind West Croydon station.

I was eighteen and still at school. I had had my go at Hamlet, tearing several passions to tatters in high boots and a wig that looked like a tea-cosy. Determined to become a student at the Royal Academy of Dramatic Art, and confident of success, I actually began telling people I had been awarded a scholarship. I hadn't yet taken the audition. But as I watched the skilled professionals in the Pembroke's opening production, I began to recognise that enthusiasm and wish-fulfilment on their own were not enough to ensure me a place in their profession.

The Pembroke season had started with an obscure Anouilh comedy, *Thieves' Carnival*. I had never seen theatre-in-the-round before, but found it, along with many other Croydonians, fascinating. Here was something new. The space was like a sunken boxing ring, with banks of seats on each side of the square and exits on each diagonal, plus another exit through swing-doors leading into the foyer. It held about four hundred and, since the stage area was in the centre and the audience on all sides, there was no scenery. A few chairs, a table, actors, plus lights suspended from a grid above, were enough to create the imaginative world of any play. I couldn't keep away from the place.

One afternoon I wandered into the small foyer. I was studying the glossy black-and-white photos of actors on display, when a sandy haired whippet of a man came scurrying out of the tiny box office. He had yellow protruding teeth and was carrying a number of similarly coloured envelopes under his arm. I had seen him the previous week playing the piano in a night-club scene in the current production. I had registered from the programme that his name was Les Dangerfield and that he was also the company manager. He eyed me suspiciously: 'Yes?'

I told him I was 'probably' going to Rada in October, that I'd done some acting at school and wondered if there was any chance of a job for the next couple of months. I also said I had seen *Thieves' Carnival* last week and had spotted him. He simpered foxily, 'Oh, you liked it? Not a bad little show.'

'Terrific,' I agreed.

He eyed me again and seemed to make up his mind about something. He took the envelopes from under his arm and thrust them at me: 'All right, blondie, take these up to town and give them to Clement. This is the address.' He then gave me a ten-shilling note for the fare and said, 'If Clement likes you, you can be the new ASM.'

'I'm sorry – the new what?'

'Assistant Stage Manager, ducky. Off you go.'

An hour later, having taken the train from East Croydon station, I was climbing the plush carpeted stairs of an elegant

building in Jermyn Street, just off Piccadilly. I rang the bell of
what my mother would have called a 'luxury flat', and, after a
moment, the door was opened a few inches. A tanned bespectacled middle-aged face looked through the gap. I could just
see he was wearing a white towelling bath-robe. He looked me up
and down and smiled encouragingly. 'Hello.' He made it
somehow a three-syllable word. His accent was American. This
was clearly Croydon's millionaire.

'Mr Scott Gilbert?' I held up the envelopes. 'Mr Dangerfield
sent me with these.'

Keeping the door on the chain, he put out his arm and drew
the packages through the gap. He inspected them briefly, without
opening them. He seemed delighted. 'Why, thank you,' he
smiled, then turned to call over his shoulder. 'John –' Behind him
I could see another tanned figure, younger with close-cropped
dark hair, emerging from an inner room fastening his own white
bath-robe. Clement passed the stack of envelopes to him: 'Here
are the photos, John. This young man has brought them.'

'Oh, hi,' beamed John, looking at me over Clement's shoulder.
His teeth were as white as his robe. He was American too and
seemed equally pleased. 'Hey, thanks for bringing these. You're a
prince.' They stood, one behind the other, looking out at me
through the narrow space. I didn't know what to do next.

I began: 'Er, Les, er, Mr Dangerfield said –'

'Yes,' Clement interrupted me, 'marvellous.' Then he said,
'*Compulsion*.'

'Compulsion?' I repeated blankly.

'That's right. We start rehearsals Monday. It's the British
premiere. You can do an American accent can't you?' The two
genial figures grinned expectantly at me.

I grinned back, trying not to show my joy. 'Sure thing,' I said.

It turned out that 'John' was the director of *Compulsion* and
that, while I had been on the fifteen-minute train ride, Les had
phoned Clement to suggest that I might be right for a small part
in the play.

Rehearsals did start on Monday. Most of my time was taken up
with making tea for the actors (some American, many English)

all of whom I held in awe, all of whom had great resonant voices and spoke loudly about their agents and their previous engagements. They were extremely nice to me, even when I forgot to give them their props or failed to provide them with the correct line when I was 'on the book'. I engaged them in incessant conversation about their acting lives. I had seen some of them on television. This gave them further glamour in my eyes, and made me feel it an honour to race out to the seedy sandwich shop near the station to fetch their lunch.

Compulsion was a powerful drama adapted from Meyer Levin's novel about two young students who murder a younger boy 'for kicks', to see if, as Nietzschean 'übermenschen', they can get away with such a crime. Based on the real-life Leopold-Loeb story, Orson Welles had starred in the film version as Clarence Darrow, the defence lawyer. Although the Pembroke production was short on famous names, it attracted full houses for its three-week run, and several leading critics made the trip to review it. My role (unreviewed) was Milt, student-friend of the leading characters, who were played by two amiable young actors, Barry Warren and Derrick Smee. Although I had only five lines, my function was not entirely without point. It is Milt who discovers the important clue to the killing: a broken typewriter key that eventually leads to the boys' arrest. I looked forward to my one scene every night. I tried saying the lines in different ways at each performance, which must have been extremely annoying for the other actors, and especially for John Gorrie who, as Sid Silver, newspaper man, had most of the dialogue. He never mentioned anything, though when in the seventies he had become a busy and successful television director, I suppose I shouldn't have been surprised that he never hired me.

The unexpected success of the season was a peculiar thriller called *Lady Barker's Last Appearance*. This was a translation from a Dutch play that, according to Clement, keen to give Croydon a variety of world drama, had taken Holland by storm. I was retained as assistant stage manager and general dogsbody. The star was Cruys Voorberg, a famous Dutch actor who (Clement told me) had triumphed in the Amsterdam production. The gimmick of the piece was that Cruys played no less than three parts. The audience was meant to be amazed when, at the curtain-call, it was revealed that three of the five characters, including Lady Barker herself, had been Mr Voorberg all the time. The only problem was that, here in England, it was going to be hard for the versatile Voorberg to hoodwink the audience in each role. There was an overriding vocal sameness due, under-standably, to his less than masterful command of English. But he didn't see a problem, and Clement, looking in at rehearsals, would murmur to me, 'Mart'n, isn't he marvellous. He's the Wilfrid Hyde-White of Holland, you know.'

During the rehearsal period, Cruys Voorberg (who was also the director) asked me to read-in one of his parts – a villainous doctor – while he viewed the scene from the auditorium. I read with great emphasis, holding the pauses for far too long and endowing even the most casual phrases with a deep significance. I hardly worried about the meaning, so keen was I to mime the melodramatic attitudes of Mr Voorberg and to ape his curious accent.

When the scene came to an end, Basil Lord, a humorous actor with the face of a lizard, who was playing a solicitor, winked at me. He was tall and thin, with black billiard-ball hair and a slight stoop, so that when he moved he looked like a mobile question mark. During the coffee break, Basil beckoned me over. 'That was pretty good, old chap – the way you read,' he said. ''Specially when you didn't act. I hope you get a chance to play it one day.' I was pleased he'd said that, and secretly rather agreed with him, even though I puzzled over the bit about not acting. 'Be nice to them on the way up,' I heard him joke to Clement as he loped back to rehearsal, 'you might meet them on the way down.' Twelve years later I saw Basil at a West End first night party to which I had been invited as a so-called celebrity guest. I assumed a modest expression and went up to him. 'Basil, it's so nice to see you. I've never forgotten how generous you were to me – and your helpful advice when I was a lowly ASM and you were a visiting guest-star at Croydon.' He looked up slowly and gazed at me. After a few seconds he took a sip from his gin and tonic and said, with a puzzled look in his hooded eyes, 'Sorry, old boy, I'm afraid I don't remember you.'

During performances there was no place for a prompter to hide, so my only task, apart from setting out a few props before-hand, was to ring the telephone bell in the final scene. This was vital to the plot as it was meant to be the bank manager ringing with an answer to the important question: who is masquerading as Lady Barker? On stage the phone had to be answered by the old housekeeper, played by the elegant Peggy Thorpe-Bates. Peggy was a highly skilled actress who seemed more suited to the sophistication of some of Noël Coward's leading ladies than the subsidiary role of a Dutch drag-queen's housekeeper. But she gamely fleshed out this character, making the most of her crucial telephone scene. One night I had got chatting to some of the usherettes. They could sometimes be found during Act Two in the backstage bar. I was getting on awfully well with one of them when I heard applause coming from the auditorium. The show had finished. What? Already? Oh god – I had forgotten my phone bell. I dashed to a point of vantage from where I could see the actors taking their bows, moving around the square central area like boxers acknowledging the plaudits of the crowd. As the cast made their way back to their dressing rooms, Basil Lord saw me lurking in the shadows and muttered out of the corner of his mouth, 'You'd better keep out of Peggy's way, she's after your blood.'

It turned out that while I had sat flirting the line had been said that was supposed to signal the sound of my bell. Cruys Voorberg, in the full Lady Barker outfit, had spoken the cue: 'Don't be such a fool, Mrs Burrows, how could I have embezzled all zat money?'

Peggy opened her mouth, confident that shrill ringing-tones would prevent her answering the question. 'Lady Barker –' she began.

But no. No phone bell. Just silence. And no one else who could help. No prompter. The actors were on their own. Things didn't look too good. Cruys had enough difficulty in playing three parts in one play in a language not his own. It was down to Peggy. Trouper that she was, she knew, phone call or not, they *must* somehow finish the play. I heard later what happened from David Manners, the electrician, who had witnessed the whole thing from the lighting box. He told me that, after a few ghastly moments of silence, Peggy had vamped loudly for a couple of minutes to Voorberg about the weather. Then, as still the phone failed to ring, she had swung suddenly round and, moving superbly into a phase of her career where improvisation would provide a new cornerstone to her work, she announced, 'Was that the phone?'

The bewildered Voorberg, unable to extemporise in English, merely muttered, 'Vat?'

Peggy, realising she was on her own here, then answered the question herself. 'No, it was only the wind.'

'Vat?' said Voorberg again.

'*I* know,' said Peggy, ignoring him now, '*I* know, I'll ring the telephone exchange and find out if the lines are down.'

Not bad, especially as she could hardly ring the bank, since it was nearly midnight and no one was supposed to know that the manager was actually in his office about to blow the plot wide open. Peggy swept to the silent phone. (She could not know that I was still backstage and just making a date to meet Wendy at the Pandora coffee bar at six o'clock tomorrow.) Peggy tapped the receiver imperiously several times: 'Hello, hello . . . Ah – is that the exchange? Can you tell me – oh –' Here she stopped, and with one of the most convincing displays of natural acting ever witnessed in Croydon, said, 'Oh – I think we must have a crossed line – I think – oh – *oh*, is that the bank manager – it *is*? Good heavens – I thought I recognised your voice . . . Oh you were? You were about to telephone us, were you?' And then, with a triumphant flash of her eyes at the muted Dutchman, she heaved the play magnificently back on track with her first scripted line for some minutes: 'Yes, Mr Mansfield – and how can I help you?' She had saved the evening.

Miss Thorpe-Bates was extremely forgiving to me next day – possibly not unconnected with the fact that everyone said how wonderfully she had dealt with the crisis. Many years later I found myself working with Peggy's daughter, Jenny Oulton. Jenny told me one of her mother's favourite theatrical anecdotes, a hilarious story about an off-stage phone bell that never rang and some awful ASM who wasn't there when needed.

My name did not figure in it. Like Basil, Peggy had not remembered me.

During this summer of 1960, I had finally travelled to London to audition for the Royal Academy of Dramatic Art. Since I had been telling everybody for months that I was definitely going there, it was to my huge relief when I heard I had actually been accepted. I had retched with nerves throughout my audition piece – Romeo spouting beneath Juliet's window – and had finished by throwing up in the wings as I staggered off-stage. Presumably John Fernald, the Principal of the Academy, and his fellow adjudicators decided the strange heaving and gagging sounds that leapt from my throat at the end of each line was a Croydonian interpretation of a Veronese teenager in love.

In the final week of *Lady Barker*, and two weeks before I was due to start at Rada, Clement Scott Gilbert called me into his office. Clement was one of the most charming men I had met in my brief time in the professional theatre. He never treated me as naïve or stage-struck, and would often seek my opinion of an actor or invite me to discuss some aspect of the current production. This was flattering, and encouraged me to focus my thinking about what really worked on-stage. He leant forward at his desk in the tiny office next to the hardly larger entrance foyer of the theatre. He flicked a spec of West Croydon dust from the sleeve of his elegant grey worsted suit. 'Mart'n,' he said, 'you know Bobby Atkins is going to direct *Hamlet* here, with David William as the Prince?' I did know.

I had heard of the legendary Robert Atkins, almost the last of the Shakespearean actor-managers. Over eighty years old by this time, he had been directing recently at the Regent's Park Open Air Theatre in London. Years before, he had been responsible for some of Stratford's most celebrated productions. Even in my short period on the outermost fringe of the profession, I had heard actors speak of Robert Atkins with equal amounts of affection

and fear. They all mimicked his resonant articulation, raising a
hand that quivered in beneficent tandem with the fruity throb
of his voice. I had listened enthralled to all the stories: how he
had remarked to a young actress playing Peaseblossom in *A
Midsummer Night's Dream*, when she had failed to appear in one
scene and he found her cast down on the ground in despair, head
in her lap: 'It's no good looking up your entrance – you've missed
it.' How he was passed over in favour of the young Michael
Redgrave as the reader in Stratford Church's celebration of
Shakespeare's birthday. As Redgrave approached the lectern,
Robert's fruity bass echoed scornfully around the congregation:
'Give me one cogent reason why I should not read the fucking
lesson.' And how, after glorious years as star director of the
Stratford-upon-Avon Memorial Theatre Company, he was
summoned to the office of Sir Fordham Flower, Chairman of the
Board and founder of the famous Midlands brewery, there to be
summarily dismissed from the post he loved. Bobby was silent
while Sir Fordham spoke for several minutes, thanking him for
his outstanding work and for the magnificence of his productions
and performances. Sir Fordham finally ground to a halt. Robert
said nothing. Then, taking his time, he walked to the door,
opened it with a flourish, turned and remarked gravely, 'Flower's
Ale is piss . . .'

Now he was coming to Croydon, to pack them in at various
schools matinées. Clement looked at me earnestly through his
large horn-rims. 'Mart'n, Robert is looking for a Laertes. I know
you played Hamlet at your school, you can fence, so I thought you
should audition for him.' Wow. Laertes. 'The only problem is,
Mart'n,' Clement continued, 'I'm not sure how it would work out
with you starting at Rada and rehearsing with Bobby at the same
time.' It was worth a try.

Next afternoon I walked apprehensively onto the square
Pembroke stage that was lit by one bleak working-light. I was
greeted by a stocky white-haired old boy in a dark, slightly
threadbare three-piece suit, gold watch-chain strung across his
ample middle. He wrung my hand warmly for about half a
minute. Finally letting go, he boomed, 'Well, old son, give us yer

Laertes.' I stood back, cleared my throat, noticing suddenly the lean figure of David William (Hamlet himself) sitting at the rear of the stalls, head on one side, watching me. I imagined he was thinking, with some disdain: how could this callow assistant stage manager ever share a stage with me? I avoided his gaze and turned in the direction of Atkins, who was now sitting in the front row nodding encouragingly and cupping a hand to his ear. 'Off you go, old son,' and he waved me on as if I were traffic that had stopped too long at the red light.

I launched into Laertes' Act 2 speech, where he is about to set off for France, gabbling, 'My necessaries are embarked –' Robert held up a hand. 'Take your time old son, take your time. Gently, gently.' Then, before I could resume, he rose and spoke the line himself. Double wow. The warm cello of his voice reverberating around the little theatre seemed, for that moment, to hold all one ever needed to know about the traditions of Shakespearean acting, the words themselves, and how to convey their juicy sense. It was spellbinding, larger than life, but somehow not in the least artificial. He continued the speech for a line or two more, stopped himself and, gesturing, waved me on again.

I revved up slowly, then began. I projected – gently. Didn't gabble. I thought it through. Didn't retch. I finished the speech. Suddenly feeling I ought to attempt something of Laertes' passion, I threw myself on the floor. Reaching out my hand towards the shadowy presence of David William, I spoke Laertes' dying words with a kind of strangulated intensity:

> Exchange forgiveness with me, noble Hamlet:
> Mine and my Father's death come not upon thee,
> Nor thine on me!

Finally forcing myself up on one knee, I cried out, pointing now at Robert who still stood at the edge of the stage, his hand no longer cupped to his ear, 'The King. The King's to blame!' Then I fell back onto the unswept floor, collapsed, and *died*.

Robert turned towards the rear stalls. I saw that Clement had joined David William at the back. All three exchanged a brief look, then Robert stepped forward and helped me to my feet. He put his left arm around my shoulders, grasped me by the hand with his right, pumped it even more vigorously than before and announced, 'Well, old son, I fancy we can make a Laertes out of you.' I was bemused to learn that this meant I had been offered the part.

Next day, though, I was stunned when John Fernald told me, in effect: 'It's either them or us.' He explained that I couldn't possibly start my training at Rada and be allowed to have time off to rehearse and appear in *Hamlet*. Rada or Robert, it was up to me. Bitterly disappointed, I discussed it with Clement. Attractive as it had seemed to begin my career with such a break, I sensed anyway that I was too young (and certainly without enough experience) to hold down a major part in a fully fledged production. I turned it down. I was surprised to see that my mentor was relieved: 'I think you're wise Mart'n,' he said. 'You should see Robert in rehearsal. He would have crucified you.' A few years later, when I was playing Octavius in Clement's West End production of *Man and Superman*, I reminded him of that lucky escape. Clement laughed and said, 'Oh god yes, Mart'n, and don't forget we were only paying you five pounds a week. Robert really wanted you because you were cheap.'

Two weeks later, still living at home in Croydon, I began my drama training.

The Royal Academy of Dramatic Art in the 1960s was the most prestigious of the London drama schools, and possibly still is. In the forties and fifties the Academy had acquired a reputation for turning out actors and actresses with drawing-room comedy charm and a 'Rada' voice. Now a new breed had begun to emerge. Ex-students such as Albert Finney, Peter O'Toole, Alan Bates and Tom Courtenay were already enjoying successes in plays and films that demanded regional accents and a grittier kind of playing. In 1960, Rada was precariously balanced between the older traditions of theatrical training and newer ideas of so-called naturalism, widening to embrace television and films.

The tutors I started to encounter were a remarkable group of people. Most of them seemed to be much loved by their ex-pupils, who would often drop in to a class for a visit, especially if they had just landed a theatre job or a 'telly'. The revered Clifford Turner was our voice teacher. Elegant, gentlemanly, he had a wry sense of humour and a sharp ear for wrong inflections. We learnt, with feelings of deep awe, that Sir John Gielgud himself would some-times engage him for a refresher voice lesson before embarking on a new role. Clifford soon encouraged me out of most of my schoolboy Shakespearean habits of imitation and thoughtless gabbling. He explained to us all how the actor's voice must become a natural extension of the movement and flow of the body. He would get us standing against the sides of the wide Gower Street classroom. As we slowly slid our backs down the wall, bending our knees, then up again, we would intone his favourite vocal exercises. Voice and movement synchronised. This was the first of many revelations to come.

One day he confided to us his concerns about new films set in the streets and factories of the industrial north. He worried over what he called the 'lazy' accents required. He told us that he had been anxious that one of his students of just a few years before, Alan Bates, starring in A Kind of Loving (set in Manchester) might have discarded all he had learnt about voice and speech during his time at the Academy. But, Clifford said, he had just seen Alan on television in The Cherry Orchard and, he beamed, leaning back in his chair, 'I needn't have worried. It was all still there.' He looked round keenly to see if we understood his point. We were beginning to; as actors we had to lose our worst idiosyncrasies of speech, our regional or suburban accents, and yet still be able to recall them when necessary. Bates, after employing the flat vowels of a working-class Lancashire lad, could still inhabit the fluid cultivated speech of a Chekhov translation. Courtenay could play both Billy Liar and Faustus. Finney could be equally convincing at the factory bench or in Elsinore.

After a week or two of Clifford Turner's classes, we were invited to select pieces to read aloud before the class. Foolishly, I chose his favourite poet, Keats. I embarked on the lengthy 'Ode to a Nightingale', probably the most challenging poem for even the best verse-speaker. He listened intently, expressionless. The afternoon traffic murmured its way down Gower Street beyond the high Georgian windows of the room as I moaned on, gulping for air every so often, suddenly wondering why I had chosen such a complex exercise. Clifford let me finish and I collapsed in my seat breathless and exhausted. He chortled quietly as I lay back, still gasping. 'Nice try,' he said, 'nice try.' I thought for a moment of the flame-haired Miss Fisher turning to her school-inspector lover and saying with a shrug, 'You see. You see.'

Peter Barkworth – dapper, neatly plastered fair hair, clerical grey suit, polished brown shoes – looked more like a bank manager than the highly accomplished actor he was. His classes in acting 'technique' were the perfect antidote to the generalised flamboyance that had characterised my acting attempts so far. Barkworth's aim, simple but revelatory, was to help us discover natural, untheatrical ways of behaving and speaking on stage. He encouraged us to look for methods of personalising aspects of human behaviour, of focusing points of physical emphasis in a scene by relating the action to what we were saying. It was Clifford Turner's theory from a different perspective. Hamlet had much the same idea in his speech to the players.

One day, Barkworth asked me to perform any speech I knew by heart, from any play. I chose the passage from *Julius Caesar* where Cassius persuades Brutus to join the conspiracy. I got up and acted it out it in front of the class, zipping about the room in a series of stagy moves, spouting the lines in a stilted artificial manner. Pretty good, I thought. And anyway what does Barkworth know about Shakespeare? He's a 'modern' actor. Without commenting on my efforts, Peter asked me to attempt the speech again. Why not try it sitting down this time, he suggested, perhaps while sharpening a pencil. What? What had this to do with the Bard? Still, I grabbed a pencil from my bag, got up, and started the speech again. 'Therefore, good Brutus, be prepared to hear.' I twisted the pencil in the imaginary sharpener. Stopped. Looked up. (Just a minute, this was making sense.) I continued. 'I, your glass/ Will modestly discover to yourself/ That of yourself which you yet know not of.' I looked down, gave the pencil another twist, then raised my eyes. I began to understand.

It was in Peter Barkworth's 'technique' class that we discovered how physical behaviour – slowed down, speeded up, interrupted – can change the face of the action, clarify the scene, providing all kinds of counterpoint that will be interesting for the audience and enhancing to the play. A year later I played Cassius with the National Youth Theatre, and although I wasn't actually able to justify pencil-sharpening in the streets of Rome, I found other ways of focusing the attitudes of the character. It was Peter who first made me understand that there was a great deal more to acting – even in Shakespeare – than sound and fury. He generously shared with us many acting 'secrets' of his own that he had refined over the years. He eventually collected these lectures in his remarkable book, *About Acting*.

His method of 'look, move, speak' as a way of analysing a piece of dramatic action was intriguing. We soon became adept at *looking* at a character on-stage, *moving* swiftly to the door, then *speaking*: 'Good night'. Or even more expressively: *glaring* at our fellow actor, then *raising* an arm, pointing to the door and barking: '*Get out!*' The danger in following this excellent pattern of acting advice was that in a short time we were all, girls as well as boys, in danger of becoming mini-Barkworths off-stage as well as on. We began to speak in his precise carefully manicured tones, moving swiftly about the building, pausing in doorways, uttering clipped 'Good nights' and 'Get outs' before shutting the door neatly and soundlessly behind us and stalking to the locker room to change into our tights for movement class.

We were a diverse bunch of acting hopefuls. The girls, in their leotards and tights, looked more like ballet dancers than drama students. Sarah Badel and Gemma Jones, daughters of celebrated actors, seemed cool and assured even at seventeen years old. Sarah Miles, a year ahead of us, reminded me of a beautiful lost fawn as we occasionally passed each other on the stairs, she gazing into the middle distance with the same vague, driven expression on her face that was soon to be captured so lovingly on film by directors such as Joseph Losey and David Lean.

The stairs were also the place to encounter the statuesque

American student Carol Cleveland and her diminutive friend Lynda Titchmarsh. Lynda was a gifted comedy actress who had lied about her age in order to be accepted by the Academy. She was still fifteen when she arrived from Liverpool. After Rada their careers went in unexpected directions. The dramatic actress Carol became a cult figure in the 'Monty Python' series and Lynda the comedienne metamorphosed (after early acting successes as Lynda Marchal) into Lynda La Plante, to create some of the most memorable and hard-hitting television dramas of the eighties and nineties, including 'Prime Suspect' and 'Widows'.

At first most of the men felt ill at ease in the tights we were required to wear for many classes. I had worn them on my school stage a few times but for several lads the whole idea of these odd garments (plus obligatory ballet pumps) was in total contrast to their lives up to that point. Philip Martin was twenty-three and had arrived at the Academy after several years working in a factory. He and Ian McShane (darkly handsome with his Tony Curtis quiff) looked oddly self-conscious as they walked about the building, play scripts under their arms, or grabbed a quick fag outside the canteen before mime class. They seemed like spindly figures from a Lowry canvas. Oddest of all was Greek student John Theocharis, older than the rest of us, tall, distinguished-looking, already possessing a voice of alarming resonance and power. He dressed always in a neat white shirt and tie, elegant dark jacket, and carried a bulky, businessman's briefcase. For all the world a Greek tycoon – as far as the waist. But the tights and pumps below lent his figure, as he hastened to his studies, the surreal quality of a bespectacled genie lately released from a bottle.

One morning in the locker room I encountered a chirpy lad of about my own age with a tousled mop of brown hair. He had dark insolent eyes, a Mancunian accent and a face that reminded me of a potato. He told me his name was Mike Leigh and that he came from Salford. I asked him if that wasn't where the great Albert Finney had been at school. 'Yes,' replied Leigh, and added, 'As a matter of fact, a lot of people there say I remind them of Albie.' He said this with a dead-pan delivery and looked at me closely to see how I took this remark. He seemed deadly serious.

As I got to know Mike better, I began to feel he was probably the best kind of student to be. I could see that many of us were too acquiescent in accepting our tutors' direction. In various productions we would sweep downstage (or more often upstage) testing out our new-found 'technique', filling the stage with an airy self-confidence. Mike Leigh was different. Not for him the flashy exterior, the obedient acceptance of a move or a motive. He would always ask 'why?' Why must I move here? Why should I speak in this way? Why does my character suddenly hide behind the screen? Unless there was a satisfactory explanation from the director Mike would be unwilling, even unable, to respond. He needed to perceive total truth in the moment. This didn't stop him being a brilliant comic actor: his Costard in *Love's Labour's Lost*, which we did in our final term, owed more to Stan Laurel than Stanislavsky or the Method. His search for the 'real' truth as opposed to a dramatic rendering of what only seemed to be real, contained, perhaps, the seeds of the unique work he has since created as a director and 'deviser', first in the theatre, then on television and in films. Mike Leigh's methods of working from pure, character-based improvisation have drawn amazing performances from his actors. I have always presumed this approach derives from his early insistence on asking 'why?'

On a couple of occasions, Peter Barkworth conducted some extended improvisation classes in which, having been given a certain scenario, we would invent heart-felt scenes of confrontation. These would sometimes go on for an hour, only to be curtailed as another class burst into the room, anxious to begin their own spontaneous explorations. We found a rare liberation in these exercises, often discovering that there was 'no acting required', that we were just reacting to a situation naturally. Sometimes, students who in other more formalised rehearsal conditions had been stiff and theatrical suddenly seemed released, and gave performances in these classes of surprising power and depth. Was this, too, an influence on Mike's later techniques? Had Peter Barkworth ignited an initial spark in the genius of Mike Leigh?

On Yer Way, José

November 1960

London

I discovered that Rada had an arrangement with the Royal Opera House, Covent Garden, whereby impoverished drama students could earn one pound a night by appearing there as 'walk-ons'. This was exciting news since most of us were existing on a very few pounds a week. The concession, we were told, was also extended to members of the Household Cavalry by a decree dating back to Queen Victoria. They too appeared on their nights off as soldiers, sailors, even Nubian slaves. One winter's evening I hurried towards Floral Street with a group of fellow class members including Ian McShane, Philip Martin, Richard Kane, Ralph Wilton, George Layton and Ramsay Blackwood (the only black student at Rada at the time). We had been ordered by John Fernald to report to the Opera House for its new production of *Carmen*. It was the first night and we were instructed not to arrive until after the performance had begun; there might be time for a quick rehearsal during the interval.

The stage door-keeper directed us down some stone stairs to the 'supernumeraries' room, which we were to share with our burly Household Cavalry colleagues. A little wizened man, who looked like a toupeed monkey, scuttled forward to greet us. He informed us he was Monty the wardrobe master, and we were all going to be toreadors tonight. He gave Ramsay an odd glance, then said, 'All right, girls, get your gear off an' slap that bowl on your faces.' He indicated a vat containing a gallon or so of brown body make-up, which I later learned had been known as 'bowl' from before Henry Irving's time at the Lyceum. He threw a handful of sponges at us and told us to get daubing. 'Not you, gorgeous,' he said to Ramsay, who was already going to be the darkest Spaniard in the bullring.

When we had sufficiently disguised our student pallor Monty pointed to a row of glittering outfits hanging on two long rails: 'Come on, suit of lights everyone.' As we struggled into the costumes we became aware we were being scrutinised from the other end of the room by the Household Cavalry, already dressed as *carabinieri*. They watched us with the cool contempt of old hands. McShane and most of the others looked fine – not too unnaturally tall for toreadors. But, six-foot and fair-haired, I suspected that the supercilious titter that ran round the far end was directed mainly at me. I continued to buckle my breeches. When we were ready Monty inspected us, somewhat tartly, and shrugged; he had seen it all before. 'On yer way, José,' he sighed, and led us up the stairs and along a series of corridors until we found ourselves in the cavernous wing space of this magnificent theatre. For a moment we were at a loss: humbled by its vastness. Our comfortable Gower Street cocoon seemed a million miles away. All was quiet. It was the interval. The stage was dark and empty. We still had no real idea what we were supposed to do. The massive curtain was down but we could just make out the murmur of the first night audience beyond.

An efficient-looking man wearing a dinner-jacket and carrying a clipboard appeared suddenly out of the gloom. 'Rada?' he inquired briskly.

'Yes,' we nodded.

He introduced himself as David the stage manager and reminded us that were toreadors. He consulted his watch anxiously, then gave us instructions. 'Right, chaps, you'll start here in the wings, in pairs.'

He began moving us together and shifting us around: 'Good – that's more like it.' He shunted us about, sizing us up. He placed the two most unlikely Spaniards, Ramsay and me, together at the rear of the group, then changed his mind and shoved us into the middle. He went on hurriedly, 'You'll hear the chorus on stage so listen out for your music, then you'll hear "Here they come, here they come", and on a cue from me,' (he looked at us over the top of his specs) 'you'll march on – full of pride – as they're singing the "Toreador Song", and they'll be waving, throwing flowers at you. You'll continue marching upstage and round, round again and off the other side. Got that?' We nodded earnestly. He leant across towards Ramsay and me and said, 'Remember – Spanish. Toreadors. Try and blend in.' He gave a last look round, catching sight of the disdainful *carabinieri* who were assembling a few feet away. 'Good!' He nodded approvingly towards these veterans from whom, clearly, he felt we Rada lads could learn a thing or two. He turned back to us: 'Keep the marching pace going, Rada – don't forget you've got the Cavalry coming up behind.' I caught sight of Monty mouthing something that looked like 'oops' in the background. The Cavalry towered over us. We adjusted our capes and hats and shuffled nervously, clearing our throats. David assessed us one last time, hastily moved Ramsay upstage of me and, checking his watch for a third time said, 'No time to rehearse. Good luck' and scurried away. There was a moment of dead silence. Then David's tense voice: 'Stand by, tabs, and – go!'

As the curtain rose we heard the first thrilling chords from the orchestra. The lights began to come up, brighter and brighter, bathing the huge stage in the full glaring sunshine of a Spanish afternoon. Mesmerised, we watched the fifty-strong chorus, fully bowled and gaily apparelled, turn and stare expectantly into the wings: 'Here they come, here they come,' they intoned. They meant us. We cleared our throats. I sniffed. We were ready. The music swelled. This was it. Wasn't it? We heard David suddenly yelling, 'Go Rada – go *toreadors*!' And then, in our dazzling suits of lights, we stepped out proudly, flamboyantly – surely a credit to our movement teacher, Madame Fedro – as we made our Covent Garden debut.

It was strangely uplifting: the chorus all around, Bizet's music, the flowers, the kisses, all of it for *us* as we marched across that mammoth arena, the focus of every eye in the House. And, as the 'Toreador Song' soared into the blue cycloramic sky, I found myself joining in. I couldn't help it. I had to. I just *had* to sing. 'Toreador, la, la la la la *lah* – toreador, toreador.' Forgotten were the yodelling difficulties of my childhood. I felt marvellous. Here I was, on the stage of one of the greatest theatres in the world, completely on song. Sublime. Ian McShane and Philip Martin, no longer Lowry matchstick-men but authentic Spanish bull-fighters, strode ahead of me; Ramsay Blackwood moved in lissome syncopation alongside and, with the Household Cavalry's finest bringing up the rear, we marched and marched – and I sang my heart out until we reached the far side and made our flower-bedecked exit.

In the wings I was turning to my chums to say wasn't that *incredible* when I felt a hand on my shoulder. It was David, his face inches from mine, whispering but somehow shouting, 'What the *hell* do you think you were doing?'

I genuinely didn't know what he meant. While the gut-wrenching drama of the bullring moved inexorably towards its conclusion a few yards away, I looked at him blankly: 'What?'

'You were *singing*,' he screamed quietly. 'You're not here to *sing*. You're from Rada. You should know better. *Idiot!*'

As José plunged the knife into Carmen's heart and Bizet's electrifying orchestration reached its heart-rending climax, I could feel myself returning to the real world. I said: 'I'm sorry David. I really am. I'm afraid I got carried away.'

McShane winked at me as we started to make our way back to the basement. 'Olé, Jarvo,' he said.

Towards the end of the first term I was surprised to receive a phone call from the new company manager at the Pembroke Theatre-in-the-Round. He asked me to drop by for a chat. Terence Fitzgerald was an urbane ruddy-faced character who reminded me of an elongated Billy Bunter. Probably no more than thirty-five, he had an avuncular way of addressing you, rather in the manner of a kindly High Court Judge who felt that you – the prisoner at the bar – at least deserved to be treated with courtesy. A rotund stomach protruded from his thin frame, as if he had thrust a cushion under his red-striped shirt in order to play

Falstaff at short notice. Like Clement Scott Gilbert, he was never to be seen without a suit and invariably sported a yellow or pink spotted bow-tie. He was unfailingly polite to me; I assumed that Clement had not bothered him with the tale of my Peggy Thorpe-Bates debacle.

'My dear young Martin,' he beamed. 'We have some stars coming down to do the Christmas show, so we need somebody clever and splendid such as your good self to look after them.' I soon learned this actually meant, 'We need a cheap dogsbody, are you free?' I certainly was. The vacation was coming up, it was a fiver a week and the affable Terence had hinted there might be a couple of small parts for me as well.

On the last day of term I raced from Gower Street to the Soho rehearsal room where the readthrough of Croydon's musical version of Charles Dickens' *A Christmas Carol* was about to take place. I found that I was an ASM, under the crisp authority of twenty-two-year-old ex-paratrooper, Jon Finch – who looked like a film star and eventually became one. But I had indeed been cast in two roles. The first was the turkey seller in the opening number. Jon plonked a sheet of music in front of me. 'That's your bit of the song,' he said brusquely. I stared at it. And at the accompanying words:

> Come along Mister, come along do –
> Here's a prize-winning turkey that's made for you . . .

'All right everyone, off we go!' Immediately the musical director was thumping away on the piano and the entire company (who had only met each other minutes before) launched into the opening chorus, sight-reading the music and offering, in golden song, their Christmas wares. It sounded great: the baker, the pastry cook, the wine merchant and then – oh – the turkey seller. I could see from the script that my solo was coming up – but the notes on the sheet meant nothing to me.

Despite my recent moments of *Carmen* euphoria, a feeling of helplessness engulfed me. I was back at the junior school concert unable to produce a yodel – and now here was my cue and there was no way I could sell my turkey. I was just turning to the director to mutter, 'I'm sorry, I don't sing –' when I heard from behind me a rich, almost operatic baritone, peddling a turkey on my behalf in full-throated ease. The voice belonged to John Baddeley, the young actor playing Dick Wilkins. He had apparently noticed my nervousness and, though he had a couple of solos of his own to worry about, had pitched in to save me from further embarrassment. Later he generously suggested to Clement and Terence that I should *speak* my turkey seller lines as a sort of cockney Rex Harrison. I could see the musical director wasn't too happy – he had composed the score – but I was allowed to get away with it.

My second role, the Ghost of Christmas Future, was a character I felt I could really get hold of. Although the part contained no dialogue I looked forward, every night, to my one scene. Jon Finch, in charge of the dry-ice machine, ensured that the stage was covered by a low-lying cloud so that my feet were hidden from view. It seemed that this huge cloaked figure, a hood obscuring its face, was floating slightly in space as it moved towards the cringing Scrooge and pointed, inexorably, to the future. Scrooge, in the person of Laurence Hardy, would then grab me by the shoulders, crying, 'Oh Spirit, Spirit, say this is not so. Tell me this is not the future.' Miraculously, the phantom would crumple in his hands and there would be nothing left but the cloak, falling empty to the ground.

The effect on the audience was gratifying. The trick worked like this: under Terence Fitzgerald's tuition I had spent hours constructing a large head-shaped cage made of chicken wire. In preparation for my entrance I held this contraption above my own head on a steel rod, with one hand. Jon Finch then placed the voluminous cloak over the top of the cage so that the hood concealed all but the shape of the wire head. The illusion was of a ghostly monk, eight feet high. In my other hand, inside one of the lengthy sleeves, I held a huge flesh-coloured false finger (on a stick) which emerged, when raised, to point towards the future. Because of the heat engendered by the heavy serge I wore only underpants. The cunning of the operation was that when

Scrooge grasped my shoulders and began to shake them he was, in reality, taking hold of the base of the chicken wire beneath the cloak. At this moment I would sink swiftly to the ground while Scrooge still seemed to be wrestling with the fearsome creature. As he reached the climax of his speech he would let go; cloak and cage fell on top of my crouching form beneath the swirling mist, the lights blacked out, followed by applause. In the dark I would gather up cloak, cage and finger, and make for one of the exits.

One particular night everything seemed to be going right. As the *sprechstimme* turkey seller I had managed to speak my lines absolutely on the beat for the first time. And now, after a speedy costume change, here was the mute Christmas Future, spookier than ever, floating on the dry ice. Even the feet and ankles of the nearest audience members were lost in the seeping mist. Perfect. The wraith wafted silently towards centre-stage. Implacably it raised a cloaked arm and pointed its great digit. From the interior of the fetid outfit I heard Scrooge cry out, felt him grasp the wire. Expertly I dropped down – false finger and all. He relinquished his hold, the whole thing crumbled away, the audience gasped, the lights went out and from my position on the floor I heard the applause.

As usual, I scooped everything up and felt my way along the side of a raised block of seats towards the exit. But tonight was different. I couldn't locate the wooden panelling that normally acted as my guide. With my bundle under one arm, I groped along – stretching out with my free hand for clues. At last – something. Thank God, the lights would be on again any second. Suddenly I heard shrieks and giggles. I felt legs, knees. 'Get off!' somebody cried. I realised what had happened. In the blackness I had taken a wrong turning and was now heading along one of the front rows. I daren't turn back or I'd be caught like a rabbit in the oncoming headlights of the next scene. I floundered on, the screams and giggles becoming louder. Then, thankfully, something solid. I shoved – and, with a clang and a crash, half fell through some sort of gap and hit the ground. The bundle broke my fall. I could hear full-blown laughter now. As I began to pick myself up, I was stupefied to find that I had actually burst my way through the emergency exit doors at the side of the auditorium. I was on the pavement in the street outside the theatre and most of the audience could see me through the open doors. I could see *them*. They were pointing me out and cackling hysterically. This was a comedy bonus they hadn't expected: a crazed-looking youth standing under a lamp-post in his underpants. As I sprang forward to close the double doors the audience burst into spontaneous applause for the second time.

I snatched everything up again, moved swiftly round the outside of the building and, ignoring the searching glances of several passers-by, walked up the alley to the stage door. It was locked. I rang the bell and stood shivering until, finally, it was opened by the courteous Terence Fitzgerald. There was a curious expression on his face as he stood back to allow this near-naked, goose-pimpled apparition – carrying a pile of old clothes, a load of chicken wire and a gigantic finger-on-a-stick – to re-enter the theatre. 'My dear Martin,' he exclaimed with ineffable good manners, 'do come in!' But I sort of knew that, despite his unfailing civility, he had to be thinking, 'Here really *is* a prize-winning turkey.'

At the start of our second year I was disappointed not to get the part of Bassanio in *The Merchant of Venice*. I played instead the elderly Doge. A few days after our three public performances in Rada's Vanbrugh Theatre, I received a letter from a well-known agent of the time, Gerald Welch, congratulating me on my performance and inviting me to come and see him with regard to future representation. Thrilling. When I walked through the door of his office the following week, callow, eager and nineteen years old, he paused in the act of rising from behind his desk to greet me and sat down again sharply. 'No, no,' he said, 'they've sent the wrong one.' I stopped halfway across the room. He was heavy, grey-haired, in a blue blazer and flannels. He looked like the sort of man who might have retired early from the army and was now secretary of a Home Counties golf club. 'What's your name?' he asked brusquely. I told him. 'No, no,' he said again as I hovered in the centre of the room, 'I wanted the chap who played the old boy. The Doge of Venice.'

Not knowing what else to do I pulled his letter from my pocket and held it out, assuring him that it was indeed I who had been the Doge.

He looked at me in a sort of blinkered disbelief, then shook his head. 'No, no,' he said, for a third time. We didn't seem to be getting anywhere. 'Yes, yes,' I considered replying, but before I had decided anything he said, 'I wrote to you because I thought you were an older actor. Mature student sort of thing. But I see you're just a boy. We want older actors. Sorry.'

There seemed little else to say or do. He picked up some papers on his desk and it was clear I was dismissed. I thought, this is very curious. If he had been so comprehensively convinced by my doddering Doge, why, on discovering it had been merely a character performance, did he not now think me worth pursuing? I stood my ground for a moment, looked at him hard, stalked to the door, turned and said, in a clipped Barkworth voice, 'Thank you. Good morning.' I felt, as I closed the door sharply behind me, that Peter would have been proud of me.

I combined my two years at Rada with membership of the National Youth Theatre. In the early sixties, the NYT was still merely the 'Youth Theatre'. Although the majority of its members were from the London area, it was already attracting wider attention as a group of young people, many still at school, who performed Shakespeare with extraordinary energy and commitment. Its founder, Michael Croft, had been an English teacher at Alleyn's School in south London, where he produced the annual play. The school itself had been founded by Edward Alleyn, one of Shakespeare's star actors. Croft's methods of casting were interesting. He would often recruit the most vociferous football-playing ruffians from the playground and transfer their toughness and teamwork to the school stage, where they would find themselves appearing as fighting lords, rebellious nobles, Trojan warriors. Mark Antony's previous experience was more likely to have been as centre-half on the football field than swotting in the school library.

Croft soon built up a remarkable band who became so dedicated to acting Shakespeare under his leadership that they persuaded him to put on a production in the school holidays. Croft agreed. The Toynbee Hall on the south side of the River Thames was hired and a teenage *Henry IV, Part One*, with David Weston a persuasive Falstaff, became almost required London theatregoing. Critics such as W. A. Darlington in the *Telegraph* and Harold Hobson in the *Sunday Times*, urged their readers to travel to Southwark to see it. In a couple of years the Youth Theatre's reputation had grown, and in August 1959 Croft was offered the Queen's Theatre, Shaftesbury Avenue, where he directed *Hamlet* with Richard Hampton as the moody Dane and Hywel Bennett an astonishingly convincing Ophelia. (It was another year before the girls arrived.) I had seen this production and came away with a mixture of awe and envy. I applied immediately for an audition. A fortnight later, still in my last year at school, I received a summons.

I met the legendary Michael Croft for the first time in a sleazy rehearsal room underneath a block of council flats behind Victoria station. He was a stocky, bear-like man, thirty-nine years old, with curly hair already greying at the sides. He had a pugnacious chubby face, small piercing eyes and a pursed mouth that seemed permanently set in a wry half-smile, as if he were about to break into derisive laughter at the lunacy of the world. Or at the absurdities of the Arts Council, who consistently refused to recognise the value and importance of the work he was doing with young people.

As I entered the scruffy room, Croft was seated in the centre of a half-circle of rickety metal chairs, flanked by three or four Youth Theatre members. Clearly these were lads who had graduated from the playground. They all seemed to be dressed in black leather jackets and motorcycle boots. I stood there uncertainly in my school blazer and cavalry twills. A fair-haired boy of about my age whom I had seen playing Rosencrantz, flicked ash from his cigarette and nodded at me casually. This was Simon Ward who, along with Ian McShane, John Shrapnel, Hywel Bennett, Helen Mirren and Michael York, was to form the nucleus of the Youth Theatre company over the next few seasons.

Croft rose from his chair and greeted me with a hearty handshake. 'Well, Martin –' he said. There was a crisp northern edge to his voice. He could have been a fighting lord himself. He told me to sit down. I drew up one of the battered chairs. He asked me what I had been doing and I told him about my love of Shakespeare and acting and my hopes of getting into Rada. 'Ah yes, Rada.' The sardonic mouth and slightly rolled 'r' made me wonder if he disapproved of that mainstream establishment. In fact, I discovered later, two of his leading actors, Jane Merrow and David Weston, were already at the Academy and Simon Ward and Hywel Bennett would soon be following them. I learned too that John Fernald, Rada's principal, regarded Croft's productions with some admiration – even if they contained rather more blood and guts than the supposed refinements of Rada's bona fide drama training. No Barkworth pencil-sharpeners here. I knew the next Youth Theatre production was to be a modern-dress *Julius Caesar* and I told Croft I had prepared a speech of Cassius. 'Ah yes, Cassius. Splendid, Martin . . .' he said, in the same amused tone. Again I wasn't sure of his attitude.

As I got up I noticed how many chunky concrete pillars there were in the room. They seemed to be holding up the entire building. I moved to a space near the centre. I had been practising in my bedroom for the last week and the combination of speech and movement that I had put together had seemed logical and fluid: cross over to the bed, try to persuade Brutus to join the conspiracy, swing up to the chest of drawers, stalk away with nostrils aquiver when Brutus won't listen, turning my back on him. Then swiftly cross over to look out of the window, where the washing was flapping on the line in next-door's garden. Pretty good I thought.

It didn't work out quite like that in this subterranean echo chamber. I started off all right but, when I made my first pre-planned move, I found myself stuck directly behind one of the great concrete pillars. I was completely hidden from Croft's view; indeed from all the others except Simon Ward who, by leaning slightly to his left, which he did, was the only one who was able to judge how my mysterious Cassius was shaping up so far. Not too well.

Nevertheless, I kept talking, speaking louder to compensate for the unfortunate masking problem. I just couldn't seem to move. I felt utterly rooted. All I could do was continue the speech, projecting madly, until my next 'bedroom' move. This got me out into the open for a couple of lines. Then, as if thrust by some unseen hand, I moved four paces to the right, to be obscured once again by another floor-to-ceiling pillar. I heard my voice rising an octave and bouncing off the walls. I hammered away until my bedroom template allowed me to emerge, still talking, and (thanks to the memory of next-door's washing) fling myself upstage, before turning sharply, in plain sight of my audience.

There was suddenly silence in the room. I sat down coolly. Simon's face was inscrutable. He and the other black-jacketed boys looked at their motorcycle boots. They drew on their cigarettes. Nobody spoke. Croft tapped himself thoughtfully two or three times on his barrel chest, a gesture I was to see him make a hundred times in the future. Tap, tap, tap. Before the image of Miss Fisher and the Forest Woodman could fully materialise, Croft, accompanying his tapping with a slow nodding of the head, regarded me for some moments and said, 'Cassius, yes, well Martin, very good.' Tap, tap, tap again. Then – 'Yes, very self-effacing.' Then, with a final double tap and a nod, he invited me to join the company.

A year later I actually played Cassius on a Youth Theatre tour of Italy. Luckily our set had no pillars.

The success of Croft's productions meant more seasons in the West End and invitations to tour abroad to play major theatres in Paris, Amsterdam, Berlin, Brussels and Rome. It was an exhilarating double life: music, movement, mime and technique during the Rada term, and gutsy verse-speaking in the holidays. 'Now then, Martin,' Croft would say if I tried too much 'look, move, speak' in rehearsal, 'none of your Rada tricks here.' Back at the Academy, as I swashed and buckled with Sheila Gish, Mike Leigh and Gemma Jones in *The Country Wife*, our canny director Ellen

Pollock would sweetly suggest I toned it down, took my hands off my hips and 'spoke with a little more finesse'. Between these disparate approaches I began, vaguely, to draw together some craft-strands of my own. Then, in the spring of 1962, Croft asked me to play the Duke of York to Simon Ward's Richard II on a tour of Holland.

I had discovered the existence of this play ten years earlier at my grandparents' house. It had been at the period when, aged nine, I had embarked on my doubtful adventures with the Forest Woodman. One November evening, after tea, I had been browsing through Grandpa's bookcase. I idly picked out his *Complete Works of Shakespeare*. It fell open at *Richard II*, Act 2, Scene 1, and the first words I saw on the tissue-thin page were:

> This royal throne of kings, this sceptred isle,
> This earth of Majesty, this seat of Mars,
> This other Eden, demi-paradise . . .

I began to choke with an emotion I didn't quite understand. But, as I read on, there was something extraordinary in the power of those words and images that leapt instantly on to a screen in my head I hadn't even known was there. Words and phrases were turning into pictures, beamed out in full colour: 'sceptred isle', 'precious stone', 'silver sea'. And then: 'like to a tenement or pelting farm'; 'inky blots'; 'this blessed plot, this earth, this realm, this England . . .'

I wasn't sure what a lot of it meant, who was speaking or why. But, oddly, tears were starting to run down my cheeks. When I heard Grandma and Grandpa coming back from the kitchen having done the washing-up, I brushed the tears away, closed the book and replaced it between *Whitaker's Almanac* and *Games and Pastimes*. By the time they came into the room I was sitting at the table, ready for the usual game of cribbage. I felt strangely happy.

At seven o'clock I set off on the twenty-minute walk home with an extra Lyons mini-roll and two digestive biscuits ('to keep me going', as Grandma had put it). Those discovered images seemed inside me and all around. It was raining: 'small showers last long while sudden storms are short'. I stuffed the chocolate roll into my mouth: 'with eager feeding food doth choke the feeder'. There were no pelting farms in South Norwood (I wasn't really sure what a pelting farm was anyway), but there was certainly a tenement or two. I walked quickly past them, rounded the 'blessed plots' of the allotments and the wat'ry Neptune of Norwood Lake, then up the hill towards home.

I was certain, as I entered the cul-de-sac and headed for our green front door, that Shakespeare knew everything there was to know – about me, about Norwood, about our little world, even about the inky blots of history homework.

And now, a decade further on, I had secured the challenging role of the ancient Duke of York in *Richard II*. I would be projecting some of Shakespeare's greatest words, beating out glorious iambics and delivering the Grand Old Duke to his Dutch devotees. And I wouldn't be sliding up and down the wall of Clifford's classroom while doing it. I would be centre-stage at the Kleine Komedie, one of Amsterdam's finest theatres. Here was also the perfect opportunity to assess my work-in-progress in the technique classes: certainly the way I saw the part there would be room for a lot of look, a great deal of move and a tremendous amount of speak.

I considered first the Duke's appearance. He is Richard II's uncle and therefore old enough to be his father. Simon Ward's father. Hmm. During our rehearsals in London I concentrated on the old Duke's walk, and decided that at his age he should have a stick. My thinking never got much beyond the fun of actually being able to move around with this useful prop. It could be used for prodding courtiers into action, for beating on the ground to emphasise a point or even tapping one of the fighting lords jocularly on the buttocks. Tap, tap, tap. Perhaps the Duke had gout? Although the rate I scudded across the rehearsal room berating Northumberland and castigating the King suggested otherwise. I was pleased to find that Chris, our designer, agreed with my feisty approach. He added heavy robes and breeches with cloak, gloves, belt, boots and chains. Splendid.

The part also gave me an opportunity to practise my make-up
skills. I decided to try out some of the tricks I had learnt from the
chipper little man at Rada who had introduced us to the wonders
of Leichner and Max Factor. I felt I knew something of this already,
having watched Ernie Gibb at our school plays. Now, backstage in
Amsterdam with half an hour to go before curtain-up, I was applying more crow's feet around my eyes than I had lines in the play. I
etched some crimson stripes into the indentations down the sides
of my nose. I mixed in a little No. 16 to suggest gauntness, and
highlighted my cheekbones with the pasty cream-coloured No. 5.
I drew a grey line under my lower lip for emphasis, dimpled my chin
for nobility, darkened my lashes to make my eyes appear larger,
blackened my brows and reddened my nose. Taking a powder-puff,
I gave my entire face a liberal dusting of talcum. I then attached the
moustache, riveting it painfully to my upper lip with spirit-gum,
topping off the whole thing with the silvery, slightly balding wig. I
looked at myself in the mirror. I tried out a line or two in the thin
projected voice I had chosen for the Duke:

> . . . be it known to you
> I do remain as *neuter*.

I looked again at my reflection. There was something vaguely
familiar about this white-headed figure with the multi-coloured
face. Who was it?

At that moment Michael York came into the room to wish me
good luck. He stopped short for a second, mouth just a fraction
agape, as he saw me turning towards him. Then, with typical good
manners, he thrust out his hand and shook mine heartily. He was
playing my son, the handsome Aumerle. I wished him good luck,
too. Ian McShane, my fellow Rada student, adjusted his quiff in
the mirror to a marginally more medieval height. He was playing
a darkly glamorous Henry Percy. 'Good luck, Jarvo,' he threw
over his shoulder as, with the same swagger that has distinguished
a hundred 'Lovejoy' episodes, he made his way towards the wings.
I'd had exciting chats with both Michael and Ian during the long
hours of the technical rehearsal. All three of us had confided our

hopes and ambitions. I had said how I wanted to be able to play character parts, good ones of course, like this one. They both looked thoughtful and said nothing.

Ian told us with perfect candour that he wanted to get into movies. I nodded enthusiastically: 'I'm sure you will, Ian,' I said, 'because you're bloody good-looking.' His features broke into an easy smile. He regarded me for a moment, quiff on one side, gazing at the railway network of my make-up. He winked (I wasn't sure whether at me or Michael) and said, 'You're not so bad yourself, Mart.' Then, over the tannoy came 'Beginners, please'.

I gathered up my stick, belt, gloves, cloak and we filed out of the dressing rooms, making our way towards the stage. We knew it was a full house out front; the idea of a teenage company of young Shakespeareans was appealing to young Dutch audiences. We had heard and seen the crowds that had been gathering around the theatre all day. In the corridor I bumped into Simon and wished him luck. He smiled smoothly. I almost felt he didn't need it, dazzlingly arrayed in pink and gold, courtesy of the Old Vic. I felt suddenly confident as I followed him down the stairs. I swung my stick. As we passed into the wings I caught sight of myself in the long mirror just by the entrance. It was then, as I adjusted my wig one more time, that I realised who it was I resembled: Lady Barker, as played by the Wilfrid Hyde-White of Holland. No time to worry about that now.

The show turned out to be a near-riot. This was an exuberant audience, reacting spontaneously and energetically to everything we did. Simon scored a notable triumph and the applause that greeted Richard's more quixotic behaviour would not have disgraced the Beatles or a Rolling Stones concert of a few years hence. My own performance, I felt, went well. I was jeered at, certainly, but that, I told myself, was an excellent reaction to the character. There were cheers when Bolingbroke was banished. There were whistles when McShane threw down his gage. Sighs when Michael York, in blue tights, strolled coolly across the battlements. There were even laughs when the Duke of York doddered, waved his stick and proclaimed that he would remain neuter.

Then it was all over. Flowers were strewn on the stage. We

took a dozen curtain-calls. The audience wouldn't let us go. In the dressing rooms, as we removed our costumes (plus, in my case, wig, beard, moustache and heavy make-up), we could hear the crowds outside the stage door, still laughing, still giggling, still cheering.

Simon was one of the first to make his exit, running the gamut of Dutch girls whose boyfriends seemed perfectly happy for them to reach out to touch him and take him off to one of the many night-clubs surrounding the adjoining square. McShane appeared next and some of the crowd broke away, encircling him, urging him to sign programmes, backs of hands, stomachs, pleading with him to join them. Michael York emerged, modestly shaking his head and smiling as he received the same treatment.

It was my turn. I came out of the stage door walking quickly, face stinging a little from the spirit-gum. I looked around. Modest but expectant. The cheers and cries subsided. Nobody seemed interested and then, suddenly, the screams were renewed and a great wave of acclamation arose as Hywel Bennett and Robin Ellis were spotted behind me. Somehow our fans had missed me. Never mind. I knew what to do. Under cover of the ovation for Hywel and Robin I took the opportunity to nip back inside for a moment. Then, as the applause began to quieten, I sauntered out, not hurrying this time, grinning a little, waving. Nothing. Nothing at all. They weren't interested.

Twenty minutes later I was sitting in a quiet bar near the canal with Geoff Hutchings who had played John of Gaunt. Despite the fact that he had spoken the wonderful lines that I had discovered at Grandma's ten years before, he too had been passed over by the fans. We raised our Dutch beers in a melancholy toast. It was then that I made a mental note to adjust some of my recent thinking. I decided that although I still wanted to play character roles, I'd better not want to play them all the time. And if I *did* play them, I'd better not dodder around like Cruys Voorberg in full drag. I could see, as I watched my friends being feted by the fans, how much fun it was to be recognised by your audience.

In 1962, a man called Yat arrived at Rada. We were told he was

Swedish and had been a well-known dancer with the Ballet Jooss. If he had a surname we never learnt it. He was simply Yat. John Fernald, determined that his drama school should receive all the benefits of modern thinking (even if he himself preferred the safer traditions of music and movement) had invited Yat to give classes in his own theories of physical expression. Our group were to be the guinea-pigs.

Yat had demanded that we subject ourselves to his authority for two hours every afternoon, at the expense of some of our other classes. No more mime from the stately Miss Phillips, who sat in a black costume and matching hat, beaming sedately as we moved about the room in small groups creating our mute scenarios. We would then present our mimes to her – rather as if we were party guests, and she some kind of beatific hostess. No more John Broom, the balding young man with a wicked smile who seemed to come nearest to being able to help us understand the relationship between our physical behaviour in life to move-ment on-stage. And no more Madame Fedro, who had been a dancer. She had a peppery mittel-European temperament and was adored by her students. She made us act out scenes that we had been rehearsing for other classes or for productions in the Vanbrugh Theatre, and would then comment on how we could make our increasing physical awareness work to the advantage of the character and the play. And here was Yat entering our class-room accompanied by his teaching assistant and interpreter, an English actor in his thirties called Christopher Fettes. Their faithful labrador, Johnny, was by their side.

Some of us had seen Christopher give a physically assured though vocally indifferent performance as one of the lovers in A Midsummer Night's Dream at the Regent's Park Open Air Theatre. At close quarters, he had a permanent, sardonic expression on his face. He managed to convey to us all, over the next weeks, a feeling that we were wasting our time in wanting to become actors. He made us nervous if we heard he had attended any of our performances. He seemed world-weary, with none of the warmth of John Broom, the fire of Madame Fedro, the delight of Clifford Turner or the concern of Peter Barkworth. Neither he nor Yat ever seemed to know our names. Some years later Christopher became the principal of a London drama school, where he and Yat developed their theories into a highly successful approach to drama training.

Yat himself seemed only marginally more approachable than cool Christopher. He was a small lithe man in his late forties, with close-cropped greying hair, high Slavic cheekbones tinged with red, and a vulpine mouth. 'Yat the rat' rose instantly to my mind on his first entrance. When he spoke to us – in short impenetrable sentences – I felt we were taking part in one of those uncompromisingly severe Ingmar Bergman films. We were as far from Shakespeare, 'look, move, speak', even Amsterdam, as was possible to imagine.

The canine member of the trio, Johnny, would also be present every afternoon. He seemed a fine example of their methods as he padded up and down the room, occasionally stopping to inspect one or other of us as we lay groaning on the floor, trying to understand these gruelling exercises that had apparently made perfect sense to European modern-dance troupes of the 1930s. Johnny, having toured the room, would then return silkily to the front of the class. Lying down between his two masters, he would stretch out his nose on the polished wooden floor and gaze at us as if to say, 'It's this easy.'

Yat's method, we were told, was based on movement theories developed in Europe by the dance theorist Rudolf von Laban. We had to spend long periods lying on the floor, alternately raising and lowering our legs, holding them excruciatingly in the air for extended periods. We would then stagger to our feet and attempt to do the same kind of thing with our arms. At four o'clock we lurched from the room, aching and exhausted. Our other tutors would wonder, as we arrived listlessly for our next class, what exactly Fernald had taken on. It was certainly true that Yat's regime of constant exercise tuned us up, but as we rarely did anything new and hardly moved from our designated spot in the room, though this was a movement class, none of us felt we were getting anywhere. Even the tactful Peter Barkworth asked where we thought it was all heading. None of us knew.

One day, after only an hour of what Yat and Christopher termed 'floor-class', we were amazed to hear them ordering us to get up and to sit down. Like prisoners in a concentration camp given an unexpected reprieve, we obeyed gratefully and grabbed chairs. We sat down and waited. This was to be Yat's first written-theory class. It seemed to consist of analysing words and phrases he and Christopher employed to describe physical actions in the floor-classes and then applying them to actual speeches from plays. We began to see his point – to some extent. If the action of a leg rising from the floor then swiftly kicking out had been described as 'wringing-going-flicking', then we could accept that certain attitudes of characters within a play could be pinned down in a similar way. Yat invited us to select passages from anything we might be studying in another class and to define each line or half-line in terms of 'strong', 'weak', 'wringing', 'flicking', 'bound', 'free', and so on. On the face of it this didn't seem so different from what we had brought to our work with Madame Fedro or John Broom. Yat told us we now had to perform our chosen speech to the class, making sure we adhered to this new 'actioning' of the words. The effect was alien. For most of us, a speech that we had worked on with, say, Clifford or Peter that had just started to make some kind of psychological sense, now became suddenly estranged. Phrases that under Yat's supervision we defined as 'light' or 'heavy', now fell from our mouths in the barking or bleating tones of an animal that had just been taught to speak. Lines that had begun to sound natural or 'real' in a current production, now contained all the humanity and spontaneity of a speak-your-weight machine. Now it was me.

I had chosen 'This royal throne of kings' from *Richard II*. In Yat terms, I thought, this could perhaps be redefined as one long yearning nostalgic whinge. I decided to perform it in this manner, partly, I must confess, to get a few laughs from my classmates and partly, in my arrogance, to show both Yat and Christopher (Johnny too, if he had a nose for the Bard) that theirs was no way to approach Shakespeare. The rules of Shakespeare were all in the verse. The action was in the iambics. Take care of the sense and the sounds will take care of themselves. I got up and recited the speech, applying each new 'actioning' gear-change and ending on a great 'wringing' moan.

I sat down. The class, aghast, held their breath. Christopher looked at me coolly then turned to Yat for his comment. Johnny blinked and closed his eyes. Yat gazed at me for a moment dispassionately and then remarked, in the longest sentence he had spoken all term, 'There you are, Martin, you can do it, that was very good.' I didn't know what surprised me more: the fact that he thought my rendition was good when I thought I was being deliberately bad. Or that he knew my name.

That night, Sarah Badel went home and told the whole story to her father, the great Alan. His opinion was that these classes were a waste of time. Next morning she informed Fernald she would not be attending them any more. Fernald, fearful of appearing not to be giving wholehearted support to his new star tutor, delivered an ultimatum: unless she continued to attend Yat's classes she could not remain at Rada. So Sarah entered the theatrical profession a few months ahead of most of us. In a short time she was starring in her first television play – her co-star, Peter Barkworth.

The next to go was Ian McShane. After his Youth Theatre successes (including a saturnine Casca on the Italian tour) I wondered if he was now finding Rada a bit parochial. Certainly, in an extraordinary verse play, *Domitian*, written by ex-student Brian Spink and directed by Fernald himself, Ian was given only a minor part. Somehow I had landed the title role of the crazed Roman emperor while McShane and John Hurt were sidelined – John as a soldier and Ian as a slave. John was fairly equable about this, having had his fair share of leading parts. Ian was less happy (as who would not be) to carry the emperor's water bowl, bow humbly and return to the dressing room. He was not encouraged, I am sure, by my own overweening delight in being, for the first time, leading man. One night during the interval I asked him if he wouldn't mind bowing a little less sardonically when I made my first entrance. Later I overheard him sounding off about it:

'Bloody hell! Who does Jarvo think he is?' Good question: Jarvo thought he was the emperor of Rome.

Suddenly McShane was offered the central role in a new British film, *The Wild and the Willing*, and departed to become a film star, his early ambition fulfilled. We were all deeply impressed when he returned to see us a few weeks later, dressed in a stylish sheepskin jacket and Italian shoes. Our envy knew no bounds when we learned he was being paid £2000 for the film.

It was many years before Ian and I worked together again. When I guested on his popular series, 'Lovejoy', I noticed that some of his fellow actors were much in awe of him. I wondered, as we filmed together in Suffolk, if he might suggest I bowed meekly as I handed him an antique water jug. But no, the fiery Ian was charming. Though, when I reminded him of our Youth Theatre chats and that I had said he was 'bloody good-looking', he seemed not to remember his generous reply.

Domitian was not a success. The miniskirt (with blue bathing trunks beneath) in which I spent most of the play made me feel strangely vulnerable. Even Gemma Jones' comment that it was the trunks she liked most about my performance seemed a touch hurtful. But then she never pulled her punches. In the previous term's production of a John Arden play, *Live Like Pigs*, she and I had been challengingly cast as tough, middle-aged, northern gypsies who hurled abuse at one another. As the grizzled Sailor Sawney I strode around in a battered donkey jacket, putting on my best imitation of Wilfrid Lawson – the wonderful old actor who had originated the part. Gemma had invited her matinee-idol father, Griffith Jones, to see a performance. Next day she told me, 'My father thought you were awfully good.' I blushed – praise indeed from a professional actor. And a famous one too. 'There was only one thing,' Gemma went on, 'he couldn't actually understand a word you said.'

The *Domitian* audience could understand only too well what I was saying as I paraded in my little skirt and gold wig, proclaiming that I was going to murder my father Vespasian and my brother Titus. The trouble was that nobody seemed to care, and by Act 3 many of even my most loyal friends had disappeared to drink coffee at Olivelli's in Store Street. There, echoing the comments of the water-bearing McShane, they asked each other in appalled tones, 'Who the hell does he think he is?'

At the end of the summer term, some of my Rada tutors had enough confidence in me to give me the Vanbrugh Award and the Silver Medal. Gemma Jones won the Gold Medal. This prize insulated me a little against a final comment from Yat. He called me aside one afternoon and told me I had not done well in his class. He shook his head sadly. In his undulating Swedish accent he said, 'Maybe you have the possibility to be a photographic model.' He shrugged, then added, 'But not an actor.' Even this remark was not enough to burst the balloon of confidence that Rada had managed to inflate on my behalf. It was buoyant enough to cushion me against a worrying thought: I had no agent.

As we took part in our Finals productions, to which many influential agents and producers were traditionally invited, we began to watch the letter rack in the Gower Street entrance hall with a combination of hope and despair. The only letter I had received, several months ago, was from Gerald Welch, the agent who only wanted older men. Without representation, we knew it was difficult to get started. As I monitored the rack for more replies, I could see that many of my friends were receiving envelopes bearing such logos as 'London Management', 'Al Parker', or 'Fraser and Dunlop'. None for me, however. Not even after what I had thought of as a minor triumph of character acting in *The Country Wife*; I had played Mr Horner, that most devilish despoiler of women.

Since no letters arrived, not even from the regional repertory companies to whom I had been writing, I accepted an offer from Michael Croft. He had asked me to appear in one more Youth Theatre production, *Henry V*. This was to be at the Sadler's Wells Theatre and he wanted me to play Henry. Simon Ward would be the Chorus, Robin Ellis was Pistol, Neil Stacy the Archbishop of Canterbury. Among the English troops, Kenneth Cranham and Timothy Dalton could be found waving swords and cheering their hearts out at Harfleur, at which they died bravely – then, alive again, fighting equally courageously at Agincourt.

Katherine, Princess of France, was played by an excitingly named girl from the north, Valerie Pickup. In the last couple of years, Croft had somewhat reluctantly opened the Youth Theatre's doors to girls. He had felt, probably, that the early fun of a group of enthusiastic London lads who wanted to put on a play in the holidays had been superseded by national and now international celebrity. Everything was getting out of hand. 'Girls,' he used to say, tapping his chest, 'girls can be a problem.' In fact they were the making of the Youth Theatre and Croft soon recognised this. From 1960, when Jane Merrow and Mary Grimes had joined as Portia and Calpurnia, plus thirty more who cheered jeered and jived in the Forum crowd, Croft's company was no longer just a boys' club, high on the Bard. Although its greatest female star, Helen Mirren, was still at school in Essex, and her outstanding debut as an eighteen-year-old Cleopatra two years away, it was clear that girls were here to stay.

Henry V was both a triumph and a disaster as far as I was concerned. Henry is an enormously challenging part for a young actor. It requires a range of skills apart from the obvious one of actually committing the part to memory. It begins with the slow burn of the opening scene with the bishops, followed by the first explosion at the French messenger. Then there's the unmasking of the traitors before setting sail from Southampton; Harfleur; 'The Breach' – a huge strain on the voice, yelling above the tumult, if you are *really* to persuade those weary soldiers to have one more go at the walls – the night before Agincourt and the huge soliloquy on the agonies of kingship; the St Crispin's Day speech next morning; the battle and its aftermath; the wooing scene. I played Henry again on radio fourteen years later, with Angela Pleasence as Katherine and Paul Scofield as the Chorus, and only just managed it vocally then. Here, in a large theatre, with no experience of how to pace myself for a three-hour performance of such a part, I seemed to be tired all the time with barely enough voice to get through it all.

I was also having hair problems. Possessing such a shock of fair hair has, all my life, presented difficulties. It is so identifiable, and it just won't comb into a fringe – which was what was required for

Henry. Croft told me to get it cut. So I went round the corner from the theatre one lunchtime, to a barber near the Angel, Islington, and he wielded the scissors. Hopeless. It stuck out like the edge of a haystack over my brow. I looked more like the village idiot than King of England.

When I returned, Croft did a good deal of tapping and shook his head: 'No, Martin, no. That won't do. You'll have to try it the other way.' I went to the dressing room and attempted to comb it 'the other way'. What other way? There wasn't one. It was so short it wouldn't do anything except just sit there. I ended up putting grease on it and more or less forcing it back. Now I looked like Basil Lord.

We opened, and the reviews followed – my first in a major role. Although Bernard Levin in the *Daily Express* was generous in his praise, other critics were not. Harold Hobson expended many column inches in the *Sunday Times* faulting my verse-speaking, and mentioned that if I had indeed attended Rada, even won awards, he hoped it was not at that august institution I had been taught to 'ogle the audience'. This I took to be a comment on the wooing scene, which ended in a fairly inept dance where, certainly, I raised my eyebrows to Katherine in mock embarrass-ment at my clumsy attempts at the high lavolta. I admired Hobson enormously as a writer on theatre and was depressed that he had been so especially critical of my efforts. I had to wait until 1976, when I played Arnold in *The Circle* at the Haymarket Theatre, for his eventual endorsement of my work.

In the autumn of 1962, on the day of our last performance of *Henry*, I had a phone call from a man called David Scase. He ran the Manchester Library Theatre, a leading repertory company, and was offering me a season of plays starting in a fortnight's time. Also, he was going to be doing his own production of *Henry* after Christmas. Aha. I felt my balloon of self-confidence reinflate a little. Yes, why not? Admittedly, it wasn't Stratford, or a movie contract such as Ian McShane had already secured. But let's not forget, I told myself airily, I was a Rada prizewinner. I had a few Turner and Barkworth tricks up my sleeve. And I was the youngest actor ever to play Henry in London. So with no agent, and a clutch of mixed notices, I floated up to Manchester.

David Scase was an energetic bearded Londoner of about forty. He had been Joan Littlewood's stage-manager at Stratford East in the fifties and his no-nonsense approach meant there was little discussion on how to approach our work – it was very much 'get on with it and none of your Rada ways here'. Not so very different from Croft's attitude, but, when we began rehearsals for *Twelfth Night*, I suspected he would rather be directing a cockney comedy. We did in fact do Bernard Kops's *Hamlet of Stepney Green* later in the season and I could see he loved every minute of it, falling about all over the theatre, choking with laughter at the Jewish jokes. But *Twelfth Night* was a school set book, and apart from the evening performances we did a schools' matinée every day. Shakespeare made money.

Except for the young actor Paul Webster who, much to my envy, had been cast as Sir Andrew Aguecheek, I was the only newcomer. I had rather hoped to be cast as Aguecheek myself. I felt, at the time, I could have done it. I certainly didn't recognise what a difficult though satisfying part it is until finally I played it for Peter Hall twenty-five years later. Most of the company had been together since the season had begun a month earlier and were appearing in another play at night. I felt somewhat outside the group after rehearsals were over each day. Aguecheek, married to a French teacher, disappeared home and I made my way back to my first theatrical digs: Mrs Daniels in Daisy Bank Road.

Scase cast me as Sebastian, twin brother to Janet Suzman's Viola. This is always a tricky pairing and it's rare to find an actor and actress who can acceptably be mistaken for each other, not only by other characters but, importantly, by the audience. We were not such a couple. The old hair problem surfaced again. It became clear that my thick stack could not easily be crammed under a short chestnut wig in order for me to resemble Janet more closely. 'It would be easier,' said Cathy, the pale overworked designer, as Janet, David and I stood in a dressing room trying to sort this out, 'if we got Janet a wig that looks like Martin's hair.' I watched in the mirror as Janet, undisputed leading lady of the company, did a swift double take, narrowed her eyes and looked closely at the top of my head. It is to her credit that she didn't refuse on the spot. Instead she smiled tightly, picked up a pair of scissors and came towards me. Holding them up to my head, she cut a substantial chunk from somewhere under the top layer and handed it to Cathy. 'Give this to the wig people,' Janet told her. 'His colour will be a devil to match.'

She was right. When her wig arrived in time for our dress rehearsal we were summoned on-stage for a costume parade. We stood side by side, the Illyrian twins. Our costumes were identical – so far so good. Height, not so good: Janet, elegantly proportioned, a perfect height for an actress, probably five feet five; Martin, six feet and gangling, shifting uneasily in his new boots. Hair: Martin, his own blond thatch lacquered a little – 'to stop it bouncing,' Cathy had suggested – Janet, her locks hidden beneath what looked like one of those cleaning mops that can be detached from its handle and hung out to dry. Janet was right. The colour had been hard to match – in fact, impossible. The wig-makers had come up with what looked like peroxide mixed with a dose of crème de menthe. Scase, seated in the stalls, peered up at us for a moment then shrugged helplessly. We were left to shuffle off-stage as Sir Andrew came bouncing on in his flaxen wig for inspection. This was more like it. David and Cathy shrieked with delight and said it was just right – hilarious, they added. I looked back from the wings. It didn't seem much different from poor Janet's.

Any faint hope that our twinning might be taken seriously by the hordes of Manchester schoolchildren who packed into the theatre every afternoon was swiftly discounted at the first performance. As Janet and I turned towards each other in the final moments of recognition and Janet spoke the moving words, 'Do I stand there?' a great wave of teenage tittering broke out from the audience and a young voice yelled, 'Bloody silly!' whereupon the titters escalated into full-scale laughter with harassed teachers hushing and shushing all over the place.

Several members of the cast had recently trained at the Bristol Old Vic School, though none were as new to the profession as me. I sensed they were watching me with a certain amount of suspicion. I was learning at first hand something I had only heard about: ex-Rada students were regarded as arrogant and superficial and there was a traditional mistrust felt towards them by rival graduates from Bristol. I'm surprised that Donald Gee, Charles Thomas, Janet Suzman and other company members didn't clobber me as I strutted around pretending a fearful indifference. When fan mail started to arrive from schoolgirls who had attended Twelfth Night and I made a bit of a show of answering them all, it was amazing that my fellow actors didn't pick me up bodily and chuck me into the Manchester Ship Canal.

One of the most approachable of my new colleagues was a bald bespectacled actor from Sheffield. His natural authority, coupled with a welcoming concern that I should fit in and get to know the ropes, made me respect him very much. My regard increased when I heard he had recently toured Australia in another production of Twelfth Night in which Vivien Leigh had starred. But when he told me he was to play Orsino I was stunned. How could this middle-aged actor possibly become the passionate romantic Duke? 'You're Orsino?' I blurted out. Gently he told me that he was twenty-three, only two years older than me, and that he had started to lose his hair as a teenager. Sorry, I said. His name was Patrick Stewart. He was an excellent Orsino. After years at the Royal Shakespeare Company he found his greatest success in a seven-year run of the American television series 'Star Trek – The Next Generation', where he became an icon to sci-fi fans – the most recognisable bald-headed actor in the world.

Our next production at the Library Theatre was The Princess and the Swineherd, in which Scase promoted me to leading man. This was the company's Christmas play, a slightly fey fairy-tale with elements of traditional pantomime. I was the young Prince Dominic who prefers pottering in the garden to dealing with affairs of state. Patrick was cast as my evil brother and swanned about the stage in a costume of villainous black, thigh-length leather boots and a Charles II wig of dark ringlets. This time my own hairstyle owed more to Ian McShane than to any remote period of history. I spent a long time in the dressing room with comb, brush, water, lacquer and Brylcreem, before lowering my straw hat on to my head at a rakish angle so as not to destroy the delicate structure of the quiff.

Whatever the weaknesses of the play, I was always assured of one laugh from the audience as I made my first entrance, holding out a cucumber: 'Look, father, twelve inches long and not a kink in it!' The reaction was never stronger than on the first performance when the earnestness of my delivery, having no inkling that the place was going to erupt, meant that I (and Desmond Stokes as the king) had to wait for what seemed minutes until the guffawing subsided and we could continue the scene. In subsequent performances the audience's response to that line, though considerable, was never as stupendous. It was a good lesson. Even when you know a laugh is likely to occur, never show that you know. If you do, it might not come. Communication between actor and audience is not unlike telepathy – your slightest vibes will be picked up. If you are truly 'earnest' the laugh will be one hundred per cent. If you inadvertently let the audience sense that a 'funny line' is coming up, the reaction will be diminished in proportion to how obviously you signalled its approach. I was to learn more lessons about comedy in subsequent years – some curious ones in the Light Entertainment department of the BBC and more profound ones when I began to work with Peter Hall and Alan Ayckbourn in the eighties.

At Manchester I also learnt that cracking up with laughter oneself on-stage – corpsing – is to be avoided. 'Exquisite agony' was how Laurence Olivier described the horror of shaming oneself in front of an audience while at the same time being unable to do anything about it. As a company we were now more integrated. I could tell the older hands felt that the Rada interloper wasn't as arrogant (or as self-confident) as they had expected and could take a joke. We all agreed that the play, which we seemed to be performing interminably, twice a day, over the Christmas period, needed livening up. There was a scene in which a lovely young princess (played by Marigold Paul) discovers the Swineherd – me – outside his forest hut cooking a meal over a log fire. There are three magic pots boiling and our hero lifts the lid of each one in turn so that the princess can smell what's for lunch in the palace. As he raises the lids, enchanting fairy music emerges, the sort that princesses like, and echoes magically around the forest. It turned out that Patrick Stewart, Donald Gee and Co. were cooking up something a little different for my entertainment.

One evening, as I sat by my forest fire, Marigold asked sweetly, as usual, if she could smell what was in the pots. As usual I lifted the lid of the first one. But instead of pretty tinkling notes issuing from the loudspeaker cunningly concealed in the fake logs, out came the velvet sounds of Acker Bilk and 'Stranger on the Shore'. I shut the lid rapidly and Harry the stage-manager, who was in on the joke, swiftly stopped the music in the normal way. I suppressed a guffaw and was going to skip the next exchange with the princess, when Marigold asked innocently, 'Now the second pot, swineherd?' I looked at her. Of course, she was in on the joke too. With fearful laughter beginning to percolate inside me, I lifted the lid and the raucous full-blooded orchestration of 'Seventy-six Trombones' blared out across the stage and all around the theatre. I was laughing openly now and, as I looked off-stage and caught sight of Patrick and Donald doubled up in the wings, I knew I was lost.

The audience was puzzled. This amiable swineherd with the sculpted quiff who had been chatting agreeably to the princess, had suddenly risen from his seat by the fire and started to stagger about the stage, cackling with laughter. What was wrong? What was the swineherd up to? I was heaving now with uncontrollable hilarity. I could still see Patrick and Donald in the wings, clutching each other and looking frightened that things had gone too far. Marigold, admirably controlled throughout, raised her voice above the trombones and beckoned, to attract my attention: 'Swineherd, pray what is in the third cooking-pot?' Oh god. Still guffawing, I dived to the second one and replaced the lid, whereupon Harry, with perfect synchronicity, cut the sound dead. But before I could take control of myself, or the scene, or anything, Marigold had now (unscripted) lifted the lid of the third pot, from whence came horrifically magnified sounds of flatulence (specially recorded by Pat and Don I learnt afterwards), backed by what sounded like the syncopated rhythms of 'The Stripper', wafting across the wild forest. I lay down and roared. It was inexcusable but I couldn't help it. Tiredness was part of it, and the repetitive nature of performing the same flimsy material night after night. (It would be a long time before I discovered the joy of re-creating and freshening a performance over a long run.) So I lay there, hiccuping with unconstrained laughter, more relaxed than I had ever been on any stage anywhere. We never finished the scene. Harry lowered the lights, Marigold helped me from the floor and led me away to the wings, while the audience whispered to each other in mystified tones. Pat and Don looked white when I arrived in the dressing room, like two schoolboys who had no idea that the jape would get out of hand. They had not bargained for a cackling ninny who had lain on the floor and honked like a madman. They were most apologetic, and so was Marigold. So was I – but it took the whole interval before any of us could stop laughing, frightened though we were by what had happened. We were deeply in control for the rest of the performance. I had taught myself a lesson and now it takes a great deal more than Acker Bilk or a farting chorus to upset my concentration on stage.

A few days later, David Scase called me into his office and looked at me hard over half-moon spectacles. He had never mentioned the cooking-pot incident. It suddenly occurred to me that I was going to be fired. I knew he couldn't quite fathom me. I wasn't one of the lads, even though I had floated up to Manchester from Rada via Croft's Youth Theatre. So who the devil was I? I was a twenty-one-year-old from Croydon who had never lived away from home. Scase leant back in his chair, put his hands behind his head and said, 'Sorry, I'm not going to let you play Henry V – Pat Stewart's going to do it. I know you did it with Mike,' he went on, 'but – well, I saw it – er – we haven't talked about that yet, have we?' We hadn't, nor did we subsequently, but I presumed he had formed the same kind of opinion of my novice work as Mr Hobson had done. It was astonishing that he had hired me at all. He leant forward and put his chunky hands on the desk. 'I want you to play Pistol. Great part. It'll be good for you.'

So I hadn't been fired after all. I was relieved in a way. Although I had hoped that Scase would ask me to do Henry, I recognised that I wasn't yet really up to it. And, as he said, Pistol was a great part.

Hello Jon. How's Fleur?

June 1963

East Croydon

After having some fun with Pistol and a few other parts, I left
Manchester and returned to London. Not just to London but to
Croydon. What was it about the place? Perhaps the insecurity I
had felt at the Library persuaded me to hang on to some of the old
familiarities. Taking the boy out of the suburb didn't mean he
wasn't still to be drawn back in. I soon found myself married to
the patient girlfriend I had left behind and, before long, had a
mortgage and a three-room flat near East Croydon station.

I played a succession of parts at theatres in and around London.
They were mostly what used to be termed 'juvenile leads'. In
these roles I would bound on, often in grey flannels and a cream
shirt, grinning widely, and say things like, 'Good morning,
Mother darling, have you seen Pops?' or 'Oh, Celia, my angel,
let's live for always in boundless love.' I travelled regularly to
London for rehearsals or performances. A commuting actor.
Though scarcely a glamorous figure, I was regarded as such by
some of my fellow passengers. These were people who had been
at school with me, travelling up to town to pursue their chosen
professions as solicitors, accountants, insurance men, even stock-
brokers. I felt Bohemian and freelance as I chatted to them on the
twenty-minute journey to Charing Cross, answering their
questions about my theatrical life. Apparently it fascinated them.
I was absurdly gratified that they had seen my photo in the *Daily
Telegraph*. As far as they were concerned I was already a success

story – sophisticated, married, a sanguine young thespian. I sensed they mentioned me to their girlfriends or colleagues. 'I was at school with him, you know. Bit of a long-haired rebel he was then. Always the actor. He doesn't get the big parts but he's making his way.' At the time, their mirrored view of me seemed important to my sense of self. If they thought I was a racy young actor riding high, who was I to argue?

I had finally acquired an agent, an enthusiastic bubble of a woman called Liz Robinson. She sent me off to meet producers and directors and probably believed in my talent more than I did myself. She introduced me to Bernard Miles at the Mermaid Theatre who gave me the part of Prince Cosmo in *Galileo*. I had five lines and wore a swanky all-white costume. Bernard warned me it cost ten times more than I did so to be careful not to spill coffee on it. Liz even got me a featured role in a weird film called *Secrets of the Windmill Girls*. I was Mike, stage manager of the Windmill Theatre opposite Pauline Collins as a fan-dancer. I received my first insight into the mysteries of screen acting when the director, just before he yelled 'Action', gave me a helpful tip: 'Martin,' he said, 'this is a very, very emotional scene so wave your arms about a bit.' I began to receive reviews that said things like 'Martin Jarvis approaches the role of Jonathan in an inappropriate "jeune-premier" manner', or, if I was slightly luckier, 'Morris is attractively played by Jarvis'. Attractively played was how I felt about my life in the suburbs and those cheerful chats with my generous-spirited fellow commuters.

One day Liz Robinson rang excitedly to say she had arranged an audition for me. Michael Codron, she told me, the West End's newest and most avant-garde producer, was putting on *Cockade*, a play by a new writer, Charles Wood. The director wanted to see me. Next day I went along to the Arts Theatre. I had started to develop a technique for these sort of interviews. My approach was to appear to be coolly knowledgeable about the script and pretend that I shared something of the background of the character for which I was being considered. I soon found out this was a dangerous game to play. The director was a dark-bearded smoothie called Patrick Dromgoole. Since the part I was up for was a young cockney soldier, I walked on-stage to meet Patrick completely in character, greeting him with 'Wotcha mate!' Patrick, who had never laid eyes on me before, smiled expansively. He expounded about the play and the part. I responded, whenever I could get a word in, with 'Yeah', 'Smashin', and 'Gotcha!' I could tell he liked this engaging young Eastender. After ten minutes, he told me I was just the sort of young fella he wanted to play the rookie and the part was mine. That was where my problems began. I was stuck with this chirpy cockney persona. During the subsequent rehearsal period I daren't come clean and open my mouth off-stage for fear my Rada vowels would give the game away and I would be sacked. I spent most of the time avoiding the director or, when I couldn't dodge a coffee-break conversation, spoke in monosyllables. I caught him looking at me strangely several times and I knew he was wondering where the cheeky chappie who had seemed so right for the part had gone. I decided never to give myself such an identity crisis again.

In the winter of 1963, after the short run of *Cockade*, Codron gave me the small but crucial part of Franz Delanoue in Anouilh's *Poor Bitos* at the Duke of York's Theatre. I had one great scene with Bitos, played by Donald Pleasence, in which I had to produce a revolver and, after a tense confrontation, fire it point-blank into his face. I still managed, somehow, to be 'attractive' in the part, despite a savage crew-cut, dirty raincoat and what I believed to be a particularly belligerent Parisian demeanour. Pleasence was surprisingly kind to me, both on-stage and off, even insisting on my appearing with him in a television excerpt of the play. My other task in this production was to understudy (for an extra five pounds a week) the suave Charles Gray, who played Maxime, Bitos's old schoolfriend. I was twenty-two years old and relished the lip-curling dialogue: 'I loathe you, Bitos. I have always loathed you – ever since we were at school together.' Since Pleasence was old enough to be my father, I wasn't ideal casting, though I actually got to play the part when Charles Gray was taken ill. Michael Codron told me afterwards that my performance was vocally extremely assured. 'When I closed my eyes,' he said, 'you sounded exactly right.'

Generously, he didn't tell me what he thought when he opened them.

In 1965 my old mentor, Clement Scott Gilbert, mounted a revival of Shaw's *Man and Superman* in London. The old Pembroke in Croydon had been demolished after four years to make way for a road-widening scheme. Clement had rented the the Arts Theatre as a stepping stone to transferring the production to a major West End theatre. An intense young Canadian, Philip Wiseman, having had some successes on television, was hired to direct. Somehow, after two auditions and no doubt some nudging from Clement, I was offered the excruciatingly difficult part of Octavius Robinson. This is probably Shaw's most unplayable young man and even the fact that Octavius and I seemed to share a certain youthful ingenuousness didn't seem to help. Clement was presenting the play in conjunction with Peter O'Toole and we had heard that the great, rabble-rousing O'Toole himself was to play the leading role of Jack Tanner opposite his then wife Siân Phillips. It turned out that a few weeks before we were due to begin rehearsals O'Toole was offered a film with Audrey Hepburn and that Jack was now to be played by the smouldering Alan Badel, father of my old Rada friend Sarah. Alan was already something of a legend when I first met him in the Swiss Cottage church hall where we had our readthrough. Once more I felt out of place. There was something vaguely ludicrous in my inhabiting the role of Octavius, since he was supposed to be contemporary with Tanner. It seemed to be the Maxime/Bitos problem all over again. During coffee breaks or at lunchtime, various members of the cast would approach me with well-meant suggestions that I should consider growing a beard. Old Marie Lohr, one of the great pre-war actress-managers and still a powerful leading lady in her late seventies, suggested a few make-up ideas that might add gravitas. Siân Phillips suggested a small moustache. All their friendly concern only made it clearer to me that I was too young to get away with the part.

The only person who seemed unconcerned at the disparity between us was Alan himself. But he had problems of his own. He told me, many years later, that he had felt he was really too *old* for Tanner. He had the utmost difficulty in learning Shaw's lines, he said, and that, for him, everything throughout the short rehearsal period had been resolutely focused on committing the huge part to memory. Shaw, like Wilde, is enormously difficult to learn. Many of the speeches are set pieces that depend for their apparent naturalness on knowing absolutely where you are aiming when you begin the speech and driving right through to the conclusion of what can, initially, seem a tortuous journey. Building in false pauses and so-called natural breaks doesn't help. I was reminded of this recently when preparing *The Doctor's Dilemma* at the Almeida Theatre. The great medical 'discussions' in that play only really became accessible to the audience when we were able to dive from the top board, as it were, and, with plenty of breath in reserve, keep swimming to the other end. It's very easy to drown in Shaw for lack of oxygen.

I noticed, as we continued our work on *Man and Superman*, how wary some of my fellow actors were of Badel. I had heard the stories – how 'difficult' he was, how he didn't suffer fools gladly, how he 'ate directors for breakfast'. Surely it would have been less frightening to have been working with Peter O'Toole. I was already aware, from my friendship with Sarah, of Alan's razor-sharp perception about the whole business of acting, his need to understand the mind of the writer, his forensic obsession with the details of the text. Even after we had opened I found it inhibiting, as I crept past Alan's dressing room on my way to the stage, to meet a beady eye looking out for me and to hear the throaty voice exclaim, 'Aha – Martin, come in a minute. I think I can help you.' In fact he did. Every point he raised was relevant and encouraged me to think about my acting and how it related to Octavius's function in the play. He often talked about the 'size' of performance. There was no such thing as over-acting, he believed. 'It doesn't matter how big it is,' he would exclaim, nostrils flaring, 'as long as it's filled from inside!'

'Filled with what?' I inquired earnestly.

'The *truth* of course,' he replied, tossing his head like a restive stallion.

All the younger members of the cast copied him slavishly. Some nights there would be two or three would-be Badels on stage, all of us flaring our nostrils, tilting our heads and exhaling our lines with the breathy passion we so much admired. When I considered later how crass some of my rather obvious playing of the role was, and how, after I had absorbed his various suggestions on pausing, thinking, reacting, timing, actually delving into the text for all my answers, I was amazed he hadn't demanded my removal from the cast in the first week.

There was no doubt that Alan could have crucified me for my lack of experience in such a complex role. I was too young and, technically, he was too old. But his temperament and fire were absolutely right for Tanner. Alan was fairly short and stocky; his greying hair was dyed red for the part; his voice lacked resonance in the bass notes, owing to a wartime accident in which he had been blown up in France. This had also made him deaf. Yet his effect on an audience was mesmerising. He had developed his own way of projecting the husky, breathy tones to the back of the theatre. His powerful intellect, combined with the life and force of Shaw's dialogue, really did hold audiences in thrall. His mind was like a laser beam. I could see that his reputation for being 'difficult' stemmed pretty much from being unable to suffer gladly those he considered fools.

During rehearsals, our well-meaning director suffered most at Alan's hands. Philip Wiseman, worrying over aspects of the production, would nervously flutter about, sometimes shunting an actor across to a new position, even dragging Marie Lohr like a magnificent piece of Victorian furniture from sofa to chair to chaise-longue in an effort to improve the staging. One afternoon, while we were still rehearsing at the Arts Theatre, Philip made the mistake of attempting to propel our star a pace or two backwards by prodding him with two nervous hands. Suddenly, we sensed that something odd was happening. It was as if lightning had struck. Alan, ex-army paratrooper, stood completely still, breathing in sharply. Wherever we were in the little theatre, either on-stage, grouped in the wings, or slumped in the stalls, we just stood and watched. Alan's eyes blazed. He took a sharp pace forward, grabbed poor Wiseman simultaneously by the collar of his jacket and the seat of his trousers, raised him effortlessly into the air and carried him in one sweeping movement to the front of the stage, depositing him over the edge and into the front row of the stalls. 'Philip,' Alan breathed, 'don't ever dare lay a hand on me again. Draw a performance out of me, if you will. Never, ever, try to push one into me.'.

Siân Phillips said to me afterwards, 'Of course he's mad you know, darling. Marvellous, but quite mad.' I said nothing. I had been rather impressed as I stood next to Clive Swift and Ed Bishop, watching from the back of the auditorium. I was so taken by the cool drama of the incident that, for several years afterwards, I was always on the look-out for a tactile director to whom I could at least deliver the 'draw it out of me' line, even if the personnel-carrying part of it was unlikely to be a possibility. When, three years later, the American movie director Walter Grauman did indeed push and pull me around the set of *The Last Escape* to line up his shots, he propelled me with such charm and with so many apologies ('Sorry about this, Mart'n – don't mean to use you as a chess piece but we're against the clock here') that of course I replied meekly that it was perfectly all right and that I quite understood.

Alan's deafness made him even more unpredictable. Some evenings, after we had transferred to the Garrick Theatre for a long run, I would bump into him as we made our way towards the stage door. 'Ah ha, Martin!' he would beam, with chin thrust upwards and a Gallic toss of the head (Sarah had told me at Rada, with pride, that he was half French), 'Are you ready for tonight?'

'Er – yes,' I would reply – I really was quite intimidated by him – and then follow it up with, 'How are you, Alan?'

The flashing eyes would gaze hard at me for a moment. Then he would consult his watch and say, with the keenest energy, 'Half past six.'

My inquiries were not entirely disinterested. Because of his wartime injury, any head cold would render him virtually voiceless and even deafer than usual. The brilliantly husbanded throaty whisper, which was all that remained in these circumstances, was adored by his admiring fans, especially women, who had thrilled to the intimacy of his D'Arcy and his Count of Monte Cristo on television. I am sure he developed the expressive physicality of his acting as a result of less than reliable vocality. The difficulty was that if Alan could not appear, not only were his fans disappointed but the rest of us had to perform the play with his well-meaning understudy, Leonard. Leonard was efficient – but no one could stand in for Badel. The night eventually arrived when Alan had a bad cold, probably flu. I learnt, when I arrived at the theatre, that he could not be heard at a distance of three feet. Having had an emotional meeting with Clement and Siân Phillips, conducted on Alan's side mostly in mime, he had reluctantly agreed there was nothing for it but to go back home to Lambeth and to bed.

There was a second problem. Clive Swift had just phoned in. He had been informed by his doctor that he had got mumps. Which gave us all a third problem. Especially Leonard. He was the *only* male understudy. I had heard from Joan, the stage manager, that understudy rehearsals had been particularly interesting since Shaw's great play became, every Tuesday afternoon, a one-man show starring Leonard. Clearly he couldn't reprise his day-time versatility tonight. Indeed, he was already climbing into Badel's boxy brown suit while Jean from wardrobe made appropriate adjustments. There was nobody else in the company who could possibly take on Clive's part as 'Enery Straker, the cockney chauffeur.

Clement Scott Gilbert took the decision. Somebody would have to be found to *read* the part. Though not vast, Straker is a superbly written, play-stealing role. Almost. If Clive had not had Alan himself as Tanner, he would certainly have made off with the evening, as many a Straker had before him. But nobody could snaffle a play from under the aquiline nose of Badel.

It was nearly six-thirty. Who could we get? Clement had an idea. He set off up St Martin's Lane for the famous theatrical pub, the Salisbury. We later heard that he went into the large Victorian main bar where traditionally actors, employed and unemployed, drank after a day of rehearsing or auditioning. Some even knocked back a Guinness or two before strolling across to Wyndham's or the Albery Theatre for their night's work. Clement took a look around the mirrored room. He clapped his hands and called for silence. A few gin and tonics were lowered and several eyebrows raised. Clement cleared his throat. 'Good evening,' he announced to the assembled company. 'Is there anyone here who would care to appear as Henry Straker in *Man and Superman* at the Garrick tonight?' This was an extraordinary moment even in an establishment so much beyond surprise as the Salisbury. Certainly never had a major Shavian role been placed on offer in such a way before. There was a brief pause and, as glasses and conversation were taken up again, a sandy haired man stood up and said, 'Yes. I don't mind.' His name, it turned out, was Keith Grenville. He was a rep actor, in London to try his luck. He must have thought the legend was true – the old maxim about being in the right place at the right time. Clement hot-footed him back to the theatre before he could change his mind and brought him into the dressing room I normally shared with Clive.

I told Keith I thought he was very brave to be going on in half an hour's time, with no rehearsal. He then asked me what the play was about. He'd never read it, he said. I told him he was even braver than I thought. I took the script Clement had given him and, as I underlined the words of his part, I explained as best I could who Straker was and what was expected of him. Keith seemed remarkably cool as he put on the chauffeur's uniform and knotted his tie. 'This'll be my West End debut,' he said nonchalantly.

Clement elected to make a personal announcement to the eight-hundred-strong audience. He strode out in front of the curtain. I noticed, as I stood in the wings ready for my first entrance, that sweat glistened on the dome of his tanned forehead. He cleared his throat and, for the second time that evening, began nervously, in his curiously cultured drawl, 'Ladies and gentlemen – at tonight's performance, owing to the indisposition of Mr Alan Badel, the role of Jack Tanner will be played by Leonard Woodrow.' A disappointed murmur rippled through the audience and I could hear the sharp thump of several seats bouncing upwards as their occupants departed. Clement raised his voice an octave: 'And, owing also to the indisposition of Mr Clive Swift, the role of Straker will be read by –' he glanced down at the scrap of paper in his shaking hand '– by Keith Grenville.' More seats thumped, some mutterings, then all was quiet.

The curtain rose. After a few lines of dialogue from the elderly actor John Robinson as Roebuck Ramsden, the maid entered, announced 'Mr Octavius Robinson', and, for the two hundredth time, I made my entrance. Usually this moment excited only a modicum of interest from the audience. Tonight, I sensed, was going to be different. As I came on I was greeted by an eruption of applause such as was normally reserved for Alan himself when he came bursting through the doors minutes later. Clearly the audience assumed that this pale-faced young man was one of the courageous understudies. My first line, habitually received in silence, was tonight greeted with an encouraging laugh. The scene continued in this way with best-ever reactions to my Octavius. The door opened again and Leonard leapt on to the stage in Alan's suit. I could almost hear the audience reassessing the situation – *this* is the understudy, *not* the callow young man. It was too late to applaud Leonard but they made up for it by falling about at his every utterance while freezing me out altogether. Lines of mine that each night for the last six months had gone down a treat, were now received in frosty silence as Leonard garnered warm responses in places that would have surprised even Alan.

The second act was reserved for Keith Grenville's long-awaited West End debut. He came trotting on in the full chauffeur gear, goggles and cap at a jaunty angle and carrying the book. He read perfectly. He was a riot. This had nothing to do with the generosity of the audience. It was simply that Shaw's lines and rhythms are so speakable, his ideas so superbly accessible that the 'new man' comedy of 'Enery Straker, projected instinctually and spontaneously by the actor, inevitably brings down the house. For Grenville, who had barely had time to absorb the part, the house was at his feet. He and Shaw were triumphant.

Fascinatingly, after he had had time to find out a bit more about the play, Keith's triumph was noticeably less. At the end of the week, when he had learnt the entire part, we were longing for Clive to recover from his mumps. No discredit to Keith, who had actually done an extraordinary job, but it illustrated a point often discussed by actors that if it's not possible to rehearse in depth for, say, a month, it might almost be better (sometimes) to jump in bravely and wing it.

Seven months into the run of Man and Superman something equally strange occurred on stage. I was half way through my love scene with Siân Phillips, when I felt myself starting to black out. The lights began to spin. I couldn't catch my breath. It was momentary, and somehow I was able to pull myself back and complete the scene. It happened again a few nights later. Then, with increasing regularity, at almost every performance and always at the same point of high tension in the play. It was connected with my breathing and to the fact that I now seemed to have a permanent cold. More than a cold – I really couldn't breathe properly. I had to keep my mouth open on stage like some sort of performing goldfish. It began to be a challenge to get through each performance. The fearful moment in the scene with Siân loomed larger and larger each night. I started to dread coming into the theatre, to dread getting ready and walking on to the stage. One night, as I sloped out of the stage door and down the alley into the Charing Cross Road, I overheard a theatregoer asking someone who the awful adenoidal actor was. A few nights later Clement asked me what was wrong. I told him I didn't know.

It was a great relief to me when the long run of Man and Superman finally came to a close in spring 1966. Certainly there was something wrong with my voice, but, spared the unremitting necessity to use it on-stage for eight performances a week, the pressure lessened. I was now, it seemed, just a bunged-up actor trying to get some work in television. I discovered a nasal spray in a bilious-coloured plastic bottle. Squirted sharply up the nose before filming a scene, it seemed to keep the worst of the problem at bay, allowing me to breathe relatively normally for a few hours.

One of its side effects, though, was that it removed some of the bass notes in my voice, so most of my parts around that time sounded as if they were played by a very lightweight tenor who had narrowly survived strangulation at birth. Worse still, the powerful spray produced a negative reaction after its best effects had worn off. Following a couple of days of heavy dosing, my nasal membrane became flabby and spongy and I sounded more adenoidal than before. Hardly compatible with any of the charming-young-men parts Liz Robinson was trying to get for me at the time.

Was this whole ear-nose-and-throat disaster merely psychosomatic? Somebody had told me that anxiety always arrowed-in to your most vulnerable spot – the dancer worries about her back; the athlete becomes preoccupied with his leg muscles; the singer is throat-obsessed. Was my voice my most vulnerable spot? My best thing? Right from the beginning, all those schoolboy imitations of Gielgud and Olivier had been very much to do with the voice. I remembered someone at Rada telling me that Clifford Turner had waxed lyrical to another class about 'young Jarvis's verse-speaking. Don't know where it comes from but he's certainly got a voice,' said Clifford. Frighteningly, my 'best thing' seemed to be disappearing. I became dependent on the spray.

A call came from Liz Robinson. Trendy young television producer Verity Lambert was looking for a young man to guest-star in 'The Web Planet' – six episodes of the smash-hit series 'Dr Who'. She wanted to meet me.

I sat opposite Verity in her office at the BBC and tried to look like the sort of leading actor she was seeking. I was wearing my new grey jacket and dark trousers from Harry Fenton Outfitters in Croydon High Street, pink button-down-collar shirt, maroon woollen tie, brown suede shoes. Cool. I had fired a couple of shots up each nostril an hour before and, apart from the usual disconcerting lightening of my vocal register, I didn't feel too bad. I leant back in my chair. I liked the look of Verity. She didn't seem much older than me and I knew she was one of the most powerful producers in television. She had a Mary Quant gloss about her: short dark hair sassooned into an angular bob, smoky eyes, pale face, baby-pink lips, black skinny-rib sweater and short skirt. I thought about asking her for a drink afterwards. She began explaining about Dr Who. She told me she wanted someone like me to play Hilio, the young prince of a doomed planet, who was battling to save his dying world from the onslaught of an invading force. He was noble, vengeful, ambitious, the Hamlet of his galaxy. I leant back further. 'Ah ha,' I sniffed, with Badelian pride, 'up my street.'

Verity gazed at me for a few seconds from under heavy lashings of mascara, before indicating a pile of scripts. Well, it wasn't Hamlet in Elsinore but, if I got the part, it would keep the mortgage going on the flat. She looked at me again. 'Martin,' she said, slightly soulfully, I thought, 'I would love you to be my Hilio.'

I sniffed again. Yes, I thought, I *will* suggest a drink in the BBC Club. The young guest-star and his voguish producer. I leant forward, looked deep into her eyes and said I'd be delighted to accept.

She smiled and tossed a couple of sheets of paper across the desk: 'These are the costume designs.'

I picked up the one labelled 'Hilio, Prince of the Menoptra'. I studied it. For a long time. It was basically a picture of a giant butterfly. Furry black-and-white striped body, black legs (quite a few of them). No actual face. No proper mouth. Just a black expanse of oval head above the stick-like neck. No eyes, except for two great bulbous circles goggling darkly out at me. Two antenna attachments emerged from the inky forehead. And wings, spreading outwards from the giant thorax. Prince Hilio of the Menoptra. Hamlet as insect.

'That's you,' said Verity. 'Still want to do it?'

Rehearsals took place in a church hall near the Television Centre in Shepherd's Bush. William Hartnell, the first and crustiest of all the Dr Whos, didn't speak to me very much – and didn't attend many of the rehearsals. The rest of us rehearsed each episode for a week, before recording at BBC TV Centre. There were three other Menoptra but I was the only royal one. We had to remain behind each day for special insect-movement classes after the main rehearsal had finished. Verity and her keen young director Richard were determined that this butterfly world was going to be believable. They had hired a frosty faced choreographer called Miss de Wynter to coach me and the other three in authentic Menoptrean behaviour. Her unsmiling intensity reminded me of Yat, Christopher and Johnny back at Rada. She insisted on our assuming a kind of strutting, arrogant walk that she considered appropriate to our life on the Web Planet. She decided we should hold our arms high above our shoulders, with the fingers of each hand tightly together and curved to emulate the front legs of our role models. She then had the idea that the proboscis gash of the hidden butterfly mouth could be achieved by setting one's upper lip an inch outwards whilst simultaneously stretching the lower lip wide and downwards.

A discussion naturally ensued as to how the Menoptra should speak. With difficulty, clearly. I put forward the view that our struggle for survival against the marauding Zarbi (giant ants, also played by a group of actors confronting their own problems of physical characterisation) was the main thrust of the story. Didn't we already seem rather comic, stalking about in this stylised manner? Wouldn't it be even more risible, I suggested, for us to speak as if we had no roofs to our mouths? Our coach replied tersely that she didn't see how we *could* speak naturally with stretched jaws and widened upper lips. My point precisely, I told her. There were murmurs of agreement from the other Menoptra. One of them came up with the idea that perhaps we could speak from the back of our throats in a sort of high-pitched whine and wouldn't that sound rather noble and aristocratic? Miss de Wynter saw the logic of this approach. So that's how we did it, strutting and prancing and whining as we battled to rescue our planet from the ants. Rehearsals were a nightmare.

'You're not very comfortable with this character, are you Martin?' said Miss de Wynter after we had completed the final run-through of the first episode.

'What do you think?' I sniffed.

Actually the only thing I was marginally relieved about was

that the high nasal delivery foisted upon us worked quite well in conjunction with my current cocktail of spray and catarrh.

Verity and Richard had another creative treat in store for me when I arrived at the studio to film my first entrance. They had decided that Hilio should literally fly in, wings outstretched, land on a rocky lump of molten lava and, from this vantage point, deliver his initial statement to the other assembled bugs and aphids. Before I had time to inquire how this was to be achieved, I was told to report to wardrobe. Here I was introduced to a dour man known as 'Inky' who held some sort of leather strait-jacket in one hand and a length of rope in the other. He looked like a hangman. Inky told me he was from Kirby's Flying Ballet and would I put my legs and arms through these loops. It turned out that he was responsible, every Christmas, for Peter Pan's daring flights from Never-Never Land by way of the Scala Theatre, Bloomsbury. There was nothing for it. I climbed into the harness and two dressers helped me on with my furry body, black-and-white striped leggings and long black mittens. They lowered a sort of fencing mask over the top half of my head with just enough black gauze over the goggling eyes for me to see out. Two make-up girls were simultaneously attending to the lower half of my face, painting zebra-style stripes along my nose, jaw and neck to match the licorice-allsort effect of my Menoptrean torso and legs. The eight-foot-wide wings were now lovingly attached to my back by the costume designer herself, Daphne Dare, who reminded me anxiously to be very careful going through the double-doors on to the set – and to remember to ask her personally to detach the wings at lunchtime before I went up in the lift to the canteen.

I inched my way to the studio. It was hard to move quickly, partly because of the wings and partly because of Peter Pan's constricting leather thongs that ran between my legs, across my back and chest, with two heavy metal rings emerging from the top of my thorax – ready to accommodate the high-wire attachments. 'We'll shoot this one straight away,' called Richard keenly. Oh good. Inky fiddled about behind me, hooking me up, and suddenly I was being hauled into the air. There I hung, crutch on fire, thirty feet above my molten rock, until the moment came for me to be flown down to land on my lump of lava (with only minimal wobble) and, mittened hands held high, high voice higher, exclaim to old William Hartnell, 'Ah ha, Doctor, welcome to my dying planet.'

My ambition during this six-week engagement had shrunk somewhat. My immediate goals were to be able to rehearse and perform with some sort of dignity and to resist the temptation to tell my movement coach that I had actually turned down the Royal Shakespeare Company to do Hilio. My other aim, which shows the kind of shifting strangeness that was going on inside me at the time, was to be able to park my little Austin A35 inside the main Television Centre car park. Unless you were William Hartnell, or had a tremendous backlog of film and television roles that gave you cachet with the security guard at the gate, you would be refused entry and told to drive up Wood Lane to a piece of waste ground half a mile away. You had then to trudge all the way back to the Centre. The legendary one-armed Vic held this power of veto. He stood there at the gates to paradise in his black epauletted raincoat and peaked hat, empty left-hand sleeve tucked away in his coat pocket, right arm either waving you in to one of those prized spaces or, in my case, directing me up the road to the distant wasteland.

I always made an attempt to gain entry. 'Hello, Vic,' I would grin, in my best juvenile-lead manner, 'I'm working with Bill Hartnell today. All right to drive in?'

He would give me a basilisk stare, shake his head and gesture northwards.

Sometimes I would say: 'Only going to be here a short time today, Vic.' That never worked either. Once, after he had given the usual thumb-down, I stuck my head out of the window and said, 'OK, will you ring the Dr Who studio, ask for Verity Lambert and explain that her guest-star Martin Jarvis has reported for work but you have refused him entry? Tell her I am returning home – to Croydon.' Pretty good, I thought.

Vic's hatchet face cracked momentarily into a tight smile: 'No chance,' he said, and gestured up the road.

I didn't have the guts to stick to my guns. 'It was worth a try,' I told him, as I reversed out into the street.

In the early summer of 1966, Liz Robinson telephoned, all of a twitter, to tell me that the BBC were making a mammoth serialised version of Galsworthy's *Forsyte Saga*. She had persuaded the producer, Donald Wilson, to meet me for the coveted role of gauche young Jon Forsyte. Wasn't it exciting? He had agreed to see me tomorrow. I put down the phone. Perfect, I thought. Sniff sniff.

Wilson was an urbane pipe-smoking Scot who had been, until then, Head of BBC Television Serials. He had resigned his post in order to deal exclusively with the televising of his life-long obsession, the *Forsyte Saga*. He welcomed me with avuncular charm to his clubbable carpeted office overlooking Shepherd's Bush Green and told me he had heard I was splendid as Octavius at the Garrick. It struck me then, and I still rather subscribe to the theory today, that it's often helpful if some prospective employer has heard that you played a significant part in a successful production but didn't actually *see* it. I smiled modestly. He began to expound on his favourite subject. He told me how he had, at last, after many years of negotiation, managed to get the rights to the Forsyte novels from MGM, and how it was the most ambitious BBC project ever. There were to be twenty-six episodes in all and filming was already under way. He was thrilled that Royal Shakespeare actor Eric Porter was being so brilliant as Soames Forsyte and that New Zealand actress Nyree Dawn Porter (no relation to Eric) was playing the beautiful mysterious Irene 'quite wonderfully'. One of my schoolboy heroes, the breezy Kenneth More, had the part of the artistic Young Jolyon. 'Pretty damn good cast, eh.' Donald winked at me and drew satisfactorily on his pipe. I nodded brightly. He told me that the popular young film actress Susan Hampshire had agreed to play the key role of Fleur and that, if I secured the part of Jon, her cousin and lover, I would be filming with them all at idyllic locations in Sussex and Berkshire in a month's time. I grinned and nodded brightly again. Then a chubby cheerful-looking man in his mid-thirties wearing a baggy beige cardigan bounced into Donald's room. He was introduced as James Cellan Jones, one of the Forsyte directors. I noticed he sported opened-toed sandals and no socks. Bit of a BBC rebel perhaps? He gave me a hearty handshake and said, 'You were an awfully good Octavius I believe!'

I gave a deprecating shrug and said, 'Oh, well, thanks.' So far so good.

Donald and Jim now explained the part of Jon Forsyte to me. He is young, callow, nervous, eager to please. (Me.) He's nineteen in the episode in which he makes his initial appearance with Fleur and finishes the series as a young family man of twenty-six. (Me again – sniff, sniff.) They gave me a handful of scripts to take home and said they would make up their minds in a few days.

As I walked through the door of the flat two hours later, the phone was ringing. It was Liz at the other end. 'You got it, you got it,' she carolled. 'Isn't it wonderful! They loved you. They think you are so right for Jon. They said they loved your "damp" look.' (Sniff.)

I met Susan Hampshire for the first time a few weeks later in Jim Cellan Jones' office where we had been called to read through the scenes we were to film in Sussex. She was immaculately turned out and I was fascinated by the little tartan peaked cap she wore perched at a jaunty angle on her lustrous fair hair. She had the same Mary Quant eyes as Verity Lambert. Already a successful young film star, she must have wondered why some young screen gallant wasn't cast opposite her. So did I. She put her hand into mine, shook it delicately, looked at me closely and giggled a lot. When I heard her reading her part, I realised she was perfectly cast as Fleur Forsyte. Every nuance, every inflection was Galsworthy's character straight from the books. In contrast, I felt that my own reading sounded dull, forced and unreal.

As Sue and I got to know each other during filming, I became fascinated by the wonderfully wheedling manner she adopted when speaking in the character of the many faceted Fleur. Her voice became small and clipped and bright and careful like a tiny sparkling jewel. I told her I thought it sounded marvellous and asked her where it came from. 'Oh, it's easy,' she said. 'It's the voice I use when I talk to little children and furry animals.' Of course there was much more to Susan than just the neat little voice. She had a great eye for detail. When she spotted the way I was holding my knife in an alfresco dinner scene, she suggested to me quietly (in the furry animal voice) that it might be better if I held it like this: and showed me how. My suburban slip was showing. She, by contrast, was intensely cosmopolitan. She had recently made a film in France and had fallen in love with its handsome director, Pierre Granier-Deferre. She was now engaged to him. Before disappearing to Paris every weekend to see him, she would regale me with tales of Pierre's previous marriage, how she had met him, how passionately romantic he was, how jealous he could be. Occasionally, as we continued to work on the series, Pierre would fly to England and suddenly appear, scowling, on the set. Susan would whisper to me that he could not bear to watch our more intimate scenes. I felt distinctly uneasy in some of our passionate clinches as I caught glimpses of him lurking behind the cameras, drawing tensely on a Gauloise and looking darkly across at me. Even though he could not bear to watch, it seemed to me he conquered his aversion pretty well and there wasn't much he missed. It occurred to me that, as a director and a Frenchman, he probably hated the bland way I was acting the part of the English lover and that he could have shown me a thing or two about how to make love on the screen.

All the early scenes between Sue and me were directed by the sockless Jim Cellan Jones. (David Giles directed our later episodes.) As we filmed with him in Sussex, I sensed that we were involved in something special. There were still budgetary restrictions, though (apart from my own miniscule fee). The whole thing was being shot in black-and-white, even though colour television was to be introduced to the nation only a year hence. Apparently Donald Wilson, having finally secured the rights from America, had no choice but to go ahead and make the series straight away rather than delay it for a year and lose his option. If the *Forsyte Saga* had been made in colour it would no doubt still be turning up on television screens all over the world to this day.

Budget-conscious Wilson had forbidden Jim to spend any extra BBC cash on a particular shot in which Jon and Fleur take off from a stile near the top of Chanctonbury Ring and run down the hillside, Jon singing (fairly tunelessly) 'Sweet Lass of Richmond Hill'. Jim had secretly confided to us that he wanted to shoot this scene from the air – a kittiwake's view of young love's dream far below. Since Wilson had a disconcerting habit of turning up at the location without warning, Jim cunningly waited until the conclusion of one of these surprise visits when Donald had departed back to London. Then he put his plan into action. A helicopter, hired from the RAF and standing by at Shoreham a few miles away, now appeared overhead with cameraman Tony Leggo precariously leaning out of the open hatch. Sue and I took our places at the top of the hill, Jim called 'Action', and one of the most enduring images of the *Saga* was recorded on film – the two fleeing Forsytes racing down the valley, tiny figures in the landscape, smaller and smaller as the budget-busting chopper climbs higher and higher until all Sussex is spread out below. We were told spontaneous applause burst out in the projection room two days later when Wilson and his production team viewed the rushes. He adored the sequence, and Jim, who had been prepared to pay for the helicopter himself, was congratulated and told that money would be found to cover the extra expense.

Everybody agreed that Donald Wilson had cast the ideal actress for Irene in the person of Nyree Dawn Porter. It was clear, from a conversation I had with him on location as we stood side by side in a gent's loo, that he thought so too. Donald suddenly murmured, 'Have you met your mother yet?' I couldn't, for a second, think what he meant. Everything with Donald related to his Forsyte obsession; he was referring to his leading lady. 'Your mother, Nyree, er, Irene.'

I told him I hadn't had that pleasure yet. I wouldn't be meeting her until we rehearsed the interior scenes in a few weeks' time.

Donald's eyes sparkled and his ruddy cheeks creased upwards in pleasure as he stood in front of the porcelain: 'Oh Martin, you'll love her. She's a wonderful person, Nyree, Irene. Face of an angel. Body of a peasant. You'll love her, Jon, er, Martin.'

It didn't take a rocket scientist to work out that Donald's dividing line between the Forsytes and their portrayers was wafer-thin.

When, finally, I did meet Nyree and we began to rehearse our mother-and-son scenes, I found her charming. I noticed, too, that I couldn't help behaving towards her, on and off the set, with an uncontrollable deference. I would get up when she entered the room, offer her my seat, and generally treat her like nobility – never for a moment stopping to consider that she was actually a lively ex-dancer who had come over from New Zealand with her actor husband only a few years previously to seek her fortune. The combination of her gracious demeanour and the fact that she was playing my mother in a stately grey wig, made me forget that she wasn't much older than me anyway.

Except for the exterior filming, we were required to record many of the episodes as if they were live transmissions. This meant moving from scene to scene without a break. It was another of Donald's financial strictures; there would be less time (and money) spent on editing the recording afterwards. It went something like this: I would play a bedroom scene in pyjamas and dressing gown, then dive out of them at the side of the set, leap into full evening gear while a dresser tied my bow-tie and another laced my patent leather shoes, duck under the cameras, and race across the studio floor to lean nonchalantly on the grand piano as if I had been there for ages. As Irene finished playing an exquisite *étude*, I spoke my line, trying not to sound out of breath: 'Mmm. That was so lovely, Mother.' Nyree said to me afterwards, as I bought her a pineapple juice in the BBC Club and found her a comfortable seat, 'Mart'n –' (there was just a trace of a cute New Zealand accent) '– Let me give you a word of advice.' I took the vacant chair beside her. She leant forward and put a hand on my arm. 'Mart'n – don't let them rush you.' She smiled indulgently and I thanked her with as much grateful courtesy as if she had been the magisterial Miss Phillips at Rada, old Marie Lohr at the Garrick, or my own South Norwood grandma.

Irene's second husband (my father) was played by the genial

Kenneth More – known to all as Kenny. He was an authentic British film star, though since the new wave of regional working-class movies featuring Finney, Courtenay and Richard Harris, his star had been somewhat in the descendant. I was thrilled to be working with one of my idols, the ebullient hero of *Reach for the Sky*, *Genevieve* and *The Deep Blue Sea*. Once, on a schoolboy trip to London in the late fifties, I had been walking up the Haymarket with my friend Dave Nordemann, on our way to gaze at the voguish black-and-white Angus McBean production photos outside the Theatre Royal, when we spotted a great beige Rolls-Royce coming slowly down the street towards us. The passenger window had been wound down and a tanned figure in a colourful Hawaiian shirt, arm resting casually half in and half out, was grinning and chatting loudly to the chauffeur as they purred along – Kenneth More giving his public a good look at him.

Although Eric Porter had the number one leading role of Soames Forsyte, it was Kenny who was treated very much as the star of the *Saga* (at least until the first episodes were transmitted, after which Eric and Nyree became stars in their own right). I could see that the production team were enraptured to have this hugely recognisable character in their midst and loved saying, 'Morning Kenny, Cheers Kenny, Martin, do you know Kenny?' and blushed with pleasure when he hailed them blithely, remembering all their names. I soon got the feeling that Kenny himself was much relieved to have secured the part of Young Jolyon Forsyte, though his character departed, after an affecting death scene, in my third episode.

Kenny's natural screen acting was an education for me. I watched him like a hawk during rehearsals and was intrigued to see how, with apparent truth and simplicity, he related every moment of his character's behaviour to the camera. I was fascinated by the way, in many of his scenes with the girls, he would suddenly approach them from behind and, saying something like 'Well, my darling, we must tell young Jon about this,' grasp them by the tops of their shoulders, continuing to talk and stroke at the same time. The actor as masseur. I decided it was a carefully judged method of ensuring he wasn't out of shot for too long. I could see, too, that it was an excellent way of creating a strong 'two-shot' in which he held the dominant position. Our director seemed quite happy for Kenny to create his own positions, even though his choices influenced the camera angles. Jim did attempt to suggest some alternative moves in one emotional scene that Kenny had to play with me, where my character's story line was equal in importance to his own. Kenny considered the option for about two seconds and shook his head. 'No no, old love,' he told Jim, 'the punters want to know what I am thinking. They won't have a clue if I'm over there.' He was probably right. Nevertheless, having had nearly a year of observing Alan Badel unerringly find the most effective spot on the stage at any given moment, I was ready for Kenny, or so I thought. At one camera rehearsal, during a pivotal speech of mine, I sensed him approaching from behind. 'Well, dear old Jon,' he breezed, reaching forward and placing his hands on my shoulders in an unrehearsed move. Aha. Beginning my next line, I turned and swiftly motored away in Badelian style to continue my speech from the other side of the room. It didn't do me any good. The camera, knowing where the money was, stayed resolutely on Kenny. I was out of it for the rest of the scene.

As I got to know him a little, I began to wonder if his jaunty manner might not cloak some insecurity. I noticed how nervous he was at a publicity party given by the BBC for the leading Forsyte actors to meet the press. I saw how his hand shook as he cheerfully passed me a glass of white wine, chortling, 'Come on old darling, don't be shy!' But the cameras had the perfect 'life of the party' shot. Sensing his vulnerability only made him seem more human to me. I have wondered since if that occasional shaking hand was the beginnings of the cruelly debilitating Parkinson's disease that led to his early death. I never knew what he really thought about me. He caught sight of me once as I crept round the back of the set and was in the act of shooting a couple of squirts of nasal spray up my nose. I felt like a secret drinker or a heroin addict. He glanced at me curiously, winked, then ambled away. He never referred to it.

Eric Porter's sensational portrayal of Soames was the linchpin of the entire *Saga*. His was a consummate performance in which, in his early forties, he reached back in time to play the young Soames – prim, contained, unemotional – and then, with extraordinary acting imagination, showed the character gradually ageing through the decades, before his compelling final episodes as a totally convincing, much-mellowed old man. For many years afterwards, there was one particular scene which I would always look out for on the re-runs. Not actually for another glimpse of his brilliant precision as cold-fish Soames, but a scene in which a maid takes Soames' overcoat and hangs it hurriedly on a clothes-stand before showing him into the adjoining room. As the camera pans away to follow Eric, the heavy coat, now in the corner of the screen, is seen to slide gently off its peg and fall to the floor. There is something surreal about viewing that same scene across the years. I have seen it in Spain, France, America, and always that coat sliding to the ground (unnoticed in the studio haste on the night of recording in 1966), trapped forever in the amber of television history. It won't be long now, perhaps, in an age when sophisticated special effects can refloat the *Titanic* and sail her again from Southampton to New York, before we see a colourised *Forsyte* repeat where Soames' overcoat stays, this time, wondrously on the peg.

In January 1967, when the stirring notes of Eric Coates's Elizabethan Suite for the *Forsyte Saga* began to resound in living rooms throughout the land every Sunday night, churches stood empty, there was little traffic on the streets, phones were off the hook. The nation was in thrall to the most imperial, the most leather-bound of soaps ever. On the afternoon after the transmission of my first episode, in which the newly introduced cousins, Jon and Fleur, fall head over heels in love, I was driving up Wood Lane towards Television Centre. I had an appointment to meet the director Joan Craft for a part in her production of *Nicholas Nickleby*. I stopped at the gate. Always worth a try. Vic stepped forward as usual. Before I could even begin to smile engagingly he was shaking his head and raising his one arm towards the wasteland. Then, as I was about to punch the gear-stick into reverse, he stopped. He walked forward and looked at me closely. ''Ere,' he said. 'Last night. *Forsyte Saga*. You're a bloody good artist!' He stepped back and raised the barrier. 'In you go,' he said.

Had I arrived? That seemed to be the opinion of the *Croydon Advertiser*, thrilled to find a Forsyte in their midst. Then some of the cosier women's magazines began to discover that one of the nation's newest romantic heroes was a young father of two boys, Toby and Oliver. The family had recently moved a few miles down the road to leafy Coulsdon. That damp look was 'in' and everyone wanted to know what Martin was really like, who he really was. So did Martin.

I was a busy actor. Joan Craft offered me the title role in her thirteen-part BBC 'tea-time' serial, *Nicholas Nickleby*. Before rehearsals began, I filled in time as a drug-peddling librarian in the final season of the popular 'Emergency Ward 10' series. Fame indeed. Then I went to Manchester to star in a Granada TV play about young East Berliners attempting to escape to the West across the wall. While I was there, I went back to the Manchester Library Theatre to see *The Entertainer*. Everyone in the audience was turning round and pointing me out as the fellow on telly. I grinned nervously, pretending not to notice. They jostled for my autograph in the interval. When the show had finished, I went backstage to see a couple of actors in the cast that I knew. I felt awkward, adenoidal and shy. As I was leaving I heard one of them say, 'What a shame – Martin's gone all starry.'

A few days before we began rehearsals for the Dickens serial, I decided I had better see my local GP and tell him about my nose and all the spray that was disappearing up it. He was mildly sympathetic, if a little puzzled. He suggested I should go home, dive under a towel and inhale from a bowl the steaming fumes of Friar's Balsam. Salt and water, he told me, was also effective in alleviating catarrh. He didn't think much of the nasal spray and mentioned the after effects, which I knew about only too well. He then started discussing the *Forsyte Saga* and the success that had come my way as a result.

'What are you doing next?' he inquired.

'Dickleas Dickleby', I heard myself saying. He looked at me oddly for a second then asked me which part.

'Dickleas', I told him. 'It's the bade pard . . .'

'Hmm,' he said, 'I see.'

I survived *Nickleby*, courtesy of the spray. Somehow, by balancing the doses and enduring some days of fierce reaction when it seemed I could hardly speak at all, I managed to get through the three months' work. I was deeply grateful for the help and understanding of the feisty Joan Craft who cajoled me into a performance that was less gauche than Jon Forsyte – or Martin. She would shout and scream and bully her actors; then, after each episode was safely in the can, hug us and tell us we were 'bloody marvellous!' She had no time for the kind of in-depth discussions about the character or 'motivation' that I was beginning to favour. For her it was simply a question of 'get on with it, ducky'. Whenever I attempted a Badelian discourse on the sub-text she would say, cigarette dangling from her lips, one hand thrust into the pocket of her brown slacks, the other pushing her heavy tortoiseshell specs up her forehead and into her greying hair in a gesture of despair, 'Oh for god's sake darling, we haven't got all night!'

Something strange was starting to happen. I was experiencing a sensation at the back of my scalp, as if some kind of metal skull-cap had been clamped there. The sense of its physical presence was so fierce, almost like a branding iron, that I kept trying to brush it away with my hand. This affliction would be part of me, on and off, for the next two years. Suddenly the 'cap', and my nose, seemed to be obstructing my career. I found I was testing out the severity of my nasality in the sound of every script I was given. My test piece was the opening of Shakespeare's sonnet, 'Led be dod do the barriage of drue binds/Adbid ibedibend.' ('Let me not to the marriage of true minds/Admit impediment.') I would mutter this mantra to myself before I went into rehearsal and, if I sounded as clogged as I have indicated, I would feel the metal cap tighten a little more. I had another, shorter, test piece,

'Many men, many men', and my fellow actors would regularly catch me muttering 'Beddy bed, beddy bed', as a shot was being lined up on the set. I got some strange looks.

As a result of my new-found celebrity, I had been invited to read the 'Woman's Hour' serial on radio. This was quite a prestigious engagement and the title in question was *The Last Enemy*, Richard Hillary's moving account of his wartime flying experiences, adapted into five episodes. Although the producer, Virginia Browne-Wilkinson, had been understanding (and I, in order to convince myself it wasn't happening, had pretended there was nothing wrong), it was clear that the reading sounded awful. After struggling through the first episode, I told Virginia I was suffering from a touch of hayfever and asked, hopelessly, if it noticed at all on the recording. 'Well,' she said gently, 'it does a bit.' (I later heard that she had left the BBC to become a nun.) I listened to the transmission a few days later and it was confirmed to me by someone with less tact than Virginia: 'God, you had a terrible cold when you recorded that.' Then he added, 'But you *always* sound as if you've got a cold.'

Around that time I did a reading for somebody else at the BBC. As I came back from the loo, where I had been dosing myself up with the spray, I overheard my producer sounding off to the recording engineer that she regretted hiring me: 'You give these people a chance and what do they do? They let you down. He'll never work in radio again.' The clamp tightened. I was sure she was right. The voice that I had begun to develop, following the confidence that Clifford Turner, Michael Croft, even Alan Badel had shown in me, now seemed to be disappearing. I had just about got through the *Forsyte Saga*, had sounded worse during *Nickleby* and it was now virtually impossible for me to open my mouth without ghastly sounds emerging.

A week later, in the spring of 1968, I was sitting in the consulting rooms of Pip Redding, one of the most respected ear-nose-and-throat specialists of his day. Pip was sympathetic from the start. He told me his daughter was training to be an actress, that he recognised at once the troubling nature of my condition, and understood my fear. Actors, after all, have to speak.

Over the next weeks I became a regular visitor to his clinic at Guy's Hospital. He tried everything: x-rays, allergy tests, nasal flushing.

I was still working intermittently – usually for people who didn't know that my speech had deteriorated since the last time they had seen or heard me. I was able to play the lead in a radio play – mainly because I could justify my interpretation of the character as an adenoidal axe-murderer. I even played Nelson in a BBC schools radio drama in which, before the live transmission, the director shrugged helplessly and said, 'Good luck – try giving your nose a good blow just before the red light goes on.'

It was a nightmare. The iron clamp was tightening all the time. Pip couldn't help me with that, but he attempted to deal with the rest of the problem. He was a tiny man, standing no more than four foot eleven inches in what looked like brown school shoes. His grey worsted trousers, protruding from beneath what must have been a specially made white surgical coat, were schoolboy size. His team of attendant housemen and student-doctors towered above him. None of the treatments to which Pip subjected me seemed to alter my condition, and I would leave the clinic obsessively implementing my own test, listening for any sign of improvement: 'Beddy bed, beddy bed,' I muttered as I waited for the Coulsdon train at London Bridge station and then was forced to look up and wave gaily at a carriage full of giggling schoolgirls who had spotted me and were calling out 'Hello Jon. How's Fleur?'

A day or two later I was called back to the clinic – they had something to tell me. When I arrived Pip wasn't there. Two of his team took me into a side office and told me that Pip had been studying my x-rays and thought there was something growing somewhere far up and behind the nose. 'You seem to have a tumour in both antra,' one of them told me. 'They are effectively blocking everything up.' The other one leant forward and said, 'We don't think it's a life-and-death situation.' My heart took a jump. Until that moment I hadn't even considered there might be anything malignant lurking there. Now here were two serious-eyed young doctors reassuring me that, *probably*, it wasn't life-threatening. Were they being ironic? Sending up the anxious actor? They told me that the next week Pip would see me again and would 'go in' to have a close look at the growths. A mad Dickensian picture leapt into my head that this was where Pip really scored; like a surgical Oliver Twist, he was so small he could actually be lifted up by his team and inserted into the nostril, from whence he could crawl up the nasal passage and hack away at the offending matter at the rock face.

On a bleak April day, I was seated at the end of one of the benches that ran the length of the corridor outside Pip's clinic. Two long silver rods protruded about four inches from my nostrils. I felt like some mythic creature from a Greek or Egyptian wall painting. Not quite a unicorn – a goat perhaps, or a silver-horned ram. I paid attention to my *Times* crossword. I was waiting for the local anaesthetic to take effect. Fifteen minutes earlier, Pip had explained, 'Now, Jarvis' (it was always 'Jarvis', never 'Martin'), 'you have these tumours up there in your antra. They're like great balloons and I'm going to burst them. That should give you some relief. I can't go in until it's all nicely frozen. So we place the anaesthetic on the ends of these rods, insert them –' he proceeded to do so with deft precision '– and now you can wait out there until you're numb.'

There were others waiting on the benches outside Pip's glass-windowed clinic and it was likely that more than half of them had seen me at least once a week on television during the last year, either as gauche Jon or nasal Nickleby. I sat there attending to the crossword, trying not to knock the ends of the rods on the wall at my side as I turned to avoid the eyes of twenty other patients. I could now feel the entire area of my face – mouth up to forehead and cheeks across to ears – starting to become numb. My top lip joined in the big freeze. A young schoolgirl who had been sitting on the opposite bench and had barely taken her eyes off me, now turned to her mother and whispered, 'Is that Nicholas Nickleby?' Her mother nodded meaningfully. The little girl reached down and took a book and pencil from her school satchel, then rose and came over to me. 'Can I have your autograph, please?' I put my newspaper aside and, as I wrote my

signature in her arithmetic exercise book, I engaged her in my
best Kenny More amiable chat (as far as I could with deadened
lips). What was her name? How old was she? Was she married, ha
ha? When did school break up? She seemed too excited to do
more than nod and smile as, keeping my silver rods well out of the
way, I wrote: 'To Katherine, all best wishes and lots of love
from –' and signed my name. She gave me a grateful smile and
returned to her place on the bench. She hadn't seemed in the
slightest bit disappointed that Nickleby's lips weren't quite in
sync with his words and that a giant tuning-fork glittered from his
nostrils. I saw her later in one of the consulting rooms, being sub-
mitted to a series of hearing tests. I could see (and hear) through
the window of the large room that she was unable to identify the
noise of bells being rung and buzzers being pressed.

Next it was my turn. Little Pip wiggled my prongs around and
pronounced me nicely frozen. A member of his team then
attached lengths of tubing to the ends of the rods. Pip told me the
rods were hollow and that he was 'going in', first to burst the
inflated 'balloons' that were causing all my trouble, then to cut
away the deflated detritus. He would, he explained, flush the stuff
out, and it would drain down (courtesy of the rods) along the
tubes and finally into a receptacle now being held by one of his
nurses. The whole procedure was known as the Caldwell Luc
operation. He had every hope that relief would follow.

It was all over in a few minutes. My only moment of horror
came when I opened my eyes and saw Pip tilting towards me like
some miniscule Don Quixote, wielding what looked like two
pointed lances, and neatly thrusting them up my nostril prior to
puncturing the growths deep behind my nose.

Pip seemed to have done the trick. Next day, for the first time
in more than two years, I could manage without the spray. I
mumbled the usual mantra, 'Many men, many men', and – good
heavens – it sounded all right. I extended it to 'Many men on the
mend'. Ah ha! Terrific. The relief was wonderful. Within a week
I accepted a radio play without having to find excuses to
disappear every hour to dose myself up. In the studio, the laser-
sharp ear of the microphone did not expose any ghastliness in my

speech. The play was only a run-of-the mill thriller in the 'Afternoon Theatre' slot, but the joy and release of being able to record the part of a zippy young detective without resorting to medication was such that, on completing the performance, I felt I had triumphed as Lear and Hamlet rolled into one.

Suddenly I was working again – full time. A couple of television films, lots of radio, commentaries for documentaries – the ultimate vocal exposure – and then, out of the blue, an American war movie shot in Germany and Austria, *The Last Escape*. I learnt later that the distinguished actress Wendy Hiller had been impressed with my *Forsyte* performance and had recommended me to Hollywood director Walter E. Grauman. Liz Robinson bubbled with excitement as she sent me along to the Hilton Hotel to meet Grauman and his producer from United Artists, a stony faced man called Irving Temaner. Walter turned out to be an enthusiastic anglophile who had directed a number of successful films, including *Lady in a Cage*, starring Olivia de Havilland, and the popular *633 Squadron*. We had a short chat, during which I was requested to comb my hair back off my forehead in an authentic military manner. Grauman and Temaner studied me closely, looked at each other, and expressed themselves satisfied with my sleek 1940s hairstyle. This, combined with my *Forsyte* credentials (they had seen the series on 'Masterpiece Theatre' in America) led them to offer me the part of Lieutenant Donald Wilcox, one of the film's starring roles. Liz was ecstatic and agreed a contract. A month later I left for Munich – and, I hoped, movie stardom.

Although all now seemed well with me and my nose, and even the invisible clamp had subsided to just an occasional tingle, I was taking no chances. I would be away from home for two months, so I took the precaution of including in my luggage a new fibreglass briefcase full of the various forms of medication on which I had been dependent since the onset of the growths. As I began work on the film I made sure this first-aid kit was never far from reach – a sort of nasal security blanket.

One morning, after we had been filming for about a week, I

arrived at one of the locations in the Bavarian countryside south of Munich. I placed the precious container on a shelf in the trailer that I (and several others) shared with chirpy Johnny Briggs, who was playing a British corporal. He had, over the past few days, noticed how much my mysterious briefcase rattled and had remarked more than once, "'Ere, what the hell do you keep in there?' Today I hadn't snapped the lid shut securely and, as I lifted it up, it fell open and the contents spilled out across the floor: hayfever pills, nasal sprays, bottles of Friar's Balsam, nose-drops, ear-drops, throat sprays – all the paraphernalia of my three-year ENT agony. 'Christ!' exclaimed Briggs, 'it's a fucking pharmacy!'

Stuart Whitman, known as Stu, an amiable Californian, was the star of the film. He never knew my name, but would hail me each day in gravelly tones, by the name of my character, as he arrived on the set: 'Mornin', Wilcox! How ya doin'?' He always appeared heavily tanned. One day, I overheard him telling a group of actors that he didn't like make-up on the screen: 'I always use the Stain,' he told them.

'The Stain?' one of them repeated.

'Sure. Helena Rubenstein Stain. Stays on for days. Very natural.'

Next day, I spied Johnny Briggs looking exceptionally fit and well. 'You look as if you've just come back from holiday,' I said.

'Oh, really,' he replied airily, 'yeah, Stu and I wear the Stain. We think it's much more natural than that poncy stuff you wear.'

The Last Escape was an action movie loosely based on the Werner von Braun story in which a combined British and American commando group, disguised as Nazi officers and led by Whitman, attempts to bring the rocket scientist (and his entire family) across Germany to Allied lines. It featured an 'international cast' (actors from Britain, Germany and Switzerland, plus our American star) and a great many tanks, Sten guns and explosions. I played the young second-in-command of the unit, who endangers the success of the expedition through inexperience and fear. But, in the end, Lt. Wilcox makes good by luring the pursuing Russians away from the quarry before (rather stupidly) driving his truck over a cliff and dying a hero's death. If my first lesson in screen acting had been given to me by Kenny More, my second was provided by Stu. One day, we were waiting to film in the streets of a small Bavarian town. Whitman beckoned me over. We were to shoot a complex sequence which involved his leaning out of a weapons carrier and issuing a series of orders to me, Briggs and our fellow commandos. I walked across to where he sat sunning himself in a deck chair outside his trailer. 'Hey, Wilcox,' he breathed, chewing on the wad of tobacco that he kept permanently stacked in his cheek, on screen and off, 'Listen – I gotta lotta *dialogue* in this scene. Hey, man, I don't like *dialogue*.' (He spoke almost as if it was a line from one of the many westerns in which he had appeared. *The Commancheros* perhaps, with John Wayne: 'Hey, Sheriff, there's too much goddam *wire* on this land. I don't like *wire*. And I don't like *dialogue*.') He put a huge stained hand on my shoulder and made me an offer I couldn't refuse: 'Wilcox – you take my dialogue.' I was well pleased to have my part built up in this way and, with director Grauman's approval, I spent the next half-hour mugging up almost two pages of Stu's military instructions.

We were ready to shoot. Stuart, as Captain Mitchell, hopped up into the driving seat of the weapons carrier. Johnny Briggs, still bronze with his Stain, fingered his rifle moodily. I placed one foot on the running-board of the truck and stuck out my chin. 'Action!' cried Walter – and the scene went something like this:

STUART: Right you men. Wilcox'll give you the gen. OK Wilcox.

JARVIS: Thank you, sir. Right everybody. Now pay attention. At zero one hundred hours we shall move to Point A. I shall go on ahead in the weapons carrier with Captain Mitchell and Corporal Morse. At zero one hundred and fifteen hours, when we reach map reference zero forty-five six DK, we shall take out the enemy's

> fuel dump. Then, when you get the signal, you
> men will bring up the rest of the vehicles and
> we'll rendezvous at Point B. When we reach
> Point C . . .

And so on. When I saw the film a year later I realised why
Whitman had been happy for me to take charge of all the instructions. There I was, gabbing on in the background, while the
camera dwelt much more interestingly on our captain's tanned
features: thinking, reacting, chewing, until, when my mouth
finally stopped moving, he finished the sequence in a handsome
close-up with a curt: 'C'mon, let's go.'

Less is more.

Another tip I gleaned from Stu concerned the hat problem.
Early on, he had said, 'Wilcox. We gotta work out how we're
gonna lose our hats.' He could see I looked puzzled. He explained
that in these military action movies, where everyone is in full
uniform, the characters all look alike. ''Specially,' he drawled, 'if
you gotta hat coverin' half your face. Folk don't know which one
y'are.' I watched in admiration as, in a chase across some farm
land, cameras rolling, he ducked under a wire fence, neatly
ensuring that his German officer's cap got dislodged. He spent the
rest of the film hatless but, as he told me afterwards, recognisable.
I followed his example next day and lost my hat on a windy ride
in the weapons carrier. This was real movie acting.

The morning before we finished filming, Walter Grauman told
me he wanted to insert a new scene into the action that wasn't 'er
– in the script, Mart'n'. He grinned, slightly sheepishly. I was
wary, but he reassured me: 'Don't worry, Mart'n, no extra
dialogue. I wanna shoot your parachute drop.' Ah. I nodded as
if this was a far more sensible idea. He went on, 'I want to see you
in the air, get up close to get your reaction as you're plummeting
down.'

That evening I was driven to a forest on the outskirts of
Munich. A huge crane stood in a clearing, fully extended, like a
finger pointing into the night sky. Suspended from the top hung
a parachute, artificially held open by hidden wires. Walter called

for the contraption to be lowered. I felt like the condemned man as two stuntmen bundled me into a leather harness and hooked me on to it – Dr Who revisited. On a signal from Grauman, the crane began to rise again, slowly hoisting me into Bavarian airspace. Higher and higher until I could see across the tree tops all the way south to Austria. I hung there. Everything seemed very quiet. Soon a second crane began to swing into the air. It had a platform attached to its tip, which held camera-operator Gernot Rolle. He came alongside. We were a few feet apart. I looked down. Our director's voice floated up on the evening air: 'Mart'n, in this scene try to look scared.' I opened my mouth and heard myself yell back, '*Mister Grauman, I am scared!*' But what frightened me infinitely more than vertigo was the sound of my own voice: '*Bister Graubad, I ab scared.*' I could hear that those antra balloons, so neatly excised by Pip Redding two months before, had started to grow again.

I plummeted earthwards.

'Beddy bed. Beddy bed. Beddy bed.'

At the end of a hot summer's afternoon, I sat with Pip in his clinic at Guy's Hospital. He held up the new x-rays. 'Well, Jarvis,' he said, 'you're quite right. There they are again.'

'Dab', I said. 'Whad dexd?'

'Well, I'm going to bring you straight into hospital. I'll go in through the mouth this time. Up into the antra – tally-ho – and cut the tumours out by the root. Pretty uncomfortable, old chap, but these antro-choanal things are tougher than I had supposed.'

'Everything's bloody well going wrong today,' I heard one of Pip's team exclaim angrily as I was wheeled into the operating theatre a few days later. This didn't bode well. Little Pip's elfin face appeared alongside me as I lay on the trolley, drowsy from the pre-med I had been given in the ward. 'Well Jarvis, here we go,' he said. 'Count up to ten, old chap.'

I began, 'Wud, doo, thwee –' but by the time I reached 'severd' the effect of the anaesthetist's injection had crackled through my body and brain and I was out.

I woke some hours later back in the ward. I lay there wondering where I was and how it had gone. There was an enormous pain in my throat and nose. I could taste blood on my lips and could hardly move my tongue. My mouth seemed half open and I couldn't close it. I lay there for a long time. I felt sick. Eventually I began to hoist myself up and reached across for the shiny metal bowl I could see on the bedside locker. I was going to be sick. As I grabbed the bowl and leant over I caught sight of my blurred reflection in its silver base. The most extraordinary figure stared back at me. I learnt later that, in the kind of operation I had undergone, the patient's face becomes severely bruised and swollen. To combat this, a black rubber cap is placed on his head, from which ice-cubes are suspended by strings that hang down on to the bloated nose and cheeks to alleviate the swellings. I stared again. I looked like a groggy Billy Bunter playing Shylock in the Australian outback. I was sick. As I leant back against the pillow a fellow patient in a dressing gown approached the foot of my bed. He held a small black object in his hand. He nodded in a matey fashion and said, 'Hello'. I discovered I couldn't speak. Tongue, mouth, throat, nothing worked. I grunted something.

'You're that actor,' he told me brightly. 'My wife spotted you earlier.' He held up the black thing: 'Mind if I take a picture? You're one of her favourites.' I attempted to grunt that perhaps this wasn't the best moment, but he had already lined up the shot and pressed the button: 'Thanks, Malcolm!' he called, shuffling back to his bed on the opposite side of the ward. I presume that a unique picture of Shylock recovering from his anaesthetic still resides in some treasured album, somewhere in South London.

It would be nice to record that Pip Redding's extirpation of the growths in the antra region of my face solved everything, and that I went whistling back to a revived career. It didn't quite happen like that, although his rooting out of the re-inflated balloons did leave me breathing freely again. The clamp, though, still lurked somewhere at the back of my head and would make its iron presence felt in any moments of professional or private tension.

On the day after I was discharged from Guy's Hospital, Liz Robinson engineered a meeting for me with Graham Evans, a leading television director. He was setting up a major series, The Contenders, for Granada Television, based on John Wain's novel set in the Potteries. It is the story of four schoolfriends, of their rivalry and continuing connection as they grow up and apart. The scripts were sharp and observant. Although I wasn't natural casting for an ambitious Staffordshire young man who eventually assumes control of a large factory, Graham seemed to think I was. The fact that I was now a television 'face' probably helped. I knew I was lucky to have one more chance. Here was a hard-edged character, neither a callow cuff-shooter, nor a courting Croydonian. This was different, the northern working class, a stringy fellow from Stoke whose story of upwardly mobile business ambition would make compelling television. This was to be me.

Or was it? I had reckoned without the complex nature of my co-star – a brilliant young actor called Victor Henry who now sat opposite me in a murky Manchester rehearsal room as we assembled for the readthrough of 'The Contenders'. If Graham Evans had been fooled by my apparent appropriateness (and readiness) for the part, Victor, it seemed, had no such delusions. In his five years as a professional actor, Victor, a lad from Wakefield, was enjoying a burgeoning career in which he was already being hailed as a natural successor to Finney, Courtenay, Bates and O'Toole. He had a demonic drive and a furious edge of passion that was electrifying. It was clear to those who had seen him on film or television, or had caught his recent Jimmy Porter at the Royal Court, that here was a great modern actor in the making.

I met him for the first time in that dingy room. He didn't look like an actor. He was small and wiry, with a pasty face and a mouth that seemed, in contrast, almost purple, as if he had been gorging on a bag of over-ripe plums. His tightly stretched lower lip, with neat teeth pushing from behind, gave him the look of a vehement vole as he whipped around the room, shooting glances at me, at the director, snatching up the script in his sharp fist, discarding it, darting again towards me, laser eyes flashing behind the exaggerating lenses of his wire-framed specs. Like me, Victor had had some early successes on television. Unlike mine, these

were modern stories that spoke directly to viewers about life in
the sixties, mirroring some of the sexy, druggy, rock 'n' rolling
issues of a still fully swinging decade. He had made a film or two
(as I had), but his parts were tough, angry, questing, as against the
earnestness of mine. Who knows what demons drove Victor. I
was sure, on that first day, he recognised mine. But did he?
Because of his disconcerting directness I assumed that he saw
through me completely – recognised at once my nervousness at
returning to work and how ill-equipped I was from my previous
acting experience to convey the truths that propelled this gritty
television drama. I believed, as his glittering eyes tunnelled into
mine, that he could discern everything about me. Something
which he perceived as complacency or superciliousness. Something his working-class background gave him permission to hate.
Wakefield against Croydon? As we all sat around the table with
our scripts, he mentioned that he remembered me at Rada. He
watched me keenly as I told him, unwisely, that I had no recollec-
tion of him at that time but admired his work very much. He
widened his purple mouth, fixed me with both lenses and told me,
unblinkingly, that when he was beginning the course I had been
in my final term. He had seen some of my performances, he said,
and he didn't like me. With what I hoped was a relaxed smile, I
said, 'Oh, why?'

He now put his face a few inches from mine: 'You know, all
that lardy acting.' He flexed his lower lip and went on, 'I don't
like good-looking people. I freely admit it.' I smiled weakly back
at him. I was beginning to think I must have been cleverer than
I imagined in cloaking my guilelessness at Rada. As for 'good-
looking' – I was well aware that, with too much hair, a low
forehead and baggy eyes, I had been lucky to get away with those
parts by the skin of my nasal membrane.

I wasn't ready for Victor. He had mis-read my anxiety as over-
confidence. He had decided that what he perceived as arrogance
was a threat to the purity of his approach. I certainly wasn't ready
to begin this sort of work. He could probably tell that I was ill-
equipped to take on the character I was supposed to be playing,
unprepared for the unremitting, no-holds-barred rehearsals to

come. He seemed so unerringly right in everything he said or did. It seemed his 'look, move, speak' was '*Look* Martin, *move* out of my way if you can't keep up, and now I'm going to *speak* some home truths at you.'

As we began to put the first scene on its feet he suddenly started to grill me. His onslaught came sharp and fast: 'What are you up to? What are you doing? Why are you sitting like that? Why are you so fucking supercilious? Do you think you're superior to the rest of us? Why are you such a pain in the arse?' My head was screaming and burning. Or, wait – was it, I thought for a moment, not *me* who was under attack at all? Was it my *character*, this fictional would-be prefectorial type, that he was putting to the test? I never found out. The clamp was tightening and tightening and his voice became insistent and rasping as he stood above me. My eyes closed. 'Why are you copping out?' I heard him say. 'Why are you just sitting there? Get up. Come on, get up. Fight me. Argue with me – why don't you? What's your problem? Who are you? What do you think?' Then I heard him turn to someone else in the room and say, 'It's an identity crisis, that's what it is.' He turned back: 'Are you a man or a boy? What are you doing? Why? Why? Why? Look at me.' I forced myself to open my eyes. He shoved his pale face right up against mine. I could see yellow sludges floating in the milky white of his blazing eyes as they raked my face and body, seeking answers. I had none to give. The clamp gave a final squeeze, my head seemed to implode.

I never saw my nemesis again. I never finally found out how much of it was Victor's animosity towards me personally and how much was his own relentless obsession to uncover aspects of the characters we were supposed to be playing. Whatever the answer, it was clear to me and to the director that I couldn't act with anybody at the moment. My whole brain seemed to have closed down. Next day, having left the production, I was back at home.

The words of Victor Henry would not go away. All the 'whats' and 'whys' and particularly, as I confided to psychiatrist James Willis at Guy's Hospital two days later, the phrase 'It's an identity crisis, that's what it is.' James listened closely as I told him about the iron clamp, and the whole business of the nose. He drew from me details of my Croydon confusions and how Victor's challenge, 'Are you a boy or a man?' seemed a fearful and unanswerable ultimatum. Willis suggested that my condition was not unconnected with the long anxious period in which I had lived with the tumour problem. The amount of dissembling and cover-up I had been forced into in order to keep it at bay and continue working had, even after it seemed to be resolved, catapulted me into a massive breakdown.

I spent the following weeks papering the boys' bedrooms, painting the woodwork and emulsioning the walls of the living room and kitchen. I turned the radio up loud and let 'The Archers' and 'Woman's Hour' and 'Afternoon Theatre' wash over me as I slapped the walls. Every couple of hours I paused to knock back the cocktail of drugs Willis had recommended. At first I was incapable of speaking to anyone except my children. The idea of going out of the house was worrying, and entering a shop or being in a crowd of people was enough to invite back the clamping-iron. On my weekly visits to James Willis he was able to show me that this fear was tied up with my television image, and that I had not come to terms with who I was as a person, let alone as an actor. So it wasn't surprising I found it hard to deal with pointing fingers and autograph-seeking girls. At home I was dully content to remain indoors, taking and making no phone calls, being with my children while my wife did her best to understand and protect me from the outside world.

My loyal agent, Liz, had borne the brunt of my withdrawal from 'The Contenders' and rang regularly with encouraging messages. It wasn't, she was positive, the end of my career. There was already interest in my doing another television series. Possibly a film. They want you for Jackanory. There's a West End play. None of it seemed real. On the rare occasions when I dared to venture out, if anyone approached me or pointed me out, the old clamp would tighten.

And now a new item was making some early guest-appearances: a fiery criss-crossing lattice of burning pain that leapt up my back and across my chest. Well, if you're going to have symptoms, you might as well lay them on hot and strong. The first time this new visitor made its presence felt was just as I was entering the hallway of our Coulsdon house. I had been mowing the front lawn and been driven indoors by the sudden arrival of two teenage girl fans who had somehow found out my address and had cycled miles on the off-chance of catching a glimpse of one of their television heroes. They got off their bikes and advanced up the front path, autograph books and cameras at the ready. I dropped the handle of the mower and fled inside. As I slammed the front door, leaving the panting girls to hammer on the knocker and giggle in vain, hot shafts of fire went blazing up my torso and crackled across my back and shoulders. Then, oh no, not this, a new and heavy lambast of pain burst and flared and thumped in the centre of my chest. Oh god, this is it. This is what it's all been leading up to. Heart attack. I fell like a stone to the floor, hitting my chin on the bottom tread of our newly carpeted stairs.

The boys were at their nursery school. My wife, calm in the face of this new occurrence, entered from the kitchen. She gazed down at me, eyes wide with amazement. I lay there looking up at her. 'It's my chest,' I managed to breathe out. 'Heart. I'm having a heart attack. Get the doctor.' She went into the dining room and I could hear her speaking in low tones. Oh god, I didn't want to die. After a few moments I decided I would be better off in bed. Slowly, not getting up, gently, so as not to trigger my ailing heart into a final pumping surge that would leave my devoted wife a widow and my children fatherless, I began to crawl. It was more of a slide, really, on my back. I inched, a tread at a time, head first, up the stairs, across the landing, always on my flaring back and all the while in slow motion. Finally I was in the bedroom. Like a mad limbo dancer, I snaked backwards from the floor, up the side of the bed and oh so carefully on to the soft coverlet. The journey had taken about four minutes, but I had made it. I was still alive.

The doctor arrived a few minutes later. He was perhaps ten or twelve years older than me with crinkly hair and a ruddy complexion. I vaguely remembered, as I looked up at him, that he was something to do with the local rugby club. He gave me a wink as if he might have been going to say, 'Care for a pint old boy?' He checked my pulse briefly before fishing a stethoscope from his bag and listening to various points across my chest. He gave me another encouraging wink and, breathing hard, wrapped a rubber apparatus around my arm, muttering something about blood pressure. I presumed it was mine to which he was referring, although as he stood over me in the otherwise silent room all I could hear were his rasping breaths. I could focus on nothing but the broken vessels on his cheeks. My wife stood watching from the foot of the bed. He released my arm and, with a last exhalation and a swift glance at her, he pronounced me in robust good health. Oh. I wasn't going to die after all. I was probably, it seemed, in better health than him. Good. I sat up and swung my feet off the bed. The flames subsided, the thumping ceased. The clamp released it grip. Splendid.

I left the two of them and went briskly downstairs to the dining room. I got on with some decorating. I switched on 'Waggoner's Walk' on the radio. What a relief. I slapped the paper around and began to concentrate on the parochial story line of the soap opera's current episode. I know, I thought, I could offer them something more exciting. What about a psychosomatic heart attack, with all the appearance and apparent symptoms of a genuine one? But perhaps no one would believe it.

Despite this sudden buoyancy, it took me six weeks before I found enough courage to go back to work, and two years to be free of the chemical cushioning recommended by James Willis. But I was no longer, it seemed, acting quite so strangely. The answers to some of Victor Henry's questions about identity began to emerge. First, I had to convince myself I could still act. It seemed I could. The increased self-awareness that had come my way since Victor had opened up that particular seam was probably (I only began to recognise this years afterwards) the best thing that had happened to me. I began to find my way back. Victor, sadly, did not. He was the victim of a tragic traffic accident which left him in a coma. He never recovered consciousness and died several years later.

My long-suffering agent Liz had decided to retire. I never knew whether her decision had anything to do with me and my problems. She told me Jean Diamond at London Management ought to represent me, and arranged a meeting. I met Jean a few days later and we hit it off at once; I was now represented by one of the top agents in the business. She handed me the script of a Hammer Horror movie. Suddenly I was breathing easier and could smell a fresh part.

You turn. She is beautiful.
You keys.

Teenage Prince of Denmark – note the tea-cosy wig. Whitgift School, 1960.

Below: 'Croft's Conspirators' – as Metellus with a quiff, in the National Youth Theatre's *Julius Caesar*, 1960.

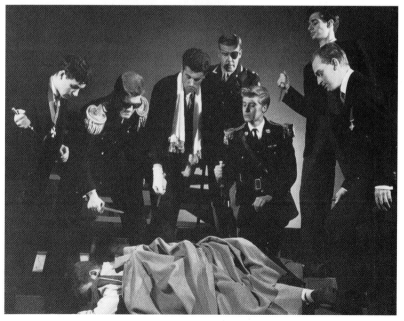

Moody acting at Rada in *Love's Labour's Lost*, 1962.

With sculpted quiff (left), Desmond Stokes (centre) and Patrick Stewart (right) in *The Princess and the Swineherd*, Library Theatre, Manchester, 1962.

As Delanoue, with Donald Pleasence as Bitos in *Poor Bitos*, Duke of York's Theatre, 1963.

With Susan Hampshire in *The Forsyte Saga*. Susan has probably just spoken in her 'little furry animals' voice. BBC TV, 1967.

Above: As Uriah Heep in *David Copperfield*, BBC TV, 1974. A vocal tapeworm.

Left: With Rosalind Ayres as Ophelia in *Hamlet* – minus tea-cosy, Theatre Royal, Windsor, 1973.

With John Collin (centre) and Stuart Whitman (right) in *The Last Escape*, United Artists, 1969. Stu has just asked me to take his dialogue.

Right: With Diane Keen in *Rings on Their Fingers*, BBC TV, 1978. 'Very wonderful,' said director Snoad.

Below: An abdicating Edward VIII in *The Woman I Love*, Churchill Theatre, Bromley, 1978.

Young-*ish* Marlow in *She Stoops to Conquer*, England, Toronto and Hong Kong, with Triumph Productions, 1978.

Right: If looks could kill … As the murderous Mr Stone in *The Business of Murder*, LWT, 1980.

Ernest Earnest and sexy Lady B. With Judi Dench in *The Importance of Being Earnest*, National Theatre, 1982.

Below: The pride of John Galliano. As Hector in a ra-ra skirt, with Brewster Mason in *The Trojan War Will Not Take Place*, National Theatre, 1983.

Above: 'Smug vicar', Ayckbourn's monstrous Rev. Gerald Gannet in *Woman in Mind*, Vaudeville Theatre, 1986.

Sleepless nights in *Exchange*, with Rosalind Ayres as Lena, Vaudeville Theatre, 1990.

Below: With a ghostly Just William, 1992.

Speaking after the beep with Michael Frayn, 1997.

Violet Elizabeth meets Just
William. With Miriam
Margolyes at the BPI Gold
Disc Awards, 1998.

Right: Overdressed for
California. As Tom in David
Hare's *Skylight*, Los Angeles,
1999.

November 1969

London

In *Taste the Blood of Dracula* I was cast as whey-faced Jeremy, the less interesting of two reach-me-down horror heroes. I was immediately sent to a sinister dentist's surgery (run by a father and son) in Belsize Park, for a fang fitting. They thrust me into the chair, told me to open wide, and forced wax into my mouth. Standing over me like Frankenstein and Igor, they watched and waited until they had got their impression. When we began filming I was told by our Hungarian director, Peter Sasdy, that my fangs were only for the Japanese version of the movie. 'When Lucy unexpectedly bites you,' he said, 'you too will show fangs. But only for Japan. They like it that way.'

The giggle-factor on the set was high. In the scene where Lucy lures Jeremy into the garden at night and savages him in the neck, I found it difficult to maintain a professional cool. The problem was that Isla Blair had been directed to turn and whisper seductively, 'Kiss me, Jeremy,' without disclosing her fangs. To do this with mouth firmly shut was challenge enough for any actress. But then, as I moved in for the snog, she had to throw her head back, open wide and reveal all. The only way to show your fangs is to stretch your mouth into a vast smile. This Isla did so perfectly that I couldn't help wanting to smile back. And laugh. That, plus the ventriloquial 'Kiss me, Jeremy', rocked us both into hilarity. Several takes were ruined. Count Dracula himself, played by the impeccable Christopher Lee, was not amused as he lurked behind Isla, waiting for the camera to whip-pan to his final reaction. He suggested darkly that we leave the set until we had control of ourselves. He was right, of course.

Having recovered, we completed the sequence with a close-up of my shocked response. Suddenly, nothing was funny any more. I was now confronted with a tricky acting exercise. What do you do when you realise your girlfriend is a vampire? Peter Barkworth hadn't covered that one at Rada. Look, move, scream? I tried my best, but felt that whatever I did just wasn't right. Or enough. Next day, Sasdy told me he was disappointed. He played back the scene for me. I saw what he meant. It all looked very tame, as if I was reacting to something quite ordinary, like a fly on a cake or mud on the carpet. I recalled Alan Badel's advice, 'It doesn't matter how big it is, as long as it's filled from inside.' We reshot the sequence. This time I pulled out all the stops. I rolled my eyes and goggled in horror like a silent-movie actor. Sasdy shouted, 'Not bad, you're getting there. Let's go again.' After two more takes, in which I felt I was now Henry Irving as Hamlet seeing his father's ghost for the first time, Peter called 'Cut!' and moved on. I could tell he wasn't satisfied. When I eventually saw the film it was apparent that my shock-horror reaction was still run-of-the-mill. Only just large enough. I have admired since how actors like Peter Cushing and Vincent Price, experts in the genre, can play this kind of thing on a monumental scale, yet never appear to be going over the top. They are always true to the situation, however extraordinary it may be. Their screen behaviour is always filled from inside.

Christopher was similarly believable as Dracula. When I consulted the script one day, I was surprised to see how few scenes he was in and how sparse his actual dialogue. He was hardly ever on the set. We filmed day after day without meeting him. One morning, I sensed a different atmosphere. The crew moved about with anxious faces. The make-up people seemed nervous. I asked a wardrobe assistant what was happening. 'Dracula arrives today,' was the reply, as she scuttled away with a clean white shirt and scarlet-lined cloak over her arm. An hour later everything went quiet. Suddenly a tall cloaked figure manifested itself on the set, ready for work. Not a moment was wasted. By the end of the day it seemed as if his entire part was in the can. *Taste the Blood of Dracula* has become a cult movie. Recently an American journalist, Oscar Martínez, interviewed me about my contribution and ended by asking what I had learnt from working with Christopher Lee. Economy, I replied.

Soon I was getting the chance to tackle larger and more complex characters. Prince Andrei in the twenty-part radio dramatisation of *War and Peace* was a role I would not have been able to handle a few months before. Godfrey Ablewhite in BBC Television's classic serial of *The Moonstone* was another intricate character that I found I could inhabit with confidence. I met up again with a young dark-haired actor, Ian McKellen, whom I had first met in the sixties when we both played young military chaps in a television series based on Kipling's *Plain Tales from the Hills*. He had been a flatmate of my old Rada friend Roger Hammond and the three of us had spent summer lunchtimes soaking up the sun on the roof of Roger's King's Road flat. Ian had impressed me with his humour and modesty, but never did I perceive the power and strength that became clear to all only a few years later when he played Richard II and Edward II for the Prospect Theatre Company. This time we were working together in a television version of Terence Rattigan's *Ross*. Ian was T. E. Lawrence in a performance full of febrile charm and skilful malcoordination. My role as the blackmailer Dickinson was a long way from any of the bland toffs for which I had become known. Cool. Devious. Corrupt. I was enjoying myself. I followed this with the title role in a television production of Peter Terson's *The Samaritan*. The character Terson created in this play was fascinating to act – a man who carries other people's problems in his head and is still able, after one of his clients commits suicide, to go out to dinner with friends and have a nice time. As someone who had been carrying some weird stuff myself, I felt in tune with this odd remote man.

In the summer of 1971, I had a call from Jean Diamond. Could I, tomorrow, go to Heathrow, where a ticket would be waiting for me, and fly to Italy for a screen test? A celebrated Polish director, 'Somebody' Kawalerowicz, was interested in my playing a leading part in his next movie, to be shot at the famous Cinecittà studios.

Twenty-four hours later a taxi picked me up at the airport, buzzed me along the streets of Rome and through the elegant gates of the famous studio. We came to a halt outside a long red-brick building. The sun beat down. There were flower scents in the air. I walked up the steps. A young assistant seemed vaguely to be expecting me and showed me to a small dressing room on an upper floor. Was there a script? I asked. No, came the reply. Jersey will come talk to you.

'Jersey?'

'*Si*. Jerzy Kawalerowicz. Beeg Pole director. He want talk to you.'

I went into the room, which was almost completely bare. Just a desk and mirror and some rickety wooden chairs. I hung around for about an hour. I opened the door once or twice and peered up and down the long corridor. Nothing. No one. Suddenly a bang on the door. In comes a large grey-haired man and a smaller, dapper man. The dapper one introduces himself in a glutinous Italian accent. He is Meester Ricci. He is interpreter. And thees, he tells me, is Meester Jerzy Kawalerowicz.

Meester Kawalerowicz beams, extends his hands and sits me down in one of the chairs. He pulls up another, sits astride it with his arms resting on the back, and puts his face a few inches from mine. He talks to me, in Polish, for what seems like half an hour. After the first few minutes I realise he is explaining his film to me. I can't understand a word. Finally he draws breath and Mr Ricci, the interpreter, who has been standing to one side, swiftly grabs the third chair in the room and places it equally near to me. He sits down and leans towards me intently. I feel like Stanley in Pinter's *Birthday Party* being grilled by Goldberg and McCann.

'You,' Ricci begins, 'are Priest. Fortified.'

'Fortified?'

'*Si*. Meedle-age. Fortified.'

'Oh.' I understood. 'Forty-five.'

'*Si*. Fortified. Catholic. Italian.'

I nodded as if it was the sort of part I played all the time. 'Right.'

Ricci continued. 'You leeve in seminary. You love. You love girl. You *lust*.'

'Right.'

'But thees lust is no good. You suffer. You are in torment. You feel geelt.'

'Oh, absolutely.'

As Ricci continued, Jerzy sat there a few inches from my face studying me closely, nodding in confirmation. Then, as Ricci sat back, Jerzy leant in still further and extruded another batch of Polish. Ricci moved in fast again:

'You are in your room at night.'

More Polish from Jerzy. It was now definitely a double-act.

More explanation from Ricci: 'You dream.'

Then more Polish.

'You dream of girl.'

Polish.

'You dream of sex.'

Polish. Polish. Polish.

'Girl come into your room.'

Quiet Polish.

'She creep up behind.'

Soft Polish.

'She put her hand over your eyes.'

Loud Polish.

'You burn. With lust.'

Sexy Polish.

'And desire.'

Polish. Polish. Polish.

'You turn. She is beautiful. You keys.'

'What?'

'Keys. You keys her.'

'Oh, kiss. Right.'

Pause. Long drawn out Polish.

'You take her. She is yours.'

'Right.' I am turning my head swiftly from one to the other, not quite knowing who best to give my attention to. I actually rather wish Ricci were the director. At least I can understand what he is saying.

Finally they get up. I get up too. Jerzy grasps me by both shoulders and gazes deep into my eyes. He says something in Polish. Ricci translates: 'He say, you are so much the man.'

Ah. I nod and smile, trying to look middle-aged, lustful and celibate.

After a further outburst from Jerzy, Ricci says, 'You weel dress now. Costume in closet there.' He indicates a grubby curtain drawn across a recess in a corner of the room. 'They weel bring you to the set soon.'

They go out. I draw the curtain aside. Hanging there is a long black robe with about a hundred buttons down the front. Also a priest's biretta hat, perched on a shelf above. I get dressed. It takes me about twenty minutes to do up all those buttons. I try on the biretta and view the whole effect in the mirror. I look about as much like a forty-five-year-old Italian priest as Danny La Rue.

I sit there in my robe and hat for a long time. Flower scents and distant traffic sounds waft up from below. My stomach rumbles. I begin to nod. Jerk awake. I get up and walk outside. Look up and down the corridor. A door opens at the far end and a priest in a long buttoned gown comes out. He is wearing a biretta. For a moment I think there must be a mirror up there and this is me. But no. It is somebody else. He is dark. Swarthy. Middle-aged. He stares down the corridor at me. Then nods. I nod back. We can both see at once that we are testing for the same part. And we both know who is the more likely candidate. I wish him good luck. He beams confidently at me. '*Grazie*,' he says, and retreats to his room.

Another hour goes by. Finally someone comes and leads me to a make-up room. While my Croydon pallor is being given an Italianate coating, Jerzy and Ricci appear again and balance either side of the make-up chair. Jerzy stares hard at me in his usual manner, but before he can say anything Ricci tells me crisply there have been alterations to the scene. He says, 'You weel have blindfold.' He seems to be taking the initiative now. Perhaps he will, after all, be directing the film. Jerzy nods. Ricci continues, 'Lisa the girl weel come in behind you.'

Jerzy shrugs this time. This is definitely Ricci's movie now.

'She gently, so gently, remove your blindfold. You amaze. You turn. You see her. You keys.'

'Kiss, right.'

Jerzy now bursts out in the most vigorous Polish yet. Not at me but at Ricci. Ricci replies sharply. In Polish. Clearly there are artistic differences. They both turn back. Jerzy seems mollified at the sight of me and utters some calmer Polish. Ricci translates, though this time I have an uneasy sensation that he does not now agree with the point made earlier, 'You are so much the man.'

In a few minutes someone leads me through a door to the brightly lit set. It looks like a priest's cell. It reminds me of the dressing room upstairs. We might as well have shot the whole thing there, I am thinking, when Jerzy appears out of the darkness beyond and slaps something over my eyes. It's the blindfold. Somebody, possibly Ricci, ties it behind. For once no one speaks. I stand there. I still really have no idea what the scene is. And why the blindfold? No one has shown me a script. There doesn't appear to be one. And what about the girl Lisa?

Suddenly I hear Jerzy shout, '*Azione!*' Or is it the voice of Ricci? I'm standing there in the middle of the room with no real idea of what's going on.

Everything is very quiet. Then I hear a door open. I can smell perfume. Someone is in the room. I turn my head sharply. I am not going to let this thing beat me. I know all about improvisation. I was at Rada with Mike Leigh.

'I hear you,' I say. I'm giving a slight Italian flavour to the voice. And deep too. Fortified.

'*Buona sera.*' I hear a sultry voice from somewhere behind me. This'll be the girl Lisa.

'*Buona sera,*' I reply. Then, in some surprise, I hear myself say, 'I need you. I need you so much.' Pretty good. Mike would be proud of me. The bouquet wafts closer. I can feel her breath on the back of my neck now. Then something running up my spine.

Her fingers. And round to the front, below my neck. Oh god, she's not going to try those buttons is she? We'll be here all night. I grab her hand and hear the next part of my improvisation: 'I burn to possess you.' Swiftly she removes her hand from my grasp and the next moment she has untied my mask and is, strangely, holding it up to the light, like a trophy.

I blink and look at her. I vaguely recognise her as the well-known Italian actress Lisa Gastoni, who used to work in England some years ago. 'Bravo,' I say, still in my fortified voice, feeling that I have taken part in some sort of conjuring act. I am just thinking that I had better now take her in my arms for the 'keys' when Jerzy and Ricci also cry 'Bravo!' and it is Jerzy himself who moves in to kiss the fragrant Lisa. Ricci swiftly follows, kisses her on both cheeks and the group of people around the set break into enthusiastic applause. I sense that only a modicum of this is directed towards me. Somebody grabs my arm and leads me away like a contestant in a TV game show. Successful or not I have no idea. Presumably they've got to go through it all again with the beaming man from upstairs. Or has he already done his stuff? Who knows?

Within minutes, the vague young assistant is escorting me downstairs to the same waiting Fiat that brought me here about a hundred years ago. As he opens the car door for me, he says, 'You will be the one. I hear it from director. You are so much the man.'

Three hours later I'm at home in Coulsdon. More tanned than when I set out, but that was just the Italian make-up that I had forgotten I was wearing.

I never heard another word from the film company, though a couple of years later at a dinner-party in Kensington, I heard a woman a few places down the table saying something that made me prick up my ears: 'Oh no, my dear, never work with the Italians. A friend of mine's husband, Eric, had a terrible time in Rome last year. He's an actor you know. He was in a film made by some famous Polish person, Jersey someone. Played an old Italian priest or something. The whole thing was a nightmare. They kept him waiting endlessly and never paid him for weeks. In the end he got so fed up he broke into the labs where they develop the rushes or whatever you call them, grabbed about eight cans of film and drove out of Rome to some secret seaside destination. Just like a kidnapping. He rang the producers up and held the film to ransom. Said if the money didn't appear in his account by the next day he was going to throw the whole film into the sea. They paid up of course.'

Good old Eric, I thought. Whoever he was, so very much the man.

In 1973 I was asked to play Hamlet. Not at Stratford – they had stopped asking – not the National Theatre. Windsor. For something they called the Festival of British Theatre at the Theatre Royal. Windsor was a stalwart rep company presided over by charming old John Counsell and his actress wife Mary Kerridge. I had never met either of them, though I knew of Mary from her moving performance as Queen Elizabeth in Olivier's film of *Richard III*.

John and Mary had run the Windsor theatre for years with notable success, completely without subsidies or grants. Partly because of its nearness to London, they were able to attract well-known actors to star in well-made plays. Lately they had taken to putting on the occasional 'classic' and this year were determined to do their *Hamlet*, even if it meant risking the displeasure of their regular audience, many of whom would rather have seen productions of Agatha Christie and Terence Rattigan all year round. I was asked down to Windsor one afternoon to discuss details of the production with John Counsell. Judging by photos of past glories displayed in the plush foyer and on the walls of the red and gold auditorium, I could see it was not unusual for the Counsells to present a play which starred not only the gracious Mary herself but featured one or both of their beautiful daughters, with John as the butler or vicar. I made my way up the stairs past more photos – mostly of members of the Royal Family being humbly welcomed to the theatre by the Counsell family. John greeted me at the door of his office and, with ineffable old-world courtesy, ushered me to a comfortable sofa and gave me tea. He told me, in chocolatey tones, that he and Mary were thrilled I was to play the moody Dane. The family was thrilled, he said. The whole of

Windsor was thrilled. I began to wonder if Her Majesty herself, just up the road, was thrilled as well.

He laid his cards on the table. 'Mary will play your mother.' He said it in a sort of 'take-it-or-leave-it' tone that suggested he'd been up this road before and that others had left it rather than taken it. I said I was delighted. He beamed, revealing a set of surprisingly green teeth. Having sorted out the Queen of Denmark he refilled my cup and, in a more tentative manner, tried to sell me his daughter. What did I think, he inquired, about Elizabeth Counsell for Ophelia? I sensed that there was room for manoeuvre here and, as I didn't know her work, I couldn't be of much help. I waited for him to suggest the other daughter, or indeed himself for Polonius, but he moved on briskly to discuss possible directors. 'You can have anyone you want,' he began, waving a benevolent hand in the air and radiating goodwill like one of the Cheeryble brothers from *Nicholas Nickleby*. I was about to mutter something polite and self-deprecating when his expression changed and he exclaimed, 'Except Peter Hall! I won't have him in my theatre!' I had seen a picture of one of the young Peter's productions from the 1950s on my way upstairs. I wondered what terrible falling out there could have been for him to be banned forever from working at the Theatre Royal, Windsor. I shrugged across the table at John, as if to say Huh, I wouldn't have wanted *him* anyway, knowing perfectly well that it was unlikely that the great Peter would have any interest, at present, in helping me to play Hamlet. In any case I had my own agenda.

I had worked many times with Martin Jenkins at BBC Radio and we had a plan that one day he would direct me as Hamlet. Martin, a brilliantly gifted director, was just a couple of years older than me, with a Billy Bunter laugh and a beard that looked like a Felix Topolski illustration. Before creating an impressive list of radio productions encompassing Shakespeare, Strindberg and Shaw (and 'Waggoner's Walk') he had co-founded the Everyman Theatre, Liverpool. He went on to work at Stratford and had directed an impressive *Brand*, by Ibsen, at Nottingham Playhouse. His contract with the BBC allowed him time to work in the theatre, so I suggested to John Counsell that Martin would be my ideal director. John, relieved I thought that I was not going to plead on Peter Hall's behalf, agreed. A few days later Martin rang me to say he was on board.

This was all going very well. I had my friend as director; now I could push for my favourite Ophelia. I had just had a call from Angela Down who had been a gutsy Jo March in BBC Television's recent *Little Women*, in which I had played John Brooke. She asked if she could be my Ophelia. I was flattered. She was an excellent actress, well known on the box (always a plus with Windsor audiences) and, not that it mattered of course, I told myself, I rather fancied her. I informed her the part was as good as hers and put the phone down. The next day I was appalled to discover, on mentioning this terrific idea to Martin, that he and John Counsell had already auditioned a young actress called Rosalind Ayres. She was wonderful, said Martin, and in any case John has just offered her the part. There wasn't much I could do except tell Martin rather sniffily to 'suit himself' and ring Angela with the bad news.

The three weeks of rehearsal and three weeks of playing Hamlet were crowded with event. First of all I met Ros Ayres, who turned out to be a strong and original Ophelia. After the first readthrough I found I was more interested in finding excuses for rehearsing my scenes with her than in most of the rest of the play.

One critic described my Hamlet as 'fast and funny' and certainly I tried not to hang about in our two-and-a-half-hour version, particularly after John Counsell murmured to me that he was keen that the audience should be able to catch their last trains. Martin Jenkins, always one to whip up the pace and energy, encouraged me to let rip and, at rehearsal one morning, I decided that the closet scene between Hamlet and his mother could really take off. Having killed Polonius behind the arras, I leapt onto the bed (a touch of Errol Flynn, I thought), took hold of Mary, screamed

> Leave wringing of your hands: peace! sit you down,
> And let me wring your heart; for so I shall
> If it be made of penetrable stuff,

grabbed her by the neck and shoulders and, in the very whirlwind of my passion, proceeded to do a deal of unrehearsed damage to her neatly sculpted Home Counties hair-do. I threw her down, picked her up again, flung her across the bed, yanked her up by the shoulders, tossed her away, leapt on top of her, hoisted her up once more before giving her a violent incestuous kiss and hurling her back one last time on to the pillows. There was silence for a moment.

I was dimly aware of members of the cast watching from the stalls, mouths agape. Then suddenly,' 'Good!' cried Martin bouncing up on to the stage almost as if he might want to join in. 'How did that feel for both of you?' I looked down at the uncrowned queen of Windsor as she lay gasping and panting, hair awry, make-up smeared. She fought for more breath, caught some, pulled herself up, smoothed her tweed skirt, patted her hair back into place, and said gamely, 'Jolly good. Though I hadn't realised it was going to be *that* sort of *Hamlet*.'

I don't think I was quite certain what sort of Hamlet I was going to be. It was all pretty physical. I did tone down my worst excesses in the scene with Mary, much to her relief, although I was still fairly lusty with Ophelia in the closet scene. I found I was being zippy all round. I was certainly taking John Counsell's note about last trains very seriously. Also, I wanted time to get to know Rosalind Ayres better in the pub afterwards. I was rather pleased with what I thought was one original idea when, in the riddling farewell to Claudius as 'dear mother' in Act 4, I gave Laurence Payne a long deliberate kiss on the lips. Like Mary, I don't think he had thought it was going to be *that* sort of *Hamlet*. I told him it was all to do with 'if kisses could kill'. Equally game, he went along with it. He mentioned to me later that I wasn't quite so clever as I had thought, as he could remember Olivier planting an aggressive smacker on the king's lips at the Old Vic in 1937.

My other idea, which director Jenkins assured me *was* a first, was a way of pinpointing the moment when Hamlet crystallises details of his plot to expose Claudius. Hamlet has just seen the First Player going through his paces and has asked if his company could perform *The Murder of Gonzago* that evening. Alone, Hamlet starts to work the whole thing out in the 'rogue and peasant slave' soliloquy: 'I'll have these players/ Play something like the murder of my father/ Before mine uncle.' It seemed to me it could be a sensational moment of revelation if Hamlet had been about to say, 'I'll have these players/ Play something like *The Murder of Gonzago* –' He could pause on the word '*Murder*' and, right there, get the final startling idea of presenting a re-enactment of what the Ghost has told him of the *actual* murder; then, with the light of this amazing plan blazing in his eyes, continue: 'of my *father*/Before mine uncle.' I tried it at rehearsal and not even Larry Payne felt he had seen it all before.

Hamlet was deemed a success by those few who made their way to Windsor, though it was not without incident during its short run. On the first night, a few minutes before the performance was due to begin, Laurence Payne was handed a note brought round from front-of-house. It was apparently from acquaintances of his and basically said, 'Hi! We're here tonight in Row C. Watching you like a hawk. You'd better be good. Cheers!' Some actors never mind knowing that specific friends are out front. Others hate it. I don't much like the idea.

Over the tannoy we heard, 'Beginners, please.' Larry screwed up the piece of paper. He adjusted his crown nervously.

After the first battlements scene, the fanfare sounded (a live trumpeter borrowed from Her Majesty up the road). The entire Danish Court trooped on – about six of them – ranging themselves around the dais on which stood twin thrones. I mooched on, making my way to a small stool downstage-right where I sat down, soulfully. The royal trumpet continued to blast. Then Mary and Larry swept on, bestowing gracious glances all round. They mounted the dais, hoisted up their fur robes (chilly in northern Denmark, Martin had told the wardrobe department) and plonked themselves on their thrones. Their legs dangled just a little bit. The trumpeter finished and nipped off to the pub. All eyes were on Larry. He smiled, looked around, bared his teeth and began the great speech,

> Though yet of Hamlet our dear brother's death
> The memory be green, and that it us befitted
> To –

He paused. He leant coolly on one arm of his throne. No one stirred. He still paused. He cleared his throat. 'And that it us befitted, to – er –' he reiterated, 'er – to –' His smile lengthened into a ghastly grin, the teeth white against his Leichner tan. 'Er –'

Good old Mary leant across and muttered, out of the side of her mouth, 'To bear our hearts in grief.' Larry continued to grin. His eyes swept the waiting Court and sweat began to pour from under the brim of his crown. We knew that panic was setting in and he couldn't recognise anything familiar.

The voice of Ted, the stage manager boomed out from the prompt corner, 'To bear our hearts in grief and our whole kingdom to be contracted in one brow of woe.'

Nothing. Still Larry couldn't pick it up. The audience was getting restless now. Ted's voice boomed on: 'Yet so far hath discretion fought with nature.' He was more or less playing Claudius from the wings. I sat on my stool and attempted to toss Larry a line. He was incapable of catching it. George Benson as Polonius tried much the same thing and, with Mary like some royal ventriloquist still offering stuff through clenched teeth, there were four of us reciting different bits of the speech. It only needed Larry's friends, no doubt as promised watching him like a hawk and clearly the cause of the whole debacle, to stand up and fling him a few morsels from Row C. Finally it was Larry himself who rose. He stood for a minute in front of his throne, then, with the panache that had made him a matinée idol at the Vic in the forties, he strode forward, off the dais and marched down towards the audience. Flinging back his ermine, he thrust out his chin and tried again: 'And that it us befitted –' He stopped. It was no good. The speech had defeated him. He shook his head in disbelief at what was happening and said, suddenly, 'Oh fuck –' catching himself in further disbelief before more than the 'fu –' had reached the front row of the stalls. He then drew himself to full height, hung his head a little, looked directly out into the audience and announced, with the gravest unction, 'Ladies and gentlemen, I am deeply sorry,' and, before anyone else could say or do anything, he swung round, moved swiftly upstage, *vaulted* into the throne, began the speech again, and gave a cracking, word-perfect performance for the rest of the evening.

George Benson was a remarkable Polonius. I had worked with him in the *Forsyte Saga* and admired him as one of Britain's most skilful character actors. His unerring sense of comedy made him ideal casting. Except, our director had a theory that Polonius, deeply manipulative and politically ambitious, should eschew all the obvious humour in the part. Martin Jenkins was strict on this point during rehearsals, and became more and more cross if he found George getting laughs from the rest of us. But it was impossible for the lovable George not to find humour in many of the set pieces with which Poloniuses down the ages have delighted audiences. Throughout the first week of the run he tried his best to expunge laughs in the interests of providing our director with the cold political operator he required. Then, sadly, during the second week, George suffered a stroke and was unable to continue in the part. It was decided that Martin himself should take over the role. This he did with great aplomb, wearing a strange four-cornered hat instead of a wig, and his own horn-rimmed spectacles, from behind which he stared out like some kind of Elizabethan owl. The specs were essential as, having had no time to learn the part, he was forced to read great swathes of it from a series of hastily concocted scrolls. Most interesting of all, though, was that in stepping so splendidly into the breach, Martin forgot all about the cold politician and resolutely went for every laugh in the text. He got most of them, too.

No actor emerges from playing Hamlet quite the same as when he embarked on the role. In my case, one of the unlooked-for joys of my time at Windsor was meeting Rosalind Ayres. My first marriage ended shortly afterwards, and a year later Ros and I were married.

The Elsinore influences were apparent in my next few parts too. I scooted around the set with lightning speed and put my hands on my hips a lot. Appropriate for 'Jackanory Playhouse' but not wholly suitable for Frank Greystock in 'The Pallisers' and a suave bank robber in 'Dixon of Dock Green'. Then, in 1974, came Uriah Heep.

Joan Craft, my director on *Nicholas Nickleby*, was going to do *David Copperfield* for BBC Television. I wanted to play Uriah. It seemed unlikely casting. I discussed this with Ros, who said why not ring Joan and tell her. I picked up the phone. A minute later Joan's strident tones came zinging down the line. She was appalled: 'Oh come on, darling! How could you ever be that oily creature?' Nevertheless, Jean Diamond got working on the case and persuaded Joan that there was no harm in my dropping by to do a quick reading.

A couple of days later I was summoned to the serials department of the BBC to meet Joan and her producer, John McRae. John was an earnest young New Zealander who had been an assistant producer on *Nickleby*. He smiled doubtfully at me. Joan lit a cigarette with one hand and threw me a script with the other. 'All right, darling, let's get it over with.' I stood up. I had of course been thinking a great deal about the character of Heep over the last twenty-four hours. I had decided to obey all the descriptions contained in Dickens' narrative concerning Heep's oleaginous manner. 'He had a way of writhing which was very ugly.' I had studied the references to 'the snaky twistings of his body'. I paid attention to the author's specific instruction as to his facial expression: 'He had not so much as a smile about him . . . he could only widen his mouth and make two hard creases down his cheeks to stand for one.' With Dickens as my director I stood up and began to read:

Master Copperfield, I'm a very umble person. I am well aware that I am the umblest person going, let the other be where he may. My mother is likewise a very umble person. We live in a numble abode, Master Copperfield, but have much to be thankful for . . .

The very act of following Dickens' instructions did something strange to the words and a thin vocal tape-worm started to emerge from my mouth. John and Joan sat quietly on the sofa as I performed the scene in which this extraordinary grotesque acquaints David for the first time with the Heep family background and ambitions. They laughed once or twice but whether out of pity, encouragement or appreciation I wasn't sure. I read on, following all the clues in Dickens' narrative, before landing myself, with a final ghastly writhe, in the chair opposite them.

I glared at them defiantly. They looked at me. Then at each other. None of us spoke. John tittered nervously. Joan flicked her lighter and ignited another cigarette. Suddenly I realised they were both a little gobsmacked. This was not their courteous Nickleby. Not the decent Forsyte. Joan broke the silence by exhaling sharply and turning to John, 'Well, I don't know about you, darling, but I thought that was bloody marvellous!'

They offered me the part on the spot and it marked the beginnings of my acceptance on television, and later in the theatre, as an actor who had 'range'. From then on, thanks to the intransigent Joan, I was able to avoid many of the perils of typecasting and the graveyard of the ageing juvenile. When the series was transmitted and I was considered to be the personification of the foxy Uriah, complete with red hair 'cropped as close as the closest stubble', there was little evidence of the callow Croydonian. Clive James wrote in the *Observer* that 'to hear him speak is like putting your foot on a toad long dead'. Now that I had a voice, free from any antro-choanal detritus, I could play around with it at will.

In 1975, I received a letter from Sir John Gielgud whom I had never met. He was congratulating me on my radio performance in one of his old parts, Richard of Bordeaux, which he had listened to, he wrote, with utmost pleasure. He hoped I might be able to revive the play in the theatre. I was thrilled to have such an endorsement from the hero of my Whitgift schooldays. The part of Richard had been a huge 'matinée idol' success for Gielgud in the thirties. I had read that audiences had queued round the block to see him in this great romantic drama. I tried to follow up his suggestion but found nobody interested in reviving the play in the seventies. At least, not with me. The good news was that within a few weeks I found myself working with him in a stage recital of Milton's *Paradise Lost*, directed by the indefatigable Martin Jenkins.

We opened with a gala performance at the Theatre Royal, York, before playing at Chichester, the Old Vic and the Queen Elizabeth Hall. There were about ten of us, including Keith Michell as Satan; Peter Jeffrey, Julian Glover and me as somewhat unlikely Archangels; Ronald Pickup and Hannah Gordon as Adam and Eve. Sir John was Milton himself. We all wore dinner jackets and our first entrance was to the sonorous strains of Wagner as we took up our positions. All very serious. No laughs. The only touch of colour was the scarlet bow-ties that Martin (and the adaptor Gordon Honeycombe) had thought appropriate for Satan and his devils.

We felt privileged to be sharing a stage with Gielgud. As Milton he was given a lectern to himself, at which he stood, near to the audience, on the right-hand side of the stage. We Archangels sat further upstage on the right, ranged in a semi-circle. At appropriate moments, we rose from our chairs in a dignified manner and approached a central lectern for our pronouncements. As Archangel Michael, I was parked on the end of our row, nearest to Sir John. During the afternoon I was privy to many of his comments as he rehearsed. He was constantly worried by the fact that we were *reading* the text, though there was no way, without weeks of rehearsal, we could have committed it to memory. At one point, having delivered a great cascade of Miltonic verse from the golden throat, he immediately turned to me and muttered, 'It's all wrong, you know. I shouldn't be *reading*. Milton was *blind*.' He was worried, too, by Jenkins' mercurial direction. Sometimes, after Martin had come scurrying down from the rear of the auditorium to tell Sir John he should give more emphasis here or speed things up there, Gielgud would turn to me and murmur, 'Ah, yes, but *he* doesn't have to do it.' Once, when Gordon Honeycombe (at that time the nation's favourite news reader) suggested Sir John deliver a particular passage with more of a rising inflection, he remarked, raising an eyebrow in my direction, 'Well, I suppose I might say it like that if it were the nine o'clock news.'

The opening performance of *Paradise Lost* was a triumph though the Archangels had an uncomfortable time. Martin had insisted that we sit with our legs crossed – in unison – right over left for archangels, left over right for devils. He forbade us to follow the text in the script while our fellow actors were speaking. We must focus entirely on whoever was doing his or her stuff at the lectern. This was a good idea but it meant that, with a minimum of rehearsal, we had to be sure of recognising our up-coming cues, giving ourselves time to rise, approach the podium, open our black spring-back folders (red for devils) and get on with our speeches. On this first performance, a few pages of Julian Glover's script slipped from his folder and fell beneath my feet as he was about get up. 'Do you need them?' I asked out of the corner of my mouth.

'I'm not sure,' he muttered back.

Before I could decide whether to break the symmetry of Jenkins' directorial pattern and retrieve them, Julian had swept forward, opened his folder with a flourish and proceeded with his eight-minute speech. He was word perfect. All the more amazing since he confirmed afterwards that most of it was still lying under my chair. Eventually it was my turn. I had been waiting a long time. I had listened to all the arguments, never taking my eyes off whoever was speaking. The devils had had their say. Satan had produced the apple and now there was silence in the whole of Creation. Including the audience. Time for Archangel Michael to draw the threads of the plot together. Cleverly, I thought, I had kept my index finger firmly inside page ninety-seven of the script to ensure I had no problem in finding my place. Now, after being focused on the action, right leg crossed over left for an hour and forty minutes, my cue was coming up. I rose and stepped forward. My left leg, having been under pressure for so long, had lost all feeling and buckled under me. I limped to the podium, opened the script, and found that my finger, after resolutely marking my place, was dead too. I could not feel it. I could not bend it. It was no help in turning the pages. Thus Archangel Michael, crippled, with an admonitory digit pointing, always pointing, to the way ahead (indeed to the mayoral banquet across the road), brought our opening performance to an odd conclusion. At the reception afterwards I heard Sir John introducing Gordon Honeycombe to a local dignitary. 'This is the awful man who reads the news – no, no, the man who reads the awful news on television. Ha, ha.'

I was now moving back and forth between character and straighter leading parts on television and in the theatre. After a long run of Maugham's *The Circle*, I accepted the part of Young Marlow in *She Stoops to Conquer*, mainly because it was to be directed by Clifford Williams. He had had a number of successes, both at Stratford and in the commercial theatre, and I had admired his production of *Wild Oats*, with Alan Howard in the lead. It seemed to me that his work had a fluency about it that suggested a strong directorial hand and a genuine understanding of what the playwright was trying to say. A few days before we began rehearsals, I found myself talking to an actress from the RSC who knew Clifford well. I mentioned that I was looking forward to working with this prolific director who currently had three plays running simultaneously in the West End. She gave me an odd look and said, 'It'll be interesting for you. Especially when you discover his secret.'

Clifford's cast seemed to be a combination of RSC and Chichester talents and was to open at Billingham, in the north-east of England, before touring to Canada and then finishing up as the star attraction at the Hong Kong Arts Festival. Goldsmith's play was intriguing, and the part of Young Marlow (in my case Young-*ish* Marlow) fascinating to work on because of his stammer. Apparently a favourite play of Freud, the concept of a young man who is a full-blooded roisterer in the presence of any barmaid and becomes a tongue-tied stutterer before the lady of the house is full of exciting theatrical possibilities. I looked forward to inhabiting the duality of the part and Marlow's failure to grasp the truth of his situation.

Rehearsals began, with Diana Quick as Kate Hardcastle and Gerard Murphy as Tony Lumpkin. As the days went on, I felt I was getting no help from Clifford on how to approach the character. He said virtually nothing to me. Was I that bad? Whenever I made a suggestion or attempted to initiate a discussion of some sort, he seemed uninterested. And what about Marlow's stammer? After we had been rehearsing for two weeks, I pinned him down one Saturday morning at the end of the session and spilled out all my ideas and worries about the part. Now at last, I thought, I will hear some great notions about the play, the production and my place in it. I need help. Clifford, small, dark, head tilted upwards, short hair brushed forward, teeth slightly forward too, listened quietly. I burbled on for several minutes. When I had finished he nodded and rested the edges of his teeth on the outer roll of his lower lip. He looked at me solemnly and blinked a couple of times. 'Well, there you are,' he said. 'The fact that you've aired all those thoughts about the part tells me you'll have no problems in playing it. Have a good weekend.'

I saw my RSC friend a few days later. She asked me how I was getting on with Clifford. I told her I was amazed he had said virtually nothing to me or, as far as I could see, to any of the actors. She asked me how I felt it was going. 'Well, funnily enough,' I said, 'it's really going quite well. I seem to have got a handle on the part and –'

'The stammer?'

'Yes, the stammer's working nicely. Yes, I think it's going to be all right.'

'Good,' she nodded. 'That's how he does it. By letting you do all the work. Clever, isn't he? Good luck.'

The curious three-centre tour of *She Stoops* turned out to be a success, beginning as a slightly puzzling pre-Christmas entertainment for the citizens of Billingham, most of whom seemed to be employed on the big industrial complexes owned by ICI. In

Toronto, we played for a month in a freezing auditorium, more suited to rock concerts, in which we had to yell to be heard. From there we transferred to the humidity of Hong Kong in February. The production emerged as the toast of their newly created arts festival and we were much in demand as guests of honour at Chinese New Year celebrations and expatriate lunches. At one of these functions I learnt, in an oblique way, that Goldsmith's view of the possibilities of human error is perfectly accurate. I had been warned by one of the ladies of the Festival Welcoming Committee that we would receive a great many social invitations during our stay. We couldn't of course be expected to attend them all, she said, but one we really *must* accept (she leant on the word 'must' just a little) was luncheon at the Governor's Residence. 'We rather regard it here, Mr Jarvis,' she gushed, 'as being invited to Buckingham Palace.'

A few days later, sure enough, I was standing on the lawn of the magnificent residence on the Peak, and gazing down beyond the skyscraper-tops to the silvery waters of the South China Sea far below. There were twelve guests for lunch. The Governor and his lady moved easily among us as we sipped our gin and tonics. White-uniformed young naval officers threw tennis balls for various governmental dogs that leapt and gambolled in the February sunshine. The Governor came towards me and, with the urbanity of Prince Philip himself, asked if I was filming with Michael Caine. I told him no. The Governor's wife approached and, with a charming smile, said that they had tried to get Mr Caine for lunch but he wasn't available. Apparently Michael was on location here. I realised I must be his replacement. I told her I was appearing in She Stoops to Conquer at the festival. She smiled politely and I felt that, like the Queen herself, she probably preferred a good musical to the classics. A large man with a yellow moustache and matching suit rolled across the grass and shook me by the hand. His name was something like Hogg-Coote. He said he had seen our show and it was bloody marvellous. He waxed lyrical. 'Bloody funny play, She Stoops. One of my favourites. Thought you were splendid as Young Marlow. Played the part m'self years ago, at university. Good role. Good show. Get down, will you.' This last remark was addressed to a posse of ankle-biting Pekinese who were attacking his trouser legs.

I risked a joke. 'Pekes on the Peak,' I said.

He laughed as if it was the funniest thing he had ever heard. He wiped his eyes with a large silk handkerchief and told me, as we made our way into the dining room, that he was on leave from the British Consulate in Nepal. He panted on about Young Marlow. 'Fine young blade, eh?' He seemed almost to be reliving his lost youth. 'Couldn't do it now, old boy. Bit long in the tooth, what?' He wiped his eyes again, mopped his brow and guffawed mightily.

We took our places around the circular mahogany table. I was surprised to find myself on our hostess's left. I thought, afterwards, that was probably where Michael Caine would have been placed had he been free. On the Lady Governor's other side was my new chum, Hogg-Coote. I noticed, as she sat down, that she hung her handbag on some sort of hook beneath the table. That seemed to be the cue for us all to tuck into an odd meal of chicken and diced beetroot. I don't remember there being much else.

The Governor himself held court on the far side of the table. I talked for a few minutes to a lady from the Hong Kong Jockey Club on my left. Finally, running out of things to say, I turned to my hostess. She bent graciously towards me. She spoke mostly about Michael Caine, still clearly feeling he was our connection. I gave her a rundown on his movie career so far as I could, and we both agreed that his best performance to date was in *Sleuth* with Laurence Olivier. After we had discussed the rival merits of *Alfie*, *Zulu* and *The Italian Job* there seemed little else to say. Hogg-Coote, on her right, was just accepting a second portion of beetroot squares. She smiled and turned back to him. But then, suddenly, she said something astonishing: 'You're *fat*. Much too *fat*. You're gross. And a greedy-guts.' Hogg-Coote didn't, it must be said, seem too worried. He shovelled down his beetroot. '*Fat* as a barrel,' she resumed, before unexpectedly turning back to me for an opinion, 'don't you agree Mr Jarvis?'

How was I to answer without offence to either?

'*Fat, fat, fat,*' she persisted, emphasising the point by thumping her knees (or was it her handbag?) beneath the table. She glanced at me, almost coquettishly, and said, 'Fat as butter, Mr Jarvis. What are we going to do with him?'

It seemed I had to make a comment. I decided to speak on behalf of my corpulent new friend: 'Well, I suppose Mr Hogg-Coote is a bit too Falstaffian for Young Marlow. Perhaps he has the weight for *Old* Marlow. Or what about Sir Toby Belch, ha ha!'

This pitched it just right, I thought. I felt I had got us all out of a tight spot. I hadn't. As I finished speaking, a silence descended. It extended across to the Governor, who laid down his fork in astonishment. Hogg-Coote himself stared at me in bewilderment. Our hostess's smile retracted itself. She turned again to her right and repeated her emphatic patting movement beneath the table. I leant forward. 'I was referring' – she spoke icily – 'to Humphrey.' I saw everything. She was thumping the rump of a large over-fed labrador who, I now realised, had been lurking for some time unseen, just below table-level, between her and the unfairly vilified Hogg-Coote.

That night, back at the theatre, I thought I acted the idiocies of Young Marlow's misapprehension with an added perception.

In spring 1978, I found myself filming the part of King George VI in an American mini-series, 'Ike – The War Years', whilst simultaneously playing his brother Edward VIII in a new play at the Churchill Theatre, Bromley. The play, *The Woman I Love* by Dan Sutherland, was based on the 1936 abdication crisis. The two brothers didn't really look alike; I resembled neither of them. I was much too tall for a start, though I managed to look vaguely like Edward with judicious hair-combing and the right tailoring. The director, John F. Landry, cunningly cast a very tall Wallis Simpson in the person of the talented six-foot American actress Holly Palance. This, he assured me, would make me look smaller. To top off the illusion, he cast hugely tall actors around us, the result being that we were eerily effective onstage as the pint-sized couple.

My chief delight in the play was the opportunity of performing Edward's abdication speech every night. I had managed to get a copy of the famous broadcast by nipping into BBC Broadcasting House and gaining access to the archive where all the royal recordings were housed. Courteous BBC warnings were displayed on the walls: 'Anyone found recording this archive material will be –' what – shot? Imprisoned in the Tower? Hung drawn and quartered? No, merely '– asked to leave immediately.' Naturally, so that I could listen over and over to the tone and phrasing of that extraordinary speech, I had secreted a tape-recorder in my briefcase. Having lined up the records I needed, I sneaked the microphone into position, switched on, and risked the punishment. Since I knew that I was soon to begin filming 'Ike', I also taped several recordings of King George VI. Poignant though Edward's abdication speech was, his brother's attempts to overcome his stammer and speak, in public and on his Christmas broadcasts, was even more affecting. There was a red label on all the George VI records which stated, 'Not to be broadcast without royal permission.' I placed them on the turntable and played them one by one. It was moving to hear those unedited old vinyls as the king, with intervals of agonising length, battled to get over the hurdle of a 'p' or a 'g' that blocked his path. 'It gives me gw-great – i- i- p- p- pleasure' – the pauses seemed endless, the effort equally so and the bravery inspiring. I could hear that he placed a number of little 'i' sounds in front of certain consonants, almost like a stile to help him bridge the gap and make it across to the other side. I also heard the weak intrusive 'r', frequently used by the upper class of that generation: 'gweat' instead of great, 'vewy' instead of very. After the theatricality of the stammering Young Marlow in Goldsmith's play, I looked forward to playing the king and investigating the real-life implications of such an affliction.

Once *The Woman I Love* had opened, I began my few days shooting as George VI. None of the production team seemed concerned that I didn't look anything like him. Our American director, Boris Sagal, an energetic veteran of many mini-series and action movies, sped towards me. He put a viewfinder to his eye and adjusted the lens. Like Stuart Whitman a few years before, he insisted on addressing me by my character's name: 'OK, King, looking good. Let's go!'

The series starred Robert Duvall as Eisenhower, with Lee Remick as Kay Summersby, his driver. General Montgomery was played by Ian Richardson and Wensley Pithey was a dead-ringer for Churchill. On our first day we were to shoot the scene in which His Majesty makes a welcoming speech of introduction to the Commonwealth leaders (played by two hundred extras) before chairing a discussion on plans for the D-Day invasion. Boris suggested that we rehearse the scene before he brought everybody else on to the set. We took our places on the platform. Duvall, sharp-eyed, hatchet-faced, sat to one side, picking his teeth with a matchstick, watching us. 'OK, King,' said Boris from halfway down the empty hall, 'you start.'

With my BBC research freshly in mind, I stood up, approached the lectern and began. 'I- I- It g- g- gives me – i – g- gweat – i – i – p-p-p-leasure –'

Boris held up a hand. 'Hey, wait a minute, King. What're you doing?'

I explained that was how George VI spoke. 'He had a stammer,' I told him, 'and a funny "r".'

Boris put down his viewfinder. 'I don't care if he had a funny ass,' he exclaimed, 'you can't take all that time over your lines. We'll be here till the war's over. Now c'm on, King, move it.'

I could see his point. I did the speech again, going light on the 'r' and stammering only twice.

'Great, King. See what I mean?' called Boris. 'Now you, Monty.'

I thought Ian Richardson looked apprehensive as he stood to deliver his first remarks about the invasion. Boris raced into a new position, viewfinder to his eye. Ian cleared his throat and began, in Montgomery's clipped tones, 'It's vewy vewy important, evwybody –'

'For god's sake, Monty, what the hell's going on?' Boris bobbed up from just below us. 'What you playing at?'

Ian, who had captured Monty superbly in those five words, leant forward and said, patiently, in his own mellifluous tones, at least an octave lower than Monty's, 'But that's how he spoke, Boris.'

Boris shook his head, 'Yeah, well, not too much of that "vewy" stuff. They won't go for it in Hoboken, New Jersey.' He looked up. 'OK, Churchill –'

I detected a flicker of a smile cross the granite features of Duvall as Wensley Pithey, Winston to the life and twice as anxious, rose from his seat. Boris ducked below the platform again, viewfinder to his eye.

'Let's hear it, Winnie,' he cried.

Wensley grasped the edge of the lectern and set his lower lip in that unmistakable bulldog grimace. 'Thwoughout histowy,' he began, 'many gweat wawwiors have stwived –'

There was a crashing sound from below us. We leant forward to see that Boris had thrown himself backwards on to the polished floor of the auditorium and was lying prostrate as if in some kind of private frenzy. He held up his arms in supplication: 'I don't believe it. You British kill me. Can't we just tell the fuckin' story?' Suddenly he sprang up, leapt on to the platform and said briskly, 'OK. King, this is the deal – you can have just *one* of those doubleyous, and you stutter on *one* "p" only. Monty – you get *one* doubleyou and no stammers. Winnie – OK, you look great but don't do any of that mouth stuff. And, Bob –' Duvall took the match from his mouth and cocked an eye. 'Bob – you're fine. But don't get any ideas from these lime –' he stopped, slapped his hand on my shoulder and winked across at his star '– these classical actors.'

Sagal made one other comment to me during the day. Wensley Pithey had been concerned as to when exactly he should rise from his seat to begin his address to the assembled leaders. I suggested I gave him a kingly nod. Boris grinned and said, 'Well, King, you can if you want, it's up to you. But you're not in the shot. What the hell's the point?'

My point was actually to provide assistance to Wensley, who *was* in the shot and needed a little 'motivation'.

Boris leant closer to me and imparted a Hollywood lesson: 'Forgive me, King, but nothing matters except what the camera sees.'

He was right, of course, though all actors know that off-screen moments between characters can influence what occurs on-screen. At Wensley's request, I gave him the regal go-ahead each time he did the scene. He was grateful: 'It makes me feel like Churchill in the presence of my king,' he whispered to me between takes. It was interesting that it was the elderly British actor who was looking for 'motivation' while the American director, who might have expected us to 'feel' everything, merely wanted us to get on with it.

I chatted with Duvall while the great Director of Photography, Freddie Young, padded slowly around the set fine-tuning his lighting. We stood outside in the sunshine. Duvall drew on a cigarette and told me he was in awe of British actors. He surprised me with a compliment: 'You've done that goddam speech 'bout fifteen times from all those different angles – with that stutter – and it's on the money every time. You guys have great technique.'

I made a mental note to let Peter Barkworth know that all had not been in vain. I returned Robert's compliment by saying I thought he was terrific in the two *Godfather* films.

He grinned wolfishly, and said that Brando had been great to work with. He then asked me: 'You know Scofield? Played Thomas More?'

Of course, I replied. One of our finest actors.

He looked at me and scratched his balding head. 'Well, you know Mart'n, I've watched *Man for All Seasons* a couple of times and I don't get it. The guy's got no juice.'

Before we could continue, Boris was calling for us to shoot one more angle on the scene and I never got to explain to Duvall what I thought was so wonderful about Paul Scofield's per-formance – a brilliantly controlled piece of film acting from one of our juiciest actors. Scofield's supreme 'technique' as the dry More had fooled even so clever an actor as Robert Duvall.

In the early summer of 1978, while I was still appearing in *The Woman I Love*, I was sent some scripts for a series called 'Rings on Their Fingers'. This was a situation-comedy written by Richard Waring, which dealt with a couple who lived together (wow) and worried constantly about whether they should get married. Simple attractive stuff, made appealing to viewers by Waring's gift for capturing the way people who love each other actually talk and bicker. He structured his half-hour scripts like neat short stories or mini-plays, usually with some kind of revelation or twist, or both, to surprise you at the end. Richard was not above borrowing from himself. Some of the domestic plotlines that occurred in 'Rings' – house-hunting, promotion prospects, the boss coming to dinner – bore a remarkable resemblance to his own earlier series, 'Marriage Lines', which starred Richard Briers and Prunella Scales. Even some of the dialogue was vaguely familiar. As Waring used to say, 'If I can't plagiarise myself who can I plagiarise?' It was no surprise to me to find that he was a fan of Richmal Crompton. I could see, as I read the scripts, that the airy optimism (and tendency towards exaggeration) of his hero Oliver Pryde was not a million miles from a grown-up William Brown. I was invited to Television Centre to discuss the part.

At that time, it seemed that in order to be a BBC Light Entertainment producer, you had to have the sort of name that wouldn't be out of place in an H. G. Wells rites-of-passage novel. A witty agent, Michael Whitehall, once suggested there must be an auditioning process where would-be employees are weeded out if their names weren't sufficiently Light Ent: Jeremy Arbuthnot, no; Julian Fortescue, no; Rupert Fellowes, no; Syd Lotterby, Ray Butt, Bernie Thompson, Harold Snoad, *yes*.

It was Harold Snoad who turned out to be the producer/director of 'Rings on Their Fingers'. This was the first time I had had any dealings with this department of the BBC. All the television directors I had met and worked with in the past had been either straightforward professionals like Joan Craft and David Giles, canny operators like James Cellan Jones, or sensitive storytellers like Ronald Wilson and Waris Hussein. Harold Snoad was not quite like any of these. He had been a floor-manager, worked his way up via 'Dad's Army' and the 'Dick Emery Show'; a master of mirth. He was a bundle of bald-headed energy who reminded me of a ricocheting snooker ball as he greeted me with a chuckling barrage of nodding and winking and thanking for coming and what did you think of the scripts? 'Very wonderful, eh? ha ha! Richard Waring thinks they are anyway, ha ha ha!'

He set a chair for me, retreated behind his desk, put his feet on it and asked if I would mind reading the script to him. I didn't mind. Almost the second I began he accompanied me with a kind of extended chortle that continued even when I paused for breath. I assumed this was the Light Ent. way of making the actor feel he was getting every ounce of comedy attention.

I rather liked Snoad's method. After I had finished, he told me my reading was hilarious – in fact, he said, 'very wonderful'. His chortle level increased as he offered me the part; it virtually went off the scale when I mentioned that I would still be performing *The Woman I Love* and wasn't really free. He wiped his eyes. 'No problem, no problem,' he guffawed, thrusting his hands deep into his grey flannels. Suddenly he leant forward, deadly serious. He spoke confidentially, 'Now, I know you've done Shakespeare and all that, drama and so on.' He leant even closer. 'Well, worry not. This may be sit-com, but – in my productions, I do –' he paused so that I could ready myself for what was to follow '– I do – *drama close-ups*.' He gave a final wink, told me again I was very wonderful and that the whole of the department would not sleep until they heard I had accepted.

I played Oliver in three series of 'Rings on Their Fingers' over the next two-and-a-half years and learnt a great deal. Richard Waring had an extraordinary ear for the comedy buried in domestic exchanges. After his early success with 'Marriage Lines', he was established as television's most expert chronicler of marital disharmony. In the mid-eighties, when I worked with Ayckbourn for the first time (in *Woman in Mind*), Alan told me how much he respected Richard's writing. He had watched those early sit-coms and had admired their lightness of touch and the affectionate tetchiness of the characters. Alan's first West End success, *Relatively Speaking*, though completely original, contains influences, said Alan, that stemmed from his appreciation of Waring's writing.

When we began work, Harold Snoad hinted to me that

Richard's reputation was in need of a boost. 'Rings', which owed so much of its instant success to the sharpness of Richard's bitter-sweet scripts, provided this upsurge. He had his own office in the Light Entertainment department and the title of Script Consultant. In rehearsal, he enjoyed producing a silver flask from his inside pocket, taking a swig and saying, 'Well, back to the office – turn down a few scripts, write a few of my own!' A boozer, he seemed oddly proud of it. It became a familiar if disturbing sight to see him swigging brandy or vodka from his little flask at our morning readthroughs. He was big and broad, with a wide face, chunky spectacles and greying hair sleeked back with a touch of Brylcreem. He had been an actor for a short time early in his career, and the slim, good-looking young man in some of the photos displayed in his office contrasted surprisingly with the bloated look of a clubbable Rolls-Royce salesman.

My co-star was the darkly beautiful Diane Keen. She was landed with a tricky problem on this series, in that she had already recorded a pilot episode with another director and another Oliver. The BBC, in its wisdom, had sacked them and brought in Harold, who brought in me. Not easy for Diane. She asked me during our first rehearsal if I had ever done sit-com before. I told her no and went on, somewhat airily, to say I imagined sit-com to be rather like the theatre except it was on television. She gave me a doubtful look. 'It isn't,' she said. She herself was a veteran of the comedy series 'The Cuckoo Waltz', and had done her time on the long-running soap 'Crossroads'. 'Still,' she added, 'if it helps you to think so –' I left it at that.

She was quite right, of course. Less is more, even in the broadest of sit-coms. The comedy *is* the situation and the wrong kind of theatrical projection is out of place, despite the seductive presence of a studio audience. It's an interesting acting dichotomy, which Diane had clearly solved for herself. It's essential to be real for the cameras, while timing the laughs that come from the three hundred people watching the recording.

After three series of 'Rings', Richard's invention started to run out and we mutually agreed that it would be difficult to take the story further. He continued to write for television and had a lesser success with a series about a company that manufactured lavatory pans. He loved this kind of humour. I remember questioning him about the presence of some doubtful lines in the first scene of one of the 'Rings' episodes. 'Aha,' he chuckled, 'you can't beat a bog-roll for an early laugh!'

I was sorry when that silver flask finally brought him down in 1995. He was a remarkable observer of the ludicrousness of human behaviour. Including his own.

The reinjection of television celebrity that had come my way meant I was in demand. And identifiable. This time round I experienced none of the old problems when fingers were pointed or I was recognised in the street. There was no ducking and weaving, although I did take to my heels once when I got trapped by two hundred schoolgirls on the concourse at Euston station.

Any free time from rehearsal or filming (I had moved straight on to a Francis Durbridge thriller series, 'Breakaway') was spent in Soho among the red lights of the recording studios. As a popular *face* on television, the advertising business, with a logic all its own, had decided my *voice* was essential to the sale of their products. So I got my larynx behind Twix, the longer-lasting snack, Barclaycard, Dulux, Hertz, Cabbage Patch Kids, Wall's Pork Sausages, Martini, Holsten Pils, Allied Carpets, Daz, the Curry's Price Promise, Ford cars, Birds Eye peas, Golden Wonder Crisps, just about anything except cigarettes and fur. My repertoire included soft-sell, hard-sell, cool, warm, steely-sell, light, dark, wry, American, even Indian. ('Can you sound a bit more like yourself, Martin? Make it more Churchillian. Yeah, magic!') Sometimes, when I emerged from the recording booth, the very people who had hired me would seem almost resentful that they had to pay for what seemed to them to take only a few minutes of my time. One advertising lady couldn't contain herself in this respect when the actor Robin Bailey had finished a short session. 'Very good,' she told him, grudgingly, 'but I do think it's disgraceful the way you actors can come in here, say "Drink More Milk" or whatever, and walk away with all that money.'

Robin put his head on one side and thought for a second. 'Ah yes, my dear,' he said with utmost courtesy, 'but it's taken me twenty-five years to get into the studio.' He meant that using your voice as a totally flexible, juicy, biddable instrument, pouring information and flavour into five or ten or twenty seconds, isn't as easy as it sounds.

I agreed with him. It had taken me nearly as long to find my own way there.

One afternoon around that time I was walking towards the DeLane Lea recording studio to 'voice' a television commercial for Old Spice aftershave. My route took me along Meard Street, past an ancient Soho establishment – no longer in existence – the Golden Girls Club. It was a sunny day and a window on the ground floor was open. A golden girl sat there giving the eye to passers-by. As I drew level she called out, 'Hello, I know you from the telly. How *are* you?'

I made my first mistake by replying, 'I'm fine, how are *you*?'

She pursued the relationship by telling me her name was Diane. 'Can I have your autograph?' she asked.

'Yes, all right,' I replied. (My second mistake.)

'Come in then,' she said, 'I'll get a piece of paper.' She disappeared from view, giggling.

Third mistake: I went up the steps of the old Queen Anne house, pushed open the door and went inside. The main room was dark and smelt of stale beer. A smoky pall hung in the gloom. Two or three other slightly tarnished golden girls glanced at me from where they sat at a rickety bar. A couple of bewhiskered men leant there, silent, watching. A sailor sat alone at a table in a corner. Diane came towards me. The only paper she had been able to find was an old brown-paper bag. She held it out: 'Here you are, sign on that. Put "to Diane", will you?' I autographed the bag. 'Ta, Martin,' she smiled. I was just turning to leave when she shot out an arm and pulled me back. 'Here, give us a kiss then,' she said. Before I could react she had yanked me forward and landed a squelching smacker on my lips. I reeled away and made for the door. 'Thanks, Martin luv,' she called after me as I fled down the steps and into the sunshine again.

A few minutes later I was recording my voice-over. I was quite

pleased with the macho tones I produced to complement the
image of the bronzed surfer on screen. 'Old Spice – For men,' I
repeated on each take. 'For *men.*' The director called a halt. I
couldn't tell whether he was happy with my efforts or not – he
seemed anxious to get rid of me. It was the same with the
representatives from the advertising agency and the men in suits
from Old Spice. They thanked me vaguely and wouldn't look me
in the eye. I got the feeling they wished they'd hired Robin
Bailey. Never mind. I went into the wash-room before leaving –
and caught sight of my face in the mirror. Oh no. Around my
mouth was the indelible scarlet imprint of Diane's lipstick. I
saw it all. No wonder they weren't sure if I was their man. There
was more to come. Back at rehearsal I told the story. 'Ah yes,'
said actor John Baddeley, 'but there's a hidden agenda. You
haven't grasped its full significance. The Golden Girls Club is
notorious. I'm surprised you didn't know. Those girls – they're all
blokes.'

Soho is an unpredictable square mile. Old Spice. Golden
Wonder. For men.

BBC Light Entertainment approached me about several other
series, none of which seemed to have the charm or insight of
Richard Waring's best ideas. I had learnt by this time that no one
really knows what will be successful in comedy. Sometimes the
most unlikely material leaps up the charts. And what seems
brilliantly funny on the page or in the studio just doesn't appeal
to the viewing audience. Around this time, Ros came across a
new book by Christopher Matthew, *Diary of a Somebody*, the
fictional memoirs of a thirty-something marketing man, Simon
Crisp. She thought it would make a perfect comedy series. I read
it and nearly fell out of bed with laughter. I told Jean Diamond,
she put me in touch with the author and, at the BBC's request,
Chris and I adapted it for television. The Head of Comedy was
tremendously enthusiastic about the pilot script. 'I love it. I am
right behind it. I want to do it!' We never heard another word.
Guy Jenkin suggested to me that he write a series about
newspapers called 'The Times', so that the comedy executives at

Television Centre could walk around saying, 'I am behind "The Times", I'm right behind "The Times".'

Instead, I was sent the first three scripts of a series about two doctors. I turned it down without any qualms. It eventually ran for six successful series. So what did I know?

In 1980, after two series of 'Breakaway', Jean introduced me to George Schaefer, an elderly American who was going to direct a film version of James P. O'Donnell's meticulously researched book on Hitler's last days, *The Berlin Bunker*. Much of the material was based on the author's interviews with Johannes Hentschel who had worked for Hitler as an electrician and general maintenance man. George – mild, humorous, everybody's favourite grandfather – offered me this part. The screenwriter John Gay had developed a fascinating two-and-a-half-hour script; a special bunker was being constructed in the old Joinville Studios outside Paris, based closely on Albert Speer's original design.

Anthony Hopkins, who had been a year below me at Rada, was to play Hitler. As with 'Ike', an 'international cast' had been assembled. A Welsh Hitler (Tony), a French Bormann (Michel Lonsdale), an American Magda Goebbels and Eva Braun (Piper Laurie and Susan Blakely) and a Goebbels from the Bronx (Cliff Gorman). The two bunker stalwarts were Misch the telephonist (Michael Kitchen) and the eccentric Hentschel (me). Tony's performance was superb, quite the most accurate and powerful interpretation of the monster of the Third Reich any of us had seen. He won an Emmy Award for it in the States but, strangely, the film has hardly been seen in Britain.

Johannes Hentschel had first worked for the Führer in the Chancellery, where Hitler had presented him with a luminous watch. Hentschel had worn it ever afterwards on one wrist, still wearing his own on the other. I thought this was an interesting point and wore two watches in the part. This led to an odd moment between Tony and me.

There was an intense concentration on the set throughout filming, probably because of the extraordinary events we were recreating. Whenever Hopkins was around, the atmosphere became even more charged. His demeanour, his attitude, everything about his physical presence *was* Hitler. He was mesmerising. During the pauses for lighting adjustments he would remain in character. We tended to follow his lead. One morning we were preparing to shoot the scene in which the Führer bids farewell to members of his loyal team. He moves slowly down the line shaking each of us by the hand before retiring to his private apartment where he and Eva Braun take their lives. Final tweaks were being made for the camera. Mindful of his preference for remaining in character, as we were standing around I said quietly to Tony, 'Look.' I pulled up my right sleeve and showed him the watch. 'This is my old watch,' I told him. 'I've had it for years.'

Tony glanced at it, then at me. He looked slightly puzzled.

I pulled up my left sleeve and continued, 'This is the watch you gave me. I always wear it on this wrist. It's luminous, as you know.'

He looked at it. Then at me. The little moustache twitched. 'What do you mean?' he said.

'Well,' I replied, 'you gave it to me. I shall always treasure it.'

'I gave it you?'

I nodded.

He paused, then said, 'You mean at Rada?'

Before I could explain that I had been speaking to him in character – he Hitler, me Hentschel – we were called to our places. I watched him take up his position next to Eva Braun. He turned, ready for his final moment, still looking puzzled. Did I *really*, Adolf seemed to be thinking, when I was an impoverished drama student, give a fellow student – in a class a year ahead – a wristwatch?

Try it. Mm. See what happens.

July 1982

Waterloo

On a bright summer day, an apprehensive group of actors stood in Rehearsal Room 1 waiting for the artistic director of the National Theatre, Sir Peter Hall, to make his appearance. This was my first time here. We were about to embark on the read-through of Peter's much heralded production of *The Importance of Being Earnest* by Oscar Wilde, which would open in the Lyttelton Theatre in seven weeks' time. I was to play Jack Worthing. Judi Dench, in what was considered by some a daring piece of casting, was to be Lady Bracknell. We waited nervously for the great man. Most of the space in the room was occupied by a strange sloping construction, rather like a motorcycle display-team's take-off ramp. Thirty feet across and rising up towards the ceiling, its blue surface glittered in the artificial light. Probably something to do with the National's production of *Guys and Dolls*. This was going to get in the way unless they removed it before we began work.

Suddenly here was our director, entering the room beaming and nodding, a beneficent mandarin of the arts. We relaxed a little. Peter has an enormous gift for making you feel the whole project is only possible because *you* are a participant. Framed within the neat dark beard and moustache, his sensual mouth parted roguishly as he looked around. He greeted us individually: a kiss for Anna Massey, a hug for Zoë Wanamaker, both for Judi Dench who stood a little apart, blushing slightly and grinning like a schoolgirl who might not have done her homework. This

was her first time at the National too. Peter grasped my hand in
both of his and murmured intimately, 'So pleased you're here,
Martin. Harold's thrilled too.' Snoad, I thought? No, he meant
Pinter, whose *Other Places* we were to premiere once *The
Importance* was up and running. Five of us – Judi, Anna, Paul
Rogers, Nigel Havers and me – would be appearing in these three
short plays. Elizabeth Garvie and Zoë Wanamaker would only be
in *The Importance*. Both productions were to be directed by Peter.
The formidable Diana Boddington, stage manager and Lilian
Baylis lookalike, herded us across to a long table down one side of
the room.

We took our places. Peter sat at the head. Various others –
understudies, assistant stage managers, wardrobe people – found
seats towards the other end. We read the play through, stumbling
a good deal over the text, cowed by this great comedy. Wilde's
world was suddenly much harder to enter than any of us had
imagined. And not so funny either. We did our best. Nigel's easy
charm seemed just right for Algernon Moncrieff. Zoë read
intensely as Gwendolen without looking up from the script.
Anna, as Miss Prism, had clearly done a lot of preparation, her
script decorated with coloured markings. Paul Rogers boomed
authoritatively as Chasuble and Elizabeth Garvie sounded witty
as Cecily Cardew. I injected Jack with a light-hearted airiness
which I hadn't yet realised was wholly inappropriate. Judi read
Lady Bracknell in a soft monotone which had people at the lower
end of the table straining forward to hear. I had worked with her
twice before, once on television and once in a recital for one of
Prince Charles' charities. Her gift of total truth as an actress takes
one's breath away. I knew that until she has found the central
core of a part she remains quiet and doesn't attempt a
performance of any kind. She was very quiet today.

After we had finished, Peter grinned wickedly and told us he
admired our efforts but the reading had been theatrical and
artificial. He then talked about what he thought Wilde was trying
to get at and how we ought to approach the play. He believed
that Wilde's plays reveal unattractive aspects of the underbelly
of Victorian society; that the aphoristic banter is often his

characters' attempts to mask the truths of their real lives. The epigrams are often a cover for something more sinister. They aren't just jokes. He made so much sense in such a short time that I couldn't believe I had not seen it for myself. Peter's point was simple and, in retrospect, obvious. It became clear, too, that a seriousness of purpose on the part of the characters actually increased the comedy of the play. *The Importance of Being Earnest* is 'A Trivial Comedy for Serious People', a drama of double lives, of hypocrisy and pretence, with buried truths lurking under the skin of each character.

Having completed his introductory chat, Peter turned to John Bury, the designer, and invited him to show us the set. This is always the cue for everyone to gather round a small model and murmur appreciatively as tiny figures are moved about and bits of miniature scenery shifted to give an idea of what the real thing will look like. John rose, bulky and intimidating as any of the battlements he had created for countless Royal Shakespeare history plays. We expected him to bend down and produce his toy theatre from beneath the table. But no. He strode over to the foot of the glitzy motorcycle ramp. 'Here we are,' he said, blinking mildly behind slightly misty spectacles.

There was no model. This *was* the real thing. Instead of appreciative comments and nods there was silence. If this incline were on the public highway, I thought, there would surely be a roadside notice, 'Engage Low Gear Now.' We gazed. I knew we were all wondering how much acting could take place on a 1-in-5 gradient. And what on earth had it got to do with Oscar Wilde? I thought of a helmeted team of National Theatre dare-devils, led by Judi Dench and Anna Massey, their throbbing machines gathering speed, hitting the slope with perfect timing, soaring into the air across the tops of twenty-five London buses before landing on a similarly glittering escarpment at the other end. The Wilde Ones. I don't recall speaking for several minutes, but Judi has told me since that she remembers my exclaiming, 'Is this *it*?'

It was. As we continued to stare, John Bury explained that in the first scene there would be a carpet on the slope, on top of which would be a small sofa and a couple of chairs. That would represent the 'luxuriously and artistically furnished' morning room of Algy's Mayfair flat. Nobody spoke. 'What about the garden scene,' I inquired eventually.

John gestured up the blue hill.

'Just that?' bleated Nigel. John nodded.

'Yes, but the muffin-eating,' we cried.

'Oh, well, maybe a table.'

'On that slope?'

'Why not?'

'And chairs?'

John was getting tetchy: 'Well, we can work all that out.'

I risked a supplementary, why was the slope blue and glittery?

He harumphed a bit and said something about the lighting he would be using for the garden. 'You know, that amazing depth of colour you get in the summer when the trees throw dark shadows across the grass.'

I caught Nigel Havers' eye. We both knew you can't play comedy if there isn't enough light. 'Anyway,' I persisted, 'grass isn't blue.'

Anna Massey leant forward and whispered in my ear, 'They called him the Prince of Darkness at Stratford.'

We began work next day. The unravelling of the text with Peter was infinitely fascinating, but life on the ramp was problematic. The rich accoutrements of Algy's rooms and Jack's country mansion were represented by a few sticks of furniture whose rear legs had to be sawn down to accommodate the rake. This allowed them to appear to be standing upright. The actors, incapable of being anti-raked in the same way, were forced to adopt awkward positions, knees bent, backs arched, trying to look natural. Walking was a challenge. More challenging still was my first scene with Nigel. As promised, John Bury had carpeted the central section of the stage. Unfortunately, this did not solve the problem of how we were to move around as elegant Victorians. 'It is a very ungentlemanly thing to read a private cigarette case,' I cried at the first public performance, lunging forward and attempting to chase Algy around the so-called morning room. 'Give it back. Aaah –!' Whereupon the apartment became a giant helter-skelter as the carpet coasted down the slope towards the audience with both of us aboard, balancing precariously like two children at the fair.

Gielgud's advice on how to play Wilde is to behave as if you are taking part in an elaborate practical joke. This isn't so far from Wilde's 'seriousness', which we were discovering as we rehearsed. I was finding, more and more, that the ultimate key to John Worthing JP was his earnestness. It's all there in the text and I couldn't believe I had never spotted the clues before. At first, because he is visiting town as 'Ernest', I was tempted, as other actors before me, to present a wannabe-dilettante with almost as light a touch as the debonair Algy. Even Worthing's opening line seemed to demand such an approach. When Algy greets him with 'How are you, my dear Ernest? What brings you up to town?' he replies, 'Oh, pleasure, pleasure! What else should bring one anywhere?' Light, witty, blithe. Well, no. One morning rehearsal, taking Algy's later description as a guide ('You answer to the name of Ernest. You look as if your name was Ernest. You are the most earnest looking person I ever saw in my life.') I made my entrance. Instead of replying to Algy's inquiry in the careless manner of yesterday, I turned a serious gaze upon him and answered in tones of gravest significance: 'Oh, pleasure, pleasure!' I followed it up with deadpan solemnity, 'What else should bring one anywhere?' Not a speck of humour. Merely the logic of a country JP whose search for the hedonistic life (and a possible proposal of marriage) is a knotty problem to be solved. Peter Hall beamed like a great cat that had been waiting for this bowl of cream.

The abiding image of Lady Bracknell had been created by Edith Evans who played it in the theatre in the thirties, with Gielgud as Jack Worthing. But for most people, her performance was immortalised in the stylish film of the fifties, still shown regularly on television. Whenever *The Importance* is mentioned, anyone, it seems, can quote the inflection of Dame Edith's unforgettable delivery of, 'A hand-*baaaag*!!!???' Hers was a joyous choice, now thoroughly patented, though not necessarily Wilde's intention in the scene; he puts only a single question mark at the end of the sentence and no exclamation mark. But how to say the line any other way? Especially when the audience is waiting, eager to see and hear what another actress will do with it. If it's a carbon-copy of Dame Edith it will seem merely imitative. If it's glossed over it will be a disappointment. During the early rehearsals, Judi muttered the line and moved hastily on.

Peter decided, after a few weeks, that we would run the play. Judi, apprehensively it seemed, took her place at the top of the slope in readiness for her first entrance. Nigel and I played the scene before she came on, finding that the seriousness of purpose we had been working on was having some effect. But no one was quite prepared for the impact that Lady Bracknell was to have on us. Here was a neat, crisp, bird-like woman whose darting eyes took in the situation at a glance and whose sweet smile belied the power she wielded. This was a sexy, barely middle-aged mini-matriarch, who flirted outrageously with Algy, clearly her favourite nephew. Her voice was flute-like, her attitude to her daughter's future prettily pragmatic. A beguiling Bracknell that owed nothing to theatrical tradition yet seemed entirely the essence of Wilde's monstrous figure of controlling motherhood. Judi, before our eyes and ears, was redefining a character that had seemed almost impossible to shift from beneath the long shadow cast by Edith Evans.

The night before we gave our first public preview, Peter told me in a confiding, almost apologetic, manner that although he thought my performance had become admirably 'earnest', he still couldn't help feeling as he watched me that I still looked too – 'How shall I put it?' he said carefully. 'Too romantic. Too much like Algy.'

I didn't know what to say to this and wasn't sure where it was leading.

'I wondered,' he went on, 'whether you might smarm your hair down more and – ah – wear spectacles.'

His large lips parted in a pleading smile: 'I do think it would be wonderful,' he promised.

Before he had finished speaking I knew that he was right and, again, I couldn't believe I hadn't had the idea myself. Next night,

I presented a bay-rummed, bespectacled, almost nerdy, Ernest. The huge laugh that greeted 'Oh, pleasure, pleasure!' began a year's run in which I learnt a great deal more about the serious craft of comedy. Judi Dench's sensual Lady Bracknell was a triumph. Wearing a sharp little hat that still had room for a couple of dead birds on its brim, she continued to throw dazzling new light on the play and her character.

Even after we had been running for several weeks, Judi still confessed to being nervous of the audience's reaction. She told me that, in the scene in which she virtually interrogates 'Ernest' as to his elegibility, she dreaded the moments that lead to the hand-bag revelation. She played it exquisitely, almost coquettishly, as Ernest seems more and more of a catch for her daughter. She took notes in a tiny book and, on hearing that I had been *found* – 'Found!' (she looked up, sharp as steel, on that) in a hand-bag, she seemed not to believe what she was hearing. She repeated quietly, almost dead-pan, 'A hand-bag?' which increased the level of comedy and moved her on to the sardonic amazement of 'The line is immaterial'.

One night, about a month after we had opened, something strange occurred. We were playing the famous scene. As usual, I was planted halfway up the slope, legs and feet angled to accommodate the carpeted rake. Judi was seated centre-stage on the unsumptuous settee that tilted, on its anti-raked legs, towards the audience. Suddenly, before the historic line, and after I had announced, 'I was . . . well, I was found,' I heard Judi exclaim: 'And where was this handbag found . . . ?'

Eh? It was as if we had suffered a small time-slip. My brain raced. We shouldn't have reached this point yet, I told myself. Had I inadvertently jumped half a page? Had I given her the wrong cue? No, I didn't think so. Had she simply hurdled the line that always gave her so much anxiety? I wasn't sure. But whatever had happened, what should we do now? Should we go back half a page? Should I repeat the 'found' line so that we could swing into the hand-bag second time around? In the event we continued, both of us looking out from behind our characters with panicked eyes as the scene went on. Finally it ended and Judi made her exit. Nigel Havers came on, eyebrow raised – they'd all been on tenterhooks backstage, wondering what happened – and we played the rest of the act. As I came off, Judi was still in the wings, waiting for me. She was almost in tears. 'Oh Mart,' she said, 'what am I going to do?' I didn't know how to comfort this great actress. I still wasn't sure it wasn't all my fault anyway. She went on, 'And what about the end of the play? It's all about the hand-bag and that you were found in it – and we haven't established it at all.' I couldn't think what to say.

During the interval the six of us gathered in Judi's dressing room and spoke in low tones as if someone had died. Anna's face was the longest as she wondered, indeed we all wondered, how the end of the play would work. Lizzie Garvie opined that what did it matter and she bet most of the audience hadn't noticed the absence of the hand-bag information anyway. Privately I thought that Lizzie, though sweetly supportive, was wrong. Of course they'd all noticed. It's one of the most famous passages in English drama, and tonight it wasn't there. Without that section, the end of the play is meaningless. Diana Boddington's stentorian tones called beginners for Act 2 and we continued the evening. By the time we reached the Act 3 revelations, we were prepared for some puzzled reactions from out front. But, extraordinarily, the final section, the reference to Jack Worthing's bizarre beginnings, the story of the handbag itself and my fetching it from upstairs, went as well as it had ever gone. None of the laughs was missed and the evening ended on a note of relief from us and delight from the audience. Afterwards, at the Long Bar in the Lyttelton foyer, we spoke to various people who had seen the performance. We were astounded to find that many had been unaware that anything was amiss and that others had assumed those lines had been cut by Sir Peter. They all knew the play anyway, they told us. Canny Lizzie was right.

It was during the run of *The Importance* that Nigel Havers, perfectly cast as the blithe Algernon Moncrieff, felt it his duty to try and make me (as poker-faced Ernest) laugh on-stage. I was just about able to resist this assault, despite his best efforts. He then had a better idea. He would attempt to make me crack up while *I* was on stage but *he* was not. Actors' jokes, when explained afterwards, usually sound fairly pointless. All I can say is that, as the run continued, Nigel's attempts to make the solemn Ernest/ Jarvis explode into laughter began to seem increasingly hilarious.

There is a point in the play where, after Lady Bracknell has finished grilling poor Jack, he is left for a few moments alone on-stage. Algy strikes up the Wedding March off-stage and Jack, perfectly furious, goes to the door and shouts, 'For goodness' sake don't play that ghastly tune, Algy! How idiotic you are!' This was where Nigel decided to cheer things up. At first he just stood in the wings and looked back at me as I glared off-stage. This was all right and not particularly funny. But over subsequent performances this moment would be developed. Some nights he would be sitting there in the wings apparently cooking a meal over a prop-stove he had found backstage. Another night he would be clearing up with a dustpan and brush. Yet another night he would be locked in a passionate embrace with Zoë Wanamaker, who was waiting to re-enter as my beloved Gwendolen. I wanted to smile at all these vignettes though, as Ernest, I was just about able to quash the tide of laughter welling up inside me. But the build-up of these incidents, plus the fact that you now know something else ludicrous is about to happen, makes you want to laugh more and more. Nigel's timing was impeccable. Suddenly, one night he wasn't there at all – and that seemed inexplicably entertaining. The next night he wasn't there again and, just as I was thinking this wasn't very funny, a huge straw-filled figure of a man flew across the opening, soaring through the air before landing beyond the downstage wing. This was getting frightening. I remembered the exquisite agony of my Manchester lapse when I had lain on the floor and cackled uncontrollably. I absolutely could not let that happen again. Like most actors, I disapprove of japes on-stage and if, as a member of the audience, I spot private jokes or 'corpsing' I want my money back. And yet here I was, part of a disgraceful display.

It got further out of hand when we took the production on

tour. It seemed that the wings were now packed each night with members of the company, eager to catch this evening's 'happening' and to see whether I would finally crack. The Theatre Royal, Glasgow, was the scene of Havers' most imaginative coup. One night, as my scene on-stage with Lady B. drew to its climax and Judi Dench prepared for her exit, I could sense the other audience gathering in the wings for the off-stage drama. Judi swept out to tumultuous applause, the music struck up from upstage-right and I stalked across to shout my line at Algy. Why didn't I just stay downstage and yell from there? I don't know, the whole thing was like a magnet. I just couldn't help myself. I moved across as usual and glared into the wings. Nothing. The tension slackened for a second. But then I saw, standing in the centre of the wing-space and gazing back at me with a serious, slightly quizzical expression, not Nigel, but a strange Scotsman in full Highland regalia including kilt. I learnt afterwards that he was a friend of the stage-door keeper and that Nigel had hired him specifically for this one-night stand. That was it. I laughed out loud. I heard the crowd in the wings stifle their guffaws. I couldn't contain my own. I laughed again. Dammit. This time, though (unlike Manchester), I regained control in a second and, as Nigel sauntered onto the stage a moment later, I played the remainder of our scene with harsh deliberation. We laughed together helplessly as the curtain came down and I resolved, for the second time in my career, never to find myself in such a position again. I decided, too, to exact an appropriate revenge on Havers.

The opportunity came on the following Saturday night – our last performance in Glasgow. He and I were sharing a dressing room. On this particular evening I had already briefed the company. Judi almost hugged herself with glee as I outlined the plan. Anna, sharing with Judi, looked more doubtful. 'If it works,' she pronounced, 'it will be brilliant.'

The whole thing depended on careful timing. The show always began at seven-thirty. Usually, as the half-hour was called over the tannoy, Nigel would stroll round to the wig room where a charming young lady would put hot carmen-rollers in his hair. He would then return to our room with a head full of curlers and leave them to cook for a while. When 'five minutes' was called he would take them out carefully and brush the Wildean locks into place. Then, donning his velvet waistcoat and jacket, he would examine the whole effect in the long mirror before, as 'beginners' was called, sauntering downstairs to the stage, ready to make an elegant entrance at the start of the play. Piano music would begin, and as the curtain rose and the music finished Nigel would glide on, mopping his brow with a silk handkerchief and inquire of his butler, 'Did you hear what I was playing, Lane?'

On this particular evening I had made sure I was ready early and, while Nigel was in the wig room, I advanced the time on his watch by a quarter of an hour. Tee hee. I did the same with the clock on the wall. I had also turned the volume to 'off' on the tannoy so that the half-hour and quarter-hour calls didn't come through. The stage management had been primed. Even Diana Boddington had been amenable. One of her team had a tape of the piano music and was ready, at seven-fifteen, to play it over the tannoy. Everything was in place. A minute or two before quarter past seven, Nigel came back into our room, as usual in his curlers, and sat down to attend to his make-up. I had just turned the volume up again. I had put my frock coat on by this time and was about to slip out of the room. Other members of the company were also creeping quietly downstairs for the denouement. Nigel looked up. 'You're ready awfully early, Mart,' he remarked.

I stopped at the door. 'Well, it's nearly time,' I murmured.

At that moment, as arranged, the sound of his opening music came blasting from the speaker to the accompaniment of the stage manager's urgent tones: 'Mr Havers to the stage immediately!'

Nigel looked up, stunned. 'What?'

'Mr Havers to the stage immediately,' said the tannoy again. The music continued relentlessly.

'Oh Christ,' he exclaimed, 'I'm late!' He leapt up, still in shirt-sleeves and braces, no waistcoat or jacket and with a headful of hot rollers. As I slid from the room, I could see him tearing the curlers desperately from his hair. I made my way down to join the others.

They were all waiting in various stages of unpreparedness on the stage, their backs to the lowered curtain. As we stood there we heard the sudden clattering of feet on the stone stairs above. Then, 'Oh Christ, oh shit!' The footsteps came closer now. They hammered into the wings, paused and then, as we all watched, a pale dishevelled figure, hair upright like a cartoon of a man in shock, tottered on to the set, panting out, 'Did you hear what I was –?'

He stopped as he saw us all ranged in front of him. He stared for a moment in disbelief, then bent double in a mixture of horror, relief and hilarity. Good sport that he was, and a master prankster, he pronounced it a 'brilliant wind-up!' He then had fifteen minutes to recover fully before making his first entrance for the second time that evening.

Back from the tour a week later, Nigel burst into my room at the National, crying, 'Do you know what *they're* doing?' He sounded like Bertie Wooster presenting Jeeves with a problem. '*They're* doing another play!'

I calmed him down and asked what he meant. He told me he had just been looking at the noticeboard and had seen that Judi Dench and Anna Massey were starting rehearsals for a two-handed play called *The Crew* which would receive performances on certain nights in the National's 'Platform' series. 'How can they do this to us?' he yelped, 'they're taking on too much.' I knew what he meant. We were already short of rehearsal time for *Other Places*. He and Anna had substantial parts in the first of the Pinter plays, *Family Voices*, and he was concerned that she would now have even less time to rehearse. We confronted Anna and Judi. They told us *The Crew* was by a young writer called Nick Harrad and dealt with the lives of two lesbian truck-drivers. It was well worth doing, they felt, and somehow they would fit it in. Nick was an important new find and it was only right his first play should be given a chance.

Fair enough. The days went by. Call sheets with rehearsal times for *The Crew* continued to appear on the board. Then one evening Nigel burst into the room again: 'It's all a wind-up. There's no such person as Nick Harrad. They're not doing a play at all. The whole thing's a hoax!'

It was. On further investigation, we found that all the notices had been fabricated by Judi and Anna. Despite this discovery we could never get them to own up. Judi in particular spoke warmly in praise of Nick Harrad and how much they were looking forward to performing his play.

Next day, Nigel and I were due to appear on a BBC Radio arts programme about life at the National. It was recorded in the studio in the late afternoon, to be transmitted a couple of hours later.When the interviewer asked how we enjoyed working with Miss Dench, Nigel and I exchanged glances. I heard myself begin: 'Terrific. Not only is she doing the Wilde and the Pinter but she somehow finds time to encourage new writers.'

Nigel seamlessly took over the baton: 'In fact, she and Anna Massey are rehearsing a play by a brilliant new writer, Nick Harrad . . .'

The interviewer nodded appreciatively as we gave him details of the two tough truckers and Nick's graphic account of their life on the road. We made it up as we went along. The interviewer concluded by thanking us for providing insight into the hard-working life of two of Britain's best-loved actresses.

Two hours later we strolled into Judi's dressing room as she prepared for Lady Bracknell. Anna was there. I switched on the portable radio we had brought in. The programme was just beginning: 'And now we hear how Judi Dench and Anna Massey are encouraging new talent at the National Theatre in a play about female truck-drivers, by newcomer Nick Harrad.' Judi didn't bat an eyelid. Anna's mouth twitched momentarily, then was still. They both listened, along with half a million others, as Nigel and I talked earnestly about *The Crew*. All Judi said as the programme finished was, 'You might have got the plot right. It's clear you haven't read the play at all.'

Judi has never admitted that Nick Harrad may not exist. Visiting her in her dressing room after a show it is likely that she will say, 'Oh, Mart, you've just missed Nick, he had to dash off.' I was pleased, a few years ago, to get his credits into a writers' *Who's Who*. He was listed as being married to Judi Massey, had two sons,

Nigel and Martin, and his writing experience, apart from *The Crew*, was mostly for magazines like *Autocar* and *Motorsport*. His two film scripts in development were listed as *Keep on Trucking* and *Hairpin Bend*. Once, at a party, Judi came up to me and said that Nick Harrad was on the phone and would like a word. When I took the call it turned out not to be Nick at all. Just some imposter attempting a practical joke.

Other Places by Harold Pinter is a collection of three plays – *Family Voices*, *Victoria Station* and *A Kind of Alaska* – that all deal with aspects of memory. My part, the strange Driver, lost in his mini-cab, is in the second play, *Victoria Station*.

This was the first time I had worked with Pinter. I met him in the rehearsal room. Large face and head. Big spectacles. Humorous mouth that seemed always about to break into a mocking smile. Even the 'Hello, Martin' from the dark, slightly projected voice sounded wryly amused, as if he felt I might make him laugh at any moment or, more likely, that he might have something ironic to say to me. Despite this suggestion of humour-in-waiting, everything seemed dark about him, like Mr Murdstone. Dark voice, dark hair and brows, black polo-neck sweater, black jacket and trousers. Though, as rehearsals continued, he would sometimes appear in a pair of gigantic *white* trainers. He smoked in those days; black cigarettes in a dark holder. He would bring the holder to his mouth with one hand while, with neat synchronicity, making a sweeping motion with the other to brush away either real or imaginary ash. The brushing of the ash would often preface a point he wanted to make about the text. (We all honed our imitations of this routine: imaginary cigarette-holder, a deep clearing of the throat, sweep of the left arm down the jacket or along the leg, followed by the phrase, 'Now look here.') In rehearsal, Peter Hall and we actors would turn to him and wait for any morsel that would help us inhabit the dark corridors of his vision.

According to those who knew, Harold was more open now in explaining his work. I had heard that, in the past, someone seeking clarification from the author – 'Harold, could you possibly tell us the reason for this character's behaviour?' – had been greeted with a curt, 'Why?' I had also enjoyed the story of the actor (the young Alan Ayckbourn) who inquired why Stanley says a particular line in *The Birthday Party*. Harold replied, 'Mind your own business.' According to Anna Massey, he was much happier now about replying to questions. 'He's much more approachable,' she confided to me on the night we opened *Other Places* at the Cottesloe. 'I mean, look at your first-night card: "Love from Harold". *Love*. He'd never have written that ten years ago.'

He was totally helpful to me in my approach to the character of the Driver, although when I asked whether there really was a body on the rear seat, he eyed me quizzically and said, 'Is there a rear seat?' Actually there wasn't, as the designer had only provided the front section of the mini-cab.

'Well no, Harold,' I replied, 'there isn't.'

'Well then.'

Fair enough. I used that point when fielding the same question from intrigued audience members after performances. But you could never be sure. Sometimes there was ash on his jacket. Sometimes not. The action of brushing was the same, either way.

Working with Pinter, I often felt I was in touch with a poet or composer of music; the heart of the piece becoming clearer by exploring the possibilities in oneself and relating them to the sounds and rhythms of the text. 'Now look here,' he told us. 'This is a beat. This is a pause. This –' brushing away the ash '– is a silence. All right?'

One morning, towards the end of the run of *The Importance* in 1982, I received a call from Harold. The familiar throat-clear, then the voice, double-dark through intimate contact with the phone itself: 'Now look here, I want you as my leading man in *Tiger at the Gates*. Let's have lunch.' It seemed that he was to direct a revival of Giraudoux's great anti-war play at the National and was offering me Hector, the part made famous by Michael Redgrave in the London production of the fifties. I knew the play slightly. When I re-read it, I wasn't sure I was good casting for the rugged warrior who returns, battle-worn and weary, to a Troy that simmers on the edge of war.

Harold invited me to meet him at the discreet Soho restaurant L'Epicure. He was waiting for me at a small table next to the heavily curtained window. He even rose as I came in and shook my hand firmly. The familiar curved smile was on his lips, as if to say, 'Look, this is really rather a joke, isn't it?' We drank dry white wine and, after we had ordered, discussed the play.

The version he intended to do was the Christopher Fry translation that had been such a success for Redgrave. I had found the script moving and poetic but, somehow, very much of the fifties. I had seen pictures: Redgrave and his company swaggering in brass-plated armour and swirling cloaks, bejewelled swords glinting in the Trojan sun. An elderly actor who remembered the production told me, 'It was all very glamorous. But actually Michael Redgrave was so built up with breast-plates and epaulettes and cloaks and wrist-bands he looked like a mobile sofa.' I still had an uneasy memory of my mini-skirted Domitian.

When I dipped into the French original I found the play to be more of a gritty comedy whose effects came from the edgy exchanges of a people on the brink of a dirty war. Written between the world wars, it seemed equally about modern politics and the small, unnoticed incidents that can escalate into international conflict, as about the Greeks and Trojans. With the image of that unwieldy sofa in my mind, I asked Harold, 'Where are you thinking of setting the play?'

He looked up from his Sancerre. 'What d'you mean?'

I thought I had better be cautious. 'Well, it's – er – French of course,' I offered.

'So what?'

'Well –' I was starting to flounder. 'I wondered where you might want to place it.'

'Troy.'

'Yes, but –'

'Troy.' He was unequivocal. 'Troy, of course. Where else?'

'Er – well –' I should have given up by now. 'It's a French play. About war. Set in the thirties –'

'Look –' If he had been smoking he would now be sweeping his knee. 'It's in Troy. About Troy. I am setting it in Troy.'

'Ah. Right.' The image of that sofa with Greek antimacassars and Trojan hangings surfaced again. 'And the er – costumes?' I inquired tentatively.

He put down his glass. 'Troy. Trojan.'

'I see,' I said. 'So not modern dress then?'

The humorous mouth took on a distinctly uncurved look. 'What d'you mean?'

'I wondered, p'raps, you know, French soldiers, grubby dirty uniforms. Home from the war. Berets. Rifles. Sort of getting away from the classic look?'

He sighed and, after a pause that was more than a beat and not quite a silence, said, with infinite patience, 'Look, this is Christopher Fry's translation. The whole thing is Troy.'

I still felt we hadn't quite put our finger on what that meant in terms of sartorial turn-out. Obviously French soldiers of the thirties were no longer an option. I spelt it out: 'So, togas, armour, sandals, thongs, ra-ra skirts and all the trimmings?'

He took a sip of wine and looked at me steadily. The mouth curved. 'Yes.'

I took only a beat. 'Great. Count me in!'

As we began to block the complex patterns of Giraudoux's play, I remembered that Harold captained a cricket team consisting mainly of actors and writers. I could see how his directorial authority must have worked on the field. Standing within the taped-out square of the rehearsal space in his white trainers, he would beckon to Derek Newark (a rugged Ajax in shiny leg-guards) and move him forward to a new position behind the votive offerings. He signalled Edward de Souza towards the upstage boundary, while slinky Nicola Paget as Helen was brought in for a catch at leg-slip. As Hector, I was given more of a roving commission – a mid-field player who tried his best to prevent hostile bombardment from the opposition. I was certain now that Hector wasn't really my part. I couldn't quite achieve the element of 'crusty joy' essential to the character. My Hector was wrapped in a slightly more filo pastry. The script was a mixture of influences: a tough scatological anti-war comedy, elegantly translated in the fifties by poet and dramatist Christopher Fry, and now piloted in the eighties by Captain Pinter. Harold had decided to revert the play to a literal translation of its original title, *La Guerre de Troie n'aura pas lieu*. This turned out to be confusing. We heard of one woman who rang the box office to ask what was being performed at the Wednesday matinée. She was told *The Trojan War Will Not Take Place*. 'Oh dear,' she said, 'what's on instead?'

Everything about the production worked well. Except the costumes. The girls looked wonderful, almost timeless in classic silken gowns and, in Helen's case, a flimsy see-through number that would have had any amount of ships heading for open water. But the men . . . The older ones, those who stayed at home and discussed policy, weren't too badly kitted out. Basic togas that, with practice and some hoicking over the shoulder, even lent a little gravitas. David Rintoul as Paris looked all right in a chunky tunic with silver epaulettes and shiny armour. With his athletic physique, good looks and plenty of brown body make-up, he was an appealing war hero. Certainly not a sofa. Maybe a tough leather armchair.

Not so Hector. First of all, the hair. Robin, the designer, decided I needed a 'back-fall'. So I had to pin extra blond locks on to the back of my head. I made the mistake of looking in the mirror before the first preview: I was reminded of my sister Angela in the fifties getting ready for a night out at the Regal Ballroom, Purley. And then the gear itself. The actual armour wasn't too bad: firm, metallic, although impossible to climb into without the help of my dresser. Impossible to get out of, too, without the help of two servants, on-stage during most of my first scene. The putting-on was relatively easy. All I had to do was to stand in the middle of the room while dresser John scuttled round me, buckling and adjusting and tightening the girth. He assured me the 'line' looked good and the whole thing 'sat' very well. I didn't wholly believe him, though I knew he was in his final year at St Martin's School of Art studying fashion design. He often brought his sketches into the theatre to show me. I could see he was talented, even if, secretly, I thought some of his stuff, particularly his dress designs, a little outlandish. I wondered who would be seen dead in something like that. Clearly I hadn't looked hard enough in the mirror a second ago. I should have had more confidence in him. As I thrust a fiver into his hand each Saturday night in the best theatrical tradition, I really had no idea that his expertise and vision would make him a star designer within a very few years. So, John Galliano strapped my shin-guards over my high-heeled leather-thonged sandals, clipped my golden wrist-bands in place, thrust my sword into its scabbard, moved it a little more to the side to prevent my tripping over it and sent me on my way to the stage. Not so much a sofa. More a three-piece suite.

Five minutes later I was taking it all off again. Or rather, Peter Gordon and Andrew Johnson were. I made my entrance, full of as much crusty joy as I could muster. After a swig from a jewel-encrusted goblet held out by Peter, I began a long spiel to my loving wife Andromache about how great it was to be home and that the Tiger of War must never be allowed through the gates again. Great stuff, but not easy when you've got Peter and Andrew beavering away, attempting to unbuckle, untie and undo, now under one armpit, now the other, now behind one knee, now the other. John Galliano, trained for it, took twenty minutes to get me fully decked out; Peter and Andrew only had two to get me unshackled. Some nights they were still having trouble with one or other of my epaulettes when the lights were changing and we were supposed to be up and away. And all for what? Finally stripped down and the last shin-guard removed, I was left alone on-stage, revealed now in a periwinkle blue ra-ra skirt and uplifted sandals, the captain of some big girls' cricket team.

Harold's production, despite these difficulties, was a dynamic account of Giraudoux's drama. The fact is that *The Trojan War* is a remarkable piece of writing (and translation) and has an undeniable power. We got better and better at conveying something of its universal truth. I even found a bit more crusty joy in my performance than either Harold or I, when we set out, had thought possible.

It was during the run of *The Trojan War* that Ralph Richardson died. I had seen him in Eduardo de Filippo's *Inner Voices*, which had for a time alternated with *The Importance* in the Lyttelton. He gave a monumental performance as the patriarch of an eccentric Neapolitan family. His command of the stage was breathtaking as he moved, at eighty-one, with the ease of someone half his age. Like all great actors, he effortlessly took your eye; wherever he stood he seemed ten foot tall. I had never worked with him in the theatre, but I had seen him one day in the National canteen, alone at a table in his dressing gown, having supper before a performance. I have always regretted that I didn't ask if I could join him but instead went to sit with my own group several tables away. I had worked with him some years before in John Powell's radio production of *Much Ado About Nothing*. He had played Dogberry, I was Claudio. John, totally dedicated to his sound-picture, was not known for word-mincing when it came to telling actors what he required from them. This included his attitude to great stars. One morning he seemed to be having trouble communicating some points to Sir Ralph. It may have been Ralph's insistence on pronouncing his own character as Dogberry that worried John. Whatever misunderstanding occurred, suddenly, as the rest of us hovered near the microphone ready for the next scene, Sir Ralph's mouth tightened and he muttered something to himself. He threw his script on to a chair and, scooping up his brown trilby and light overcoat, he turned to the aghast John. 'Very well,' he said, 'you may have your view of what I can achieve. I have mine. I have never been a very good actor.' He swung round to the rest of us, bowed slightly and said, with the deepest courtesy, 'Good afternoon.' Then, placing his trilby on his head and tweaking it into position, he walked out. It took a great deal of effort from the director (and not a little tact) to persuade him back the next day.

John's production was in fact one of the most accomplished radio Shakespeares of the seventies. It struck me then that if you have a Rolls-Bentley of an actor in the studio, you must be careful not to squeeze him on to the hard shoulder. Rather, give him free rein in the middle lane. A performer of genius may spot something worthwhile that isn't on your road map.

On the evening of Sir Ralph's death, Harold Pinter came into my dressing room during the interval of *Trojan War*. He looked grave. Oh lord, I thought, he's noticed I've turned a couple of silences into mere pauses. He said, almost brusquely, 'Ralph's gone.' We knew that he had recently suffered a series of strokes, but this was unexpected. He had died at five that afternoon and the news was only now filtering through to the various television and radio stations. Harold suggested I make an announcement at the curtain call. I spent the second half of the performance trying to put my own sadness out of my head, stave off the Trojan War and work out what I was going to say to the audience. Finally, as we took our bows, I stepped forward and raised a hand for silence. I said, quite simply, that our revered colleague Sir Ralph Richardson had died a few hours ago. Immediately there came a strange sound from the audience that none of us had anticipated. It was like something from the Greek theatre, collective and spontaneous, a kind of desperate choral sigh. I asked them to join us in a minute's silence. We stood there. Then the curtain was lowered. Later, in the Green Room bar, we learnt that audiences in the Olivier and the Cottesloe had produced that same cathartic sound – an instinctive expression of shock, grief and love for a dead hero.

Although I worked with Harold again on his short film *Precisely*, it wasn't until after a performance of Ayckbourn's *Woman in Mind* at the Vaudeville Theatre, in which I was playing Gerald Gannet, that we discussed *The Trojan War* again. Harold came, almost leaping, into the dressing room. The great skipper, without referring to the performance he had just seen, grasped my hand and said, 'You were bloody good in *The Trojan War*!'

I looked at him. My mind was still somewhere in Ayckbourn's suburban garden. I adjusted. 'Thanks, Harold,' I said.

He pursued his theme. 'There was only one thing wrong with

that production. Know what it was?' His Murdstone eyes burnt
into mine. I gazed back.

'The costumes?' I offered.

'Exactly,' he said, generously, in his darkest timbre.

I thought of that Soho lunch. Of those French soldiers I had
imagined in their grubby berets. With rifles. He curved the
familiar smile before climbing down a further flight of stairs to
Julia McKenzie's room on the floor below.

I had first met Alan Ayckbourn at the National where, for a short
time, *The Importance* had alternated in the Lyttelton rep with
Alan's new play, *Way Upstream*. We hadn't got to know each
other. I was usually hurrying down a corridor to a rehearsal and
he on his way to supervise the complexities of his set, which
consisted of a real boat on a real stretch of water. There always
seemed to be problems with the technical side of this production.
We would often arrive back from one of our weeks on tour to find
there had been another flood, hundreds of gallons had leaked
from the tank, and the backstage area was drying out; a dank,
stagnant smell pervading the theatre once again. I remember
Alan telling me, shrugging in comic despair, that they had never
had this trouble in his own theatre in Scarborough, where he had
first done the play the year before.

In 1985, he sent me the script of *A Chorus of Disapproval*.
Already being performed at the National, it was soon to transfer
to Shaftesbury Avenue. Would I like to play Guy, who rises from
the ranks of a local amateur operatic society to become its leading
man? I would. But delighted as I was with the offer, I was nervous
about the singing involved. I decided to consult the production's
musical director, Paul Todd. I mentioned that, although I was all
right at making my own 'tunes', I wasn't much good at holding
anyone else's. Paul didn't believe me. 'There's no such thing as
tone-deaf,' he told me categorically. He hadn't heard my
Croydon turkey seller twenty-five years before.

Painstakingly he took me through the songs, all from *The
Beggar's Opera*, which the amateur company eventually performs
as a climax to the play. When I had finished he grinned nervously

and looked embarrassed. I could see he was re-evaluating some of his deeply held beliefs. Without totally looking me in the eye he said that 'with a lot of work' I should be able to do it. 'After all,' he added, 'Guy's singing is supposed to be naff.'

I think I knew then that this was not for me. Just to be sure, I took a second opinion. I visited a distinguished coach with the unlikely name of Chuck Mallet, who took me through a few scales, before moving on to *The Beggar's Opera* itself. Halfway through the first song I spotted the same expression of disbelief (mixed with a little pain) that I had seen on the face of Paul Todd. Chuck let me finish, then gave his prognosis. 'Well Martin, as Henry Higgins in *My Fair Lady* – you could delight us. Possibly. But as Guy – I don't think so. I'm sorry.' He didn't have to be. I didn't think so either.

A few weeks later, and much to my surprise, Ayckbourn sent me a copy of his newest new play, *Woman in Mind*. This is a frightening account of a suburban marriage, which Michael Codron was to produce at the Vaudeville the following year. They were offering me the part of the Reverend Gerald Gannet, who is slowly driving his wife (to be played by Julia McKenzie) to the brink of madness.

Ayckbourn is a remarkable director. He has been an actor himself, a stage manager, a radio producer. He understands every aspect of the theatre. Although he had been writing and directing plays at Scarborough since the sixties, he was not permitted to direct them when they first started transferring to London with starry casts. Eric Thompson and Peter Hall were preferred by the West End managements, and Alan had to sit on the sidelines. Now, in the 1980s, he was recognised as a master, whose direction of his own work was an essential part of the process of bringing it to an audience. Some weeks before we began rehearsals, I inquired whether I might be able to talk to him about the play. He suggested we meet for breakfast at the Park Lane Hotel where he was staying.

This was the first time I had really had an opportunity to have a conversation with him. It was the morning after his play about a local drama society, *Chorus of Disapproval*, had transferred to

Shaftesbury Avenue from the National Theatre. As we munched muesli opposite each other in his suite, I thought that, with his large domed head and placid face, he looked like one of those brainy schoolboys who used to win handwriting competitions in the fifties. Or appeared on Sunday tea-time television – 'And now here's eleven-year-old Alan who has written a wonderful play that takes place on the planet Mars. He's built his own scenery, too. Tell us all about it, Alan.'

There is something very calming about being in the presence of an authentic theatre genius. Like Harold Pinter, Alan Ayckbourn didn't waste words. I felt in Alan's case that those precious commodities were earmarked for more important work on his word processor after our meeting was over. I sensed he felt no need (why should he?) to explain his play to me or indeed how he proposed to approach the production. He was quite happy to chat, but it wasn't going to be in depth. I found this reassuring. Of course I couldn't resist asking some basic actors' questions: did he think Gerald might have rimless specs? Might he wear a sleeve-less cardigan? Open-toed sandals? To all these he put his great cranium on one side, nodded as he considered each point, then said, 'Mm. Yes. If you like.'

'Trousers?' I asked.

He nodded again as if this was a perfectly logical inquiry. 'Mm.'

'Grey flannel, I thought?'

He considered again. 'Mm. Big. Baggy. Good.'

I didn't ask him how to play the part. Perhaps I should have done. He knew, as I was later to discover, though he wouldn't have told me. That wasn't his style. He likes his actors to find out for themselves. Every discovery an actor makes *for himself* about the part, he told me later, is infinitely more valuable than having stuff foisted on him. When we began work on the play several weeks later I could see how, often through anecdotes and stories, he would gently nudge his actors up the correct alley or draw them back if they seemed to be heading for a dead end.

As I finished my breakfast and got up to go, he said diffidently, with a slight frown, 'Thing about my stuff – it all happens in the niches.'

'Niches?'

'Mm. Niches. Bits in between what people say. Yep.' He nodded yet again, more to himself this time than to me, as if that might sum it up reasonably satisfactorily.

I put my script, which I hadn't opened, back in my briefcase. He watched me do this, and for a moment I thought he was going to say something else. He didn't and we shook hands, both a little awkwardly. He insisted on seeing me to the lift. We nodded a couple of times more to each other, not saying much. As the lift arrived, I still had the feeling he wanted to add something. But no. The doors closed. I discovered later that, besides the script of *Woman in Mind*, I had also packed away his copy of *The Times*. It was unopened, and on the arts page was a rave review of the West End transfer of *Chorus of Disapproval*.

Gerald Gannet is a complete bastard. He's apparently your friendly neighbourhood vicar. To many he might seem a pleasant fellow, but so far as he relates to his family he is cruel, sanctimonious, narrow-minded, pompous, self-satisfied. He is driving his wife mad. Not perhaps the ingredients for a rollicking comedy. Alan of course makes all this supremely funny, before slowly twisting the knife and revealing the stark domestic tragedy that lurks in this small back garden. Julia McKenzie was superb as the long-suffering Susan, driven further and further into her fantasy world. She creates, in her mind, an alternative family: idyllic, generous and loving. These white-clad figures inhabit an alternative garden too, a green rolling estate, steeped in summer sunshine.

At first, in rehearsing Gerald, I made the mistake of presenting him as too overtly cruel, tetchy with his wife and impatient with everything around him. Wrong. Gradually, with barely noticeable nudging from Alan, I found I was beginning to invest him with a serene self-sacrificial smugness. This had started to fall into place after Alan told a story one morning about his stepfather. His mother, at the end of her tether with this man's holier-than-thou pedagogy, had once emptied a great bowl of custard over his head. As the stuff oozed down his face and neck (said Alan with a glance at me) his stepfather had sat there, lifting his eyes to heaven as if to say 'Forgive her father, for she knows not what she does.'

Alan's rehearsal methods were simple and practical. After a readthrough, he would gently 'put the play on its feet', creating a flexible template to which every actor could contribute. 'Try it,' he would say. 'Mm. See what happens.' Then he invited us to familiarise ourselves with the lines so that, as rehearsals developed, the physical and mental threads could come together naturally and fairly swiftly. We didn't have the doubtful luxury of the National's seven weeks' preparation.

I sought and found those big grey trousers, plus an old cardigan from the Oxfam shop near the Old Vic. I had gone there during a lunch break, quite forgetting I was still wearing Gerald's clerical collar. As I unearthed the maroon knitted waistcoat from the bottom of a pile and handed over five pounds, the Irish woman who took my money said, 'There now. That'll be warm on your back, Father.'

Although Gerald was starting to come alive, there was one unexpected attempt on his life. We had begun the play at Richmond and moved on to Brighton. A few days before we were due to open in the West End, an actor whom I knew slightly attended one of the Brighton performances. After the show he proceeded to tell me, uninvited, that I was playing the part quite wrongly. He suggested, with a stunning lack of tact, that I rethink my entire approach. I was intrigued. I rather admired the chutzpah of someone who didn't mind offering an unsolicited opinion. Julia, when I discussed it with her, urged me to pay no attention. But next day I thought carefully about each of my visitor's points and decided to write to him, explaining the choices I had made.

When he received my letter, on our final Saturday at Brighton, he rang, full of apologies, and said he followed my thinking absolutely. He went on to tell me that, a few years ago, someone had given *him* notes on a performance just before he had opened in London and, he said, it had almost destroyed him. I wasn't surprised. So why, I wondered, was he doing the same to me?

He was coming to see the play again, he told me, on our first night at the Vaudeville and he wished me luck. Oh lord. The benefit of this odd situation was that it had forced me to re-examine the validity of what Alan and I had developed together. Apart from an unwelcome sense of being 'watched' on our opening performance, nothing much was altered. The play was a smash hit and the production ran for nine months, to full houses. We were outstandingly well reviewed and Julia won the *Evening Standard* Award. But it did bring home to me how dangerous it can be to comment on a colleague's performance, unless specifically asked to do so. Every actor knows he wields a peculiar power over those whose work he has just witnessed. A few years later I saw this same actor in a new play. I couldn't help watching him like a hawk. I thought he looked a bit pale when he saw me at the reception afterwards. Something about the whirligig of time bringing in its revenges ran briefly through my head as he came towards me. I quashed it, looked him straight in the eye and told him his performance was absolutely superb. He beamed. He was grateful. Possibly surprised. And, I could sense, relieved. I uncrossed my fingers and went to get a drink.

Ayckbourn's note sessions on *Woman in Mind* were really unmissable masterclasses. As the run continued, he would visit his play every few weeks, rather as a caring parent might come to see his offspring at boarding school and check on their progress. His greatest concern was to observe how much things had 'moved'. A line or piece of business can subtly change or extend, night by night, so that after say twenty performances, something that took only five seconds may now be taking eight. A line that depended for its laugh on a certain casualness of delivery may now be too heavily signalled to be funny any more. And Alan's 'niches' may, through miniscule shifts of the actor's timing, no longer be quite the same size.

He was interesting about volume, too. 'Hm,' he would murmur, leaning against the dressing room wall and nodding thoughtfully, 'it's all got very loud.' There is an impulse in many actors – certainly me – to do more and more each night, to bring something extra to each performance. A scene that was initially delicately balanced can metamorphose into overprojection and, probably, overplaying. Better to try less and less.

His other concern is always over laughs. Not that there might not be enough but that there may be too many. After we had been running two months, he became anxious about a scene in which, abetted by Peter Blythe as the doctor, I attempted to erect a small card table on the patch of scrappy lawn and place a tray of sherry glasses on it. I'd been rather keen on this scene. And I enjoyed conveying the physical ineptitude of pompous Gerald. 'Hm,' said Alan, head on one side, 'too many laughs. Mm. Too funny.' I knew what he meant: this wasn't a Ray Cooney farce. Peter and I felt like naughty schoolboys finally hauled before the benevolent beak. Next night, we said goodbye to a couple of our favourite moments and the scene was immeasurably improved. Laughter, says Alan, can be your enemy as well as your friend.

I worked with Ayckbourn again two years later in his new play *Henceforward* . . . which is set in a violent world of a few years into the future. Ian McKellen had been playing Jerome, its doubtful hero. He was leaving the cast and Alan and Michael Codron asked me to take over. I had seen the production and admired the consummate theatricality that McKellen brought to the part of the obsessive composer whose commitment is first to his work, and only second to his wife and child. I discussed the character with Ian and was surprised to hear that he had not felt comfortable. He generously mentioned to Jane Asher (who originated the role of Corinna, Jerome's wife) that 'Martin will be so much better, he understands the character'. I hoped it was intended as a compliment and not his view of my own family life.

As Alan was busy most of the time in Scarborough, the excellent Alan Strachan guided me through rehearsals. *Henceforward* . . . seemed to me to contain two specific strands.

First, the story of a man whose creative urge is the single most important thing in his life. Jerome is suffering from a 'blockage' whose dramatic unplugging leads to the play's climax: he writes and performs an inspirational work, while his wife and daughter are left to the merciless fury of the urban gangs who surround the apartment. The play's other strand is pure high comedy, in which Jerome adapts his robot housemaid into a glamorous, if metallic, fiancée. From this bizarre perspective the play deals with more familiar Ayckbournian themes of domestic discord. A technical precision is demanded from the actor as Jerome operates a variety of audio and video equipment to communicate with the outside world. Every part of his living quarters is wired for sound so that he can record human voices and transform them into music. His final task is actually to compose this extraordinary piece, beginning with small sampled sounds and culminating in the entire theatre thundering to the beat of his spectacular creation. Of course the music was pre-recorded and I had to mime the appropriate fingering, synchronising every movement on the bank of dummy keyboards as the live sound was played.

Ian had already warned me of the difficulties he had experienced in learning the sequence. He had solved them with the help of the composer himself – Paul Todd – who had invented a special colour chart that Ian studied every night along with his lines. I couldn't make head or tail of it. Suddenly I had a brainwave: I asked a photographer friend, Hilary Whitehall, if she could record Paul on video. This she did from a high angle, framing the keyboard while he played the four-minute piece. Every night, after rehearsal, I put the tape into my machine at home and slavishly followed the action, hammering away on a cardboard keyboard. It took me three weeks of bruised fingers to learn it. Soon after we opened, I had more or less convinced myself that it really was me creating the 'love theme' – live – in front of the audience each night.

When I finished the run, Simon Ward was preparing to play the same part on tour. I offered him the precious video. He was less than enthusiastic: he was sure he wouldn't need it. I was surprised. Was he perhaps a trained pianist and I didn't know?

'No,' he replied, 'but surely you just sit with your back to the audience and pretend?'

'That's certainly an option,' I told him pompously, 'but I think Alan wants the audience to see every movement.'

We didn't speak any further about it. Three weeks later Simon rang. He sounded anxious. 'Look, we open on Tuesday. It's a nightmare. Those bloody robots. And that music. It's frightening. I don't suppose you could get the video to me by tomorrow, could you?'

Two years later Ros and I were invited to revive Ayckbourn's *Just Between Ourselves* at the Greenwich Theatre in south-east London. Although very different from *Woman in Mind*, it is the study of a housewife (to be played here by Susan Jameson) who is slowly descending into a comatose state while her unbearably jolly husband, busy in the garage with DIY, sees nothing amiss. The play contains even more gadgetry than *Henceforward* . . . electric drills, ladders, toolboxes, hammers, nails, screwdrivers, wires, switches, lightbulbs, plugs, a car; plus deckchairs, teacups, plates, cutlery, sandwiches, cakes – the lot. The opening scene sets the agenda as Dennis dismantles, then reassembles, wrongly, an electric kettle. Unfortunately the production was not to be directed by Alan.

I think we all sensed something was wrong when, after the readthrough, our director stroked his grey beard and announced that, at two o'clock, we would read the play again. If ever there was a case for 'putting a play on its feet' – to begin dovetailing action and words – then this was it. Still, no harm done. We thought. We had lunch. We read it again.

Next day we read it again. And again. After each reading Greybeard would stretch back luxuriously in his chair, wriggle his sandled toes and say, 'Oh, isn't it a wonderful play?' It is, but we all knew this was not the way to get it off the ground. One member of the cast muttered quietly that the reason we hadn't started blocking was that the director didn't know what to do with it. I couldn't accept this, since the whole scenario is dictated by Alan's carefully plotted text. Greybeard seemed entirely benign so, after the fourth reading, when the words were starting to swim before our eyes and Ayckbourn's niches were closing up before our ears, I approached him: 'Erm – it takes me nearly a month to learn a big part. We've now got three weeks. Oughtn't we to get this up and running?'

He smiled knowingly and unwrapped his lunch. He said he could tell I virtually knew the part already. I told him he had been fooled by the technique (acquired in radio) of lifting your eyes off the page. He shook his head, bit into a peanut-butter sandwich and pronounced, 'It'll all be wonderful'. His saintly manner was beginning to remind me of the Rev. Gerald Gannet.

We finally persuaded Greybeard to start blocking the play. Too late. We had read it too many times. The threading together of the complicated physical requirements now became enormously difficult. We felt rushed because there was so much less time. We had lost the advantage of being able to go away at the end of the first week with a pattern of 'moves' in our heads. Ayckbourn's dialogue, which normally slipped seamlessly into the brain, became, for me at any rate, unnaturally hard to absorb. We were dead in the water before we began. I rang Alan, suppressing the feeling that I was telling tales out of school. When I mentioned the interminable readings, he confirmed what we all knew: 'Hmm. That's not right. With my stuff you have to put it on its feet as soon as possible.'

We never caught up. Too much of our energy was concentrated on knowing the lines by the opening night. The technical intricacies of ladders and lights and electricity – as well as the complications of the car and the whole paraphernalia of do-it-yourself – became almost impossible to incorporate in the time available. None of us felt secure. Greybeard started to look even greyer round the gills.

The first night felt like a breech birth. Afterwards I was angry and disappointed. It took many performances before we began to seem at all comfortable. We never *felt* comfortable. I began to dread forgetting lines. At the request of the cast, Alan agreed to come to a performance. This was generous, as it is impossible for him to retain an involvement with every production of his plays;

he has to let them go. It was both exciting and depressing that, on his visit, he was able, like a brilliant surgeon, to pinpoint the problems and set us on a road to recovery. He summed up what he had seen. 'It was', he said, 'like watching the England World Cup football team come on to the pitch at Wembley with their bootlaces tied together.' He laid down guidelines for us to work on during the remainder of the run and, in the final week, we felt we were starting to get the play right. At last I was able to expunge some of the evidence of the traumatic delivery that had marred my performance. Coincidence or not, after Alan's visit we never saw Greybeard again.

I found, in working with Alan Ayckbourn, that we shared an appreciation of radio drama. I had known I was hooked on what the human voice could do, even before I first heard Gielgud and Olivier on radio and record in the fifties. In attempting to clone them vocally on my Grundig tape-recorder in front of Mr Kelly's class, I had sensed that, used in the right way (whatever that was), the voice was almost like a projector, throwing images up on to a screen in the listener's head. Like many children growing up in the fifties, I had marvelled at the variety of voices accessible to the nation via the 'wireless'. The whole family listened on Sunday lunchtimes, as wafts of roast beef and gravy mingled with the blaring signature tunes of 'The Billy Cotton Band Show', 'Ray's a Laugh' or 'Educating Archie'. We never thought it odd that Archie was a wooden dummy (we'd seen pictures in the *Radio Times*) and the vocally dextrous Peter Brough was 'doing' the voice of Archie *and* himself. We had been told he was a ventriloquist on television and that his mouth moved all the time Archie was meant to be speaking. That didn't matter to us. Brough's radio pictures were as wholly believable as those imagined by my sister and me when we listened to another kind of entertainment on Monday nights, courtesy of the Light Programme. We dimmed the lights and crouched under the dining-room table, enthralled by the eerie announcement: 'Journey Into Space'. This was followed by the sepulchral tones of the narrator as he began tonight's episode: 'Across the vast expanse of Martian desert we toiled endlessly onwards, still in search of our lost ship.' Great movies in the mind, expert voice-painting. We took it all for granted; it wasn't until the late sixties, when I went through the horrors of being unable to breathe and speak adequately, I recognised fully that without the voice the actor is lost.

At Rada in 1962, I had entered a student competition to win a contract with the BBC Drama Repertory Company. If I won, perhaps I could meet and work alongside some of my radio heroes, whose voices were as familiar to me as those of my own family: incisive Carleton Hobbs and plummy Norman Shelley, equally well-known as Holmes and Watson; gravelly Grizelda Hervey and juicy Stephen Murray; irascible Felix Felton; sultry June Tobin, entrancing Marjorie Westbury. Would I, at last, get to share a microphone with those double-barrelled doyens of the air, Howard Marion Crawford, Nan Marriott-Watson, Dorothy Holmes-Gore? act face to face, shoulder to shoulder, with Guy Kingsley Poynter and Anita Sharp Bolster? learn, finally, what Leslie Twelvetrees and Raf de la Torre actually looked like? I won second prize, an acceptable twenty-five pounds. This bought me a nifty suit from Burton's and paid my first two weeks' rent in Manchester as a fully fledged actor.

It wasn't until I had returned to London a year later and was getting going in the West End that, encouraged by an accomplished radio actor, Michael Spice, I got in touch with the BBC. I told them grandly I was available to record radio plays during the day while appearing in the theatre at night. A week later I received an offer of ten pounds to play a young soldier in a drama called *The Blank Cartridge*. My agent, Liz Robinson, ruthlessly beat them up to twelve, and so I began an almost alternative career. Now I was able to observe at first hand the techniques of these great vocal maestros, whose expertise harked back to a time when radio (the television of its day) could make you a star. During the nine-month run of *Poor Bitos* I must have recorded ten or fifteen different plays, mostly in the basement studios of Broadcasting House. I was particularly impressed with a small, bun-shaped, grey-haired woman who danced up to the micro-

phone with phenomenal energy. It was always specially lowered
to accommodate her four foot ten inches. I watched her all one
afternoon as, script in hand, she created, out of the air, a whole
world of sophistication, of heady romance and well-heeled
humour. Her voice – oh so charming, so feminine, so all-knowing
and full of wit – swept and soared and dived into the mike, and
out again, nationwide, to fire the ready imagination of her
listening fans. This elderly bundle of vocal genius was Marjorie
Westbury herself. Really she could do anything, *be* anyone she
wanted, within the radius of the microphone. She knew, *we*
knew, the moment she approached its attentive ear, that she *was*
Elvira in *Blithe Spirit*, or Paul Temple's witty young wife in the
Durbridge mystery serials.

'I'll open the window, my darling,' she would flute, 'it's such a
lovely day.' Then, cunningly retreating a pace and turning her
head (therefore her mouth) a few inches to one side, she would
emit a pretty little effort-noise as she gently opened the imaginary
casement. (The window itself was the responsibility of a chummy
spot-effects girl called Esther Rantzen, who held aloft two pieces
of wood and slid one against the other to create the sound.)
Marjorie would then turn back towards the microphone, just the
slightest bit out of breath, say 'There, Paul', before moving
forward a step for, 'Oh, darling, I do love you so.' She would lean
closer, bestow a light kiss on the back of her own hand, sigh, and
on the out-going breath whisper to the mike, in the tinkling
manner her listeners adored, 'Oh Paul, I'm so happy.'

Watching from the sidelines, having completed my own part
as a lumpy detective sergeant, I was spellbound by her skill. Her
imaginative technique, harnessed to her understanding of
character and situation, was breathtaking. The precision and
delicacy of her movements around the microphone, her
knowledge of just how much difference a retreat or an approach
would make to the depth of the sound-picture, was the start of my
radio education. Such sonic choreography was entertaining
enough to watch. When you closed your eyes and *listened*, it was
dazzling.

*

By the time I began the long run of *Man and Superman* at the Garrick Theatre in 1965, I had probably taken part in more than a hundred radio programmes. Learning from these great performers, I found I had become part of a group of younger actors who were beginning to develop their own skills. Miriam Margolyes, David Buck, Derek Jacobi, Nigel Anthony, Ronald Pickup, Kate Binchy, Patricia Gallimore, Elizabeth Proud, Prunella Scales and Timothy West were all becoming the new radio experts. The sixties was a transitional time for broadcast drama. The days were now all but gone in which plays were transmitted live on a Saturday night. Until the fifties, the cast had been required to dress for the occasion – dinner jackets for the men, long evening gowns for the ladies. Even in 1964 I was confused for a moment when, just before we were to begin recording an afternoon thriller, the announcer slipped into the studio and approached the mike. He was wearing an open-neck shirt and jeans. I still somehow expected that he would be dressed like his voice. I had never seen him before, but I recognised the dark-brown tones as soon as he cleared his throat and began, 'This is the BBC Home Service – "Afternoon Theatre".' His voice was wearing the suit.

Two of the greatest radio directors of the later sixties and beyond were John Powell and Martin Jenkins. Powell, pale and pocky faced, twelve years older than me, moved about the corridors of Broadcasting House like a permanently panicked wraith. His trim black beard and moustache encircled a mouth that always seemed wide with fear of some imminent production crisis: an actor's agent asking too much money, the music for his recording just not right, our performances all *ghastly* in some way. And, worst of all: 'Martin, why do you sound as if you've always got a cold?'

Powell was a master of radio. His method was to work in broad swathes of sound, wide stretches of audio cinemascope. One of the first to understand the new stereo techniques that were being introduced at the time, he created dramas and documentaries that depended on multi-layered aural tapestries. I became involved in many Powell productions, including his superb *Much*

Ado About Nothing, with Ralph Richardson as Dogberry and Paul Daneman as Benedick. Here, music seemed to emerge from the swaying branches of trees, arrows whizzed from left to right across the nation's sitting rooms (if you'd got stereo) and all kinds of Shakespearean verbal fireworks entranced the ear.

In 1971, John asked me to play Prince Andrei in the twenty-episode serialisation of *War and Peace*. He shared direction of the series with Nesta Pain and Ronald Mason. His own episodes were astonishing in their use of the entire spread of stereo: Russian music and subtle effects that made you *see* the Bolkonskys' country estate, the ballrooms of Moscow and the battlefield of Borodino. We had to fight sometimes to be heard above this ravishing soundscape but, rather like David Lean in the medium of film, Powell expected, and usually found, that we rose to the occasion with performances that attempted to match his own inner vision.

Martin Jenkins was a different kind of director. No less obsessed by verdant landscapes of sound, his methods sprang from a forensic investigation of the text. He chipped away at the niceties of emphasis and inflection until the actors could finalise their own contribution. The intensity of his approach was dictated by the driving pace that was (and is) the allotted time for a recording (usually three days for a ninety-minute play). Bearded, owlishly bespectacled, fixated, Jenkins was probably the most accomplished among a group of fine directors. It seemed to me that, while yielding to nobody in his respect for the old techniques (and the old actors), he was breaking through to a less traditional approach to radio. Gone, in his 'period' productions, was the rounded tone and fruity avuncularity of some of those double-barrelled doyens. In came more speed, more natural vitality, and a kind of pebble-dashing, grape-shot sense of life and fire that made productions identifiable as his own, moments after you switched on. Nothing defeated him. He liked, occasionally, to record an entire play as if it were a live performance. Once, as we prepared to record *Julius Caesar*, he bustled into the studio, glanced up at the clock and announced, 'Right, everyone. We've got one hour fifty-five minutes to get a two-hour show in the can,

so do your best and –' with a desperate last look around the cast
'– good luck – *please*!'

In 1976, he and writer/director Gerry Jones established one of
the most extraordinary radio events ever – 'Vivat Rex'. This
twenty-six-episode saga was a serialisation of Shakespeare's
history plays, with some additions by Christopher Marlowe. It
began with *Richard II*, all the *Henrys*, *Richard III* and finished,
beyond *Henry VIII*, with the little-known *Perkin Warbeck*.
Richard Burton agreed to visit the studio for one afternoon to
record linking narration that would later be distributed across the
entire series. Derek Jacobi played Richard II, Anthony Quayle
was Falstaff, Paul Scofield the Chorus in Henry V. Others
included Michael Redgrave, Flora Robson, Peggy Ashcroft,
Diana Rigg, Keith Michell, John Hurt and John Gielgud. I was
Prince Hal in the two *Henry IV* plays, and then Henry V. Since
the production was divided into hour-long episodes, it meant that
I was in seven or eight of them. So, while appearing in *The Circle*
by Somerset Maugham at night, I spent my days roistering with
Nym, Bardolph and Mistress Quickly in Studio B10, Broadcasting House. I fought and killed Hotspur at Shrewsbury, driving
him backwards into the studio river, courtesy of a blue plastic
washing-up bowl and some convincing gurgles from Robert
Powell. I rejected Falstaff, ascended the throne and stormed the
breach at Harfleur, before racing down Regent Street to the
Haymarket for my evening's work on-stage.

Because of the huge cast and differing availabilities, many
'Vivat' scenes were rehearsed and recorded out of sequence, like
a film. The radiophonic battle locations for *Henry V* were
represented by a strange chamber at the rear of the studio known
as 'the dead room'. From its ceilings and walls protruded peculiar
gauze-covered spongy wedges, like stalactites, that were supposed
to deaden the sound and provide a convincing outdoor acoustic.
The whole visual effect was of a morgue constructed by an unholy
alliance of Magritte, Miro and Boots the Chemist. During the
famous Harfleur speech, Jenkins, never satisfied with just a couple
of takes, urged me on to more and more pace, more voice, more
and more of the energy that Henry needed to whip his exhausted

soldiers into just one more attempt. Almost on my knees with tiredness myself, I thought this was taking radio beyond the brink of its possibilities. But then I forgot the graveyard of broadcasting souls all above and around; I saw only the mud, the dirt, the walls of Harfleur, the flagging troops, the glint of armour, the flashing sword in my hand. I had even flung my script to the ground after Take Four, realising I had re-remembered the lines from my first uneasy attempt at the role at Sadler's Wells in 1962. The sublime absurdity of radio behaviour did pop into my brain a few times. Particularly as my army, in the persons of some of Britain's foremost character actors, stood around between takes clutching odd pieces of metal and wood from the effects department. John Baddeley waved a poker. Timothy Bateson, as Bardolph, sported a rolled-up umbrella. Others held carving knives or forks which, as soon as the recording light glowed red, they waved and clashed a few times to represent weapons at the ready. After an hour of takes and retakes it became harder to keep up the spirit of Harfleur, and finally impossible when, in the middle of yet another attempt, I caught sight of Bernard Hepton holding up his car keys and giving them an occasional jingle as he stood, like a greyhound in the slips, ready to cheer, for the fourteenth time, at 'God for Harry, England and Saint George'.

As a result of learning how to develop radio pictures in the dark-room of my imagination, I had been given the chance to discover the art (or craft) of reading books on the air. After an uneasy beginning on 'A Book at Bedtime', when I couldn't seem to help pronouncing words with a pedantic over-accuracy, I found I had an aptitude for storytelling. It was back to Miss Fisher and the reading-aloud class at school. I sensed that my goal should be to persuade the listeners that there was no 'reader' involved. I wanted to set up a vision in their heads and make people only aware of the 'movie'.

In 1973, I offered the BBC the idea that I could adapt and broadcast some of Richmal Crompton's *Just William* stories. They accepted, and this became my 'learning zone'. With Jane Morgan as director, I tested out ways in which I could 'live inside' the author's creations by (not very subtly at first) varying my tone. I found it was possible to keep several characters at once in the air and still retain their differing vocal colours. I learnt how to dovetail the thoughts and attitudes of the characters into the way I read the narrative. I discovered for myself as a performer what I had always known as a listener – radio is the perfect storytelling medium. I am sometimes asked by Richmal Crompton fans to 'do' the voice of William for them. But William's voice is hardly characterised: it is fairly much my own natural speech and certainly not an attempt to impersonate an eleven-year-old boy. It's his demeanour, his airy view of his place in the world ('doin' good, ritin' wrongs, pursuin' happiness') that the listener is actually absorbing. In identifying with William, the voice the audience really hears is – almost – their own.

Sometimes you learn new things about your process. I was recently persuaded by a boy of about William Brown's age to say something to him in a Williamesque way. Egged on by his mother, I obliged with, 'Huh. Extra coachin' in the holidays! I bet there's lors against it. I never heard of anyone havin' lessons in the holidays. Not anyone! I bet even slaves din't have lessons in the holidays!'

The boy immediately turned to his mother and said, 'Did you see? When he talks like William he makes his mouth into a dog's bottom.'

There was something really wrong, though, when 'Listen With Mother' asked me to be their first male storyteller. Now, instead of a woman with a cosy nannyish voice, it was me who announced to the nation's pre-school tots, 'Hello. Are you sitting comfortably? Then I'll begin.' I broadcast about three stories. Then the news came: I sounded too sinister and the children, possibly their mothers too, didn't feel comfortable at all. I was replaced by the consummate Miriam Margolyes.

In learning from Miriam and other master readers – Alan Badel, Jill Balcon, Nigel Anthony, Alan Bennett, Ralph Richardson, Maurice Denham, Paul Scofield – and from tactful directors like Jane Morgan, Martin Jenkins, John Tydeman, Gemma Jenkins, Paul Kent and Pete Atkin, I have been helped, gradually, to refine my own approach. My main aim is to make a distinction between 'reading' and 'telling'. I am always hoping you will forget that you are being read to. I want to draw you into the tale itself.

I suggested to the BBC in 1974 that, with its wealth of books already recorded on tape and in its archives, it ought to issue some of them on commercial cassette. The treasure was vast: readings by Gielgud, Richardson, Redgrave, Richard Burton, Michael Hordern, Peggy Ashcroft, Edith Evans, Sybil Thorndike and many, many others. Not to mention its trove of comedy and documentary material. I was told, though, that there was unlikely to be any call for such releases and, in any case, it wasn't BBC policy to be so commercially minded. In 1988, I was pleased when they changed their minds and acknowledged that there might be a few folk calling for audio entertainment after all. The BBC set up a commercial arm, and now BBC Worldwide are market leaders in an ever-expanding industry of books on tape.

Who actually listens? Fifteen years ago, if you mentioned you were recording a book, someone was likely to say, 'Oh, for the deaf – er – I mean, the blind?' Now, everyone is listening. *David Copperfield*, unabridged, will get you from London to Glasgow and back three times. Norma Major and Terry Waite have both expressed to me the pleasure that hearing *Just William* and *Great Expectations* has given them. I have met American children who find *Billy Bunter* funnier than Daffy Duck. The woman in the dry-cleaner's prefers *Goodbye, Mr Chips* and Dick Francis thrillers. And when HRH the Prince of Wales told me he takes my recordings on his royal tours and listens to them at night, I was able to tell *him* of the woman who accosted me at the stage door of the Playhouse Theatre. 'I always take you to bed with me, Martin,' she said.

'Really?' I replied, preparing my face for a compliment.

She smiled keenly: 'Oh yes. And you know what?'

'No. What?'

'I'm always asleep in five minutes.''

In September 1989, Michael Frayn, tall, angular, windswept and beaming, met me at the stage door of the National Theatre. He and I were to join director Patrick Sandford in one of the vast rehearsal rooms to read through Michael's translation of Yuri Trifonov's *Exchange*. They had asked whether I might be interested in playing its doubtful hero, Viktor. Of course I would. Michael had previously trusted me to make a radio series, 'Jarvis's Frayn', based entirely on his satirical pieces in the *Guardian* and the *Observer*. Its success had led to other Frayn/Jarvis projects and I had also played Frank Prosser, on television, in his tragi-comedy about a sales force, *Make and Break*. Michael's extraordinary gift for revealing the humour and heartbreak of modern existence makes him the ideal translator of Trifonov. The National itself had passed on the opportunity to premiere *Exchange*, but at least had lent us a room for our meeting. In its original form, Trifonov's affecting account of modern urban life in Russia had run for eight years at Moscow's Taganka Theatre. The story is recognisable to all Muscovites as a true one, in which an ordinary family attempts to 'exchange' their miniscule one-roomed flat for a two-roomed apartment. Michael's version conveys all the bleakness and heartbreak of Viktor as he embarks on a morally dubious scheme that he hopes will gain the family a larger flat. The play is also a metaphor for the small exchanges people make in their lives; how they start off, perhaps, with certain ideals and standards and then gradually, imperceptibly, exchange them for something less uncompromising. By the end of the afternoon we had agreed that we would open *Exchange* at the Nuffield Theatre in Southampton, where Patrick was artistic director.

The part of Viktor is enormous. When not actually involved in scenes with his wife and daughter, or dealing with accusations from relations, his mistress and his office colleagues, he is narrating the play. Often he turns to the audience, mid-scene, to provide a commentary on his actions. Like Tom in David Hare's *Skylight*, he never seems to stop talking. I share Just William's view that, 'when I'm actin' I like to have a lot to do an' a lot to say,' so I was more than thrilled to have the part. Ros was to play Lena, Viktor's wife, with Faith Brook as my mother.

Rehearsals started well, but cramming in all those lines gave me an unlooked for extra problem. I couldn't sleep. Ros and I were staying at the old Polygon Hotel in Southampton, where the staff took a friendly interest in the production. They had read about the up-coming premiere in the local paper. Whenever we returned in the evenings after another gruelling rehearsal, the girls on the front desk would ask how it was going. We would smile and nod and say, 'Fine.' What they didn't know was that, every night, upstairs in Room 243, I was lying awake, glassy eyed, while Frayn's lines ducked and dived in my burning brain. The light-bulb in my head refused to switch off. I followed various instructions from well-meaning colleagues to combat the problem. I tried hot chocolate, red wine, herbal remedies, valerian tea, calcium tablets. Sometimes, it seemed, all at once. I could almost hear the reedy tones of Johnny Briggs on that Bavarian film location as he investigated my rattling briefcase: 'Christ, it's a fucking pharmacy!' Nothing worked. Certainly not the physical contortions mentioned in a book kindly lent me by Gabrielle Lloyd, who was playing my sister. Nor the tiny carton filled with something called 'algae powder' that Marcia Warren had donated. Ros found me one night at four in the morning, standing on one leg facing into a corner of the bathroom. The book said I had to stay like that for twenty minutes and then return to bed. I didn't tell her that in my waking exhaustion I had just drunk a dropperful of 'essential oils' in mistake for the 'rescue remedy' that Roger Hammond had contributed. It was hopeless. I couldn't switch off. I lay there while the marching ants of insomnia crawled over every part of me. Each day, I would stagger through rehearsals, scraping deeper and deeper down into the barrel of my acting reserves. When I returned to the hotel the girls would sweetly ask, 'How's it going, Mr Jarvis?' Grinning like a maniac, I would say, 'Oh, marvellous. Fantastic. Great fun!' Then lurch upstairs to lie, panicked and awake once more, while mad Moscow cossacked around my floodlit head.

One morning, Saturday, I leant resentfully across the still-sleeping Ros and grabbed the phone. There was nothing else for it: I had to have some proper sleeping pills. I tapped out the number of my doctor. We had another rehearsal this morning, then I could drive to London, pick up a prescription and, please god, get some sleep. 'Good morning – can I help you?' The tranquil, motherly voice made me feel calmer already. Just what the doctor ordered.

I cut her short, thanking my lucky stars that someone was actually there on a Saturday and began, desperately: 'Look – er – Martin Jarvis here. I realise the doctor isn't there, but can you help? I'm out of town rehearsing a new play. It's a nightmare.' My voice rose sharply. 'No, you see, it's ghastly. I haven't been sleeping. I can't. At all. *Please*, you must help me. For god's sake, I've had so little sleep, that I'm –' I played my trump '– I'm starting to *hallucinate!*' I flung in a final '*Do you understand? Do you see?*' I waited. Ros, surprisingly, slept on.

There was a pause at the other end. Then, in a careful tone, 'Yes – yes I do see, Mr Jarvis. But it's Eileen, down here on the front desk. You have to dial 9 first if you want an outside line.'

Aaagh! I felt my dried brain ignite in a hellish blaze. Oh god! Had I *really* just laid bare my agonies of sleep-deprivation to the placid hotel receptionist who, for the last three weeks, had shown unfailing interest in the show's progress?

She continued, her voice warm with compassion, 'Well, you obviously need a doctor, Mr Jarvis.'

This was an understatement. But for some reason I felt I had to backtrack, make it seem all right. I heard myself saying, with a jocular laugh, as if the whole thing had been some kind of actorish joke, 'Oh, no. No no. Just breakfast please.'

We opened the following Tuesday and the harsh focus that insomnia can bring to one's perceptions seemed oddly appropriate to the desolate tragi-comedy of Viktor's existence. We were a success, and the nightmare of acting so strangely metamorphosed gradually into a sweet dream. We brought the sixteen-strong company into the Vaudeville Theatre (Doreen Mantle now playing Mother) where *Exchange* ran for a ten-week season. This also cemented a working friendship with Michael Frayn, in which he has entrusted me with radio adaptations of many more of his books and plays.

This is Hollywood.
You must learn to love 'No'.

March 1994

Hollywood

Ros and I performed *Exchange* again in Los Angeles in the early nineties in a production for LA Theatre Works, directed by Robert Robinson. The producer, Susan Loewenberg, suggested that Ros and I ought to work more often in the States. Why not? we thought. New adventures.

In 1993, I had discovered that the US immigration authorities, before awarding you a Green Card so that you can work in America, require proof of your 'excellence in the arts'. This doesn't mean auditioning in front of an invited audience at the American Embassy. They demand a dossier of your film, television and theatre successes, some reviews, plus a few well-chosen 'commendatory letters'. In other words, they want to see references and a curriculum vitae. Luckily, I already had letters from Peter Hall, Alan Ayckbourn, Michael Frayn and Martin Jenkins that suited their requirements. I thought I would complete the set by asking Harold Pinter if he would write something on my behalf. Generously, he agreed and a day or two later I received his letter. It was different from the others. It simply read, 'To whom it may concern. Martin Jarvis is an actor of considerable strength. Harold Pinter.' Economic, Pinteresque. Enormously useful.

The embassy also required pictures. Ros, in searching our files, came across a photograph of me shaking hands with John Gielgud. This was not a record of any production in which I had appeared with him. It had been taken on the occasion of his eightieth birthday at a party given by Gyles Brandreth, author of an excellent biography of Sir John, and was actually a snap of me congratulating him. I included it in the dossier. After the US Embassy had finished processing my application, the picture was returned to us. I saw that a caption had been added by my creative immigration lawyer: 'Britain's foremost actor, Sir John Gielgud, congratulates Martin Jarvis on his "excellence in the arts".'

The work permit arrived and, shortly afterwards, Ros and I started to spend time in California.

By 1994, I had been dividing my time between 'Inspector Morse', 'Lovejoy', and the Peter Hall Company in England, and the newer experience of 'guest-starring' in various Hollywood television series. As well as taking on an American agent, I had been advised to hire a 'manager'. He would, I was told, be able to co-ordinate my appointments, and generally represent my best interests. He would also take up to 15 per cent of my income, even if it were my agents who actually got me the work. But, as he told me, 'Mart'n, this is Hollywood.'

Travis, my manager, was a remarkable character. One evening, soon after he had agreed to represent me, I walked into his office. This was a shady room in a slightly run-down building on the outskirts of Beverly Hills. I had gone there, at his request, to sign various contracts. Most of them, it turned out, concerned my binding agreement to pay him a proportion of my earnings. I was there to sign about eight copies of my contract for one episode of 'Murder, She Wrote' I had recently been offered.

I never got the measure of Travis. He was a porky man of no more than thirty, young enough to be my son. He had chalk-white skin that seemed impervious to any tanning. He wore black Ray-Bans – always, indoors and out. In the two years of our association I never saw his eyes. A dark Armani suit slimmed him down over a white shirt, buttoned to the top, no tie. He was straight out of *Reservoir Dogs*. Extraordinarily, he played tennis three times a week at the Beverly Hills Country Club. This sporting image seemed as unlikely as Quentin Tarantino on the

Centre Court at Wimbledon. He hardly ever smiled. His clipped speech and machine-gun delivery had no time for pauses or small talk. His usual method of business was to juggle two or three phone calls at once which made it impossible to have a coherent, uninterrupted conversation with him. When I asked on our first meeting why he had no secretary or assistant, he said sharply, 'Nobody will work with me.'

I had begun to see why. Nevertheless, I was pleased to see him that evening and delighted to be starting filming at Universal Studios next day. 'How are you, Travis?' I began.

He brushed my greeting aside: 'Yeah Mart'n, OK. We'll do all that another time.' ('Yeah Mart'n' was his preferred way of launching any exchange with me, whether face to face or on the phone.) I could see my reflection in his dark lenses as he rattled out, 'Yeah Mart'n, I'm very busy, all my appointments are behind. Everybody is very tense today. My last appointment was late. So are you. OK it's not your fault.'

I took a deep breath and reminded myself that *he* worked for *me*, not I for him. Then I remembered this wasn't Britain. I merely said, 'It's the traffic, Travis. That's why everybody is running behind. In Britain we call it the knock-on effect.'

He bridled like a teacher dissatisfied with his pupil's work, and snapped, 'Here it's the domino effect.' Swiftly, he placed a pile of paperwork in front of me. 'Now Mart'n, I want you to date all these contracts March first and sign them.' He stabbed the top page in various places. 'And initial them here – and here. You do that now. I have calls to make.' I felt I was renting a car.

He returned to his desk and snatched up one of a number of phones. Then, while I sat waiting like a Hertz customer, he began a ten-minute breakneck solo, hardly drawing breath: 'Hi, it's Travis. Did you get those scripts? No I sent them, did you *get* them? I don't care what you say, I tell you I did. No I'm not tense. I'm just saying don't talk to me like that, I'm having a terrible day. All my appointments were late. My last one was late, he's here now. Yes I do want to have lunch with you – but let's wait till you get a job. Yes I *do* want to talk with you, but I'm saying let's wait till there's something to talk *about*. G'bye. Hello it's Travis –'. As one phone slammed down another one buzzed and was snatched up straight away. 'No I'm not at all stressed out. Why is everybody so tense today? I'm not tense –'

I tried to concentrate on signing each section of the paper mountain in front of me. A third phone rang. Travis punched a button. Immediately a slow anxious voice came on the speaker: 'Oh, Travis, I'm returning your call. I'm just a little worried that –' Travis stabbed again and the voice was gone. He then picked up two phones at once, punched their pads and, after they had automatically zapped out numbers at top speed, he left brisk messages on various answer-machines. 'It's Travis call me back. It's Travis call me back.' After a few more calls, he came and stood over me like a hit man, checking my work. He fired off criticism of my efforts: 'Yeah Mart'n, you got it wrong. You shouldn't have signed those, only those.' He pulled some of the documents from the pile and held them up. 'And you shouldn't have dated those, only those.' Before I could protest that he had not explained the requirements properly, he leapt in with 'For god's sake Mart'n, don't you sign contracts in England?'

I shot back: 'Yes Travis, but not this many for one engagement.'

He returned a sharp backhand, 'Mart'n, I *have* to get you signed. Some of those contracts are your deal with *me*. I'm your *manager*. I don't want you changing your mind and leaving me. I'm not a rocket-launcher.'

What am I doing? I thought. Do I really need to be in business with this headbanger? Then a calm voice inside reminded me again this wasn't England, and he was reputed to be one of the best managers in Hollywood. I picked up another wodge and began to fill in the dates.

As soon as he saw what I was doing, Travis leapt across the room and snatched the pen from my hand, crying, '*No* Mart'n – cross all those dates out, that's *wrong*!'

I started to draw lines through them.

'No no! *Really* cross them out.' He was screaming now. '*Obliterate*! *Obliterate*! And obliterate your initials there.'

I began to do so.

'That's it,' he yelled, happier now. 'Yes. Obliterate – obliterate.'

I continued to obey.

'Then initial the obliterations,' ordered Travis.

As I started deleting and initialling, deleting and initialling, he suddenly threw himself into the chair beside me, momentarily exhausted. He panted for a second before leaping up again and saying, in a subdued tone, 'Sorry I'm abrupt, Mart'n. I don't mean to be. I'm tense.'

I looked up from my mutilated contracts, and said, I thought charitably, 'That's all right, Travis, I'm getting used to you. It's just your manner.'

He was having none of this. He spun round sharply, his milky face taut with the wrong I had done him. 'No it's *not* my manner!' He was screeching now, almost dancing with rage. 'It's just been a terrible day!' Then he changed down a couple of gears and said, 'OK, Martin, I want to sit down and talk with you.'

'Fine,' I said.

'No no, not *now*,' he flared, 'we've no time. When are you free?'

I was thinking there is no way I ever want to sit down and talk to this extraordinary man ever again. Strangely, I heard myself say, 'Thursday?'

Travis shot to his desk and riffled through his diary. 'No, not available. Friday?'

We settled on Friday, and I said I would take him to lunch. I asked if he was bored with Spago, one of LA's most fashionable restaurants, where I knew he was often to be seen wolfing a cobb salad and downing iced tea at the speed of light. Unexpectedly, his face relaxed. The quivering mouth broke into a rare smile, like a young girl being asked on a date. I could imagine the eyes almost twinkling behind the shades. 'Oh no, Mart'n,' he simpered, 'I *love* Spago. How *wonderful*.'

My turn to be brisk now. 'Good. What time?'

He clicked back into racing gear: 'Let's say one-fifteen. But I may be late. Say one-thirty. Maybe one-forty. It could be earlier, but we'll just have to deal with that. I just want to relax and hear all about *you*. Your favourite subject, Mart'n. After all, you're an *actor*.'

I stared up at him as he stood waiting for me to complete the paperwork. He had a point. If you are going to be an actor in Hollywood, *you* had better be your favourite subject. You may not be anyone else's.

Next morning, having parked my car in the 'structure', I sauntered, in the blazing heat of the San Fernando Valley, to Stage 25 at Universal Studios. I was feeling good. The powerful star of 'Murder, She Wrote', Angela Lansbury, had specially asked for me to join the cast. No audition required. I felt in demand. What's more, the elegant Carolyn Seymour was to play my wife. My role, in an episode entitled 'Another Killing in Cork', was Cyril Ruddy, a flamboyant, garrulous (possibly murderous) British actor. 'Mart'n, it's perfect for you,' Travis had told me, with typical irony deficiency.

A friendly security guard, who happened to have seen me on American television the previous night in 'Inspector Morse', met me at the door to the set. He escorted me inside, radioing importantly ahead that 'Mart'n Jarvis is here'. This is a rare accolade in a town where notices like, 'Actors – don't even *think* of parking here' are reminders that we are two a penny.

Kelly, the second assistant director, dressed in combat gear as if ready for manoeuvres, met me inside, turned me round and walked me briskly out again. I shouldn't, she told me, have come onto the sound stage yet. She showed me to my dressing room – a small hutch in a terraced row of cubicles lined up in one of the alleyways between Stages 25 and 26. Mine was next to the lavatories. 'You can get ready, Mart'n,' she said brusquely.

'Where's my dresser,' I asked.

She looked at me as if she didn't follow. 'Can't you dress yourself?' she said, and slammed the door shut. Fair enough. I turned in the tiny space to see that a suit was hanging there ready for me. A few days earlier, I had had an extensive costume fitting, in which Don, the wardrobe supervisor, had taken photos of me in about eight different outfits, most of which were suited to the bluff character of Cyril. I only needed two. I had asked why I had to be photographed in each one, and why so many. Don explained that Miss Lansbury was also the executive producer. He dropped his voice slightly and his tone became reverential: 'Miss Lansbury will view the pictures and make the final choice of what you wear.' He had added, though, that 'she will be influenced by the suit you prefer'. I mentioned that the mid-blue looked good. He nodded and said, with a slight obeisance, that Miss Lansbury would be glad to know that.

I eyed the suit hanging there in my hutch ready for my first scene. It was a peculiar tweed outfit that I didn't remember trying on. It didn't remind me of anything I had ever come across in England. It was almost orange; shreds of what looked like pieces of All-Bran sprouted from it at irregular intervals. It seemed a little over the top, even for Cyril. I later learnt from Don that, 'Miss Lansbury has decided to wear blue today. We can't have a clash, can we?'

Certainly not. After I had put on the peculiar tweed, Kelly called to march me to the make-up caravan. There, Skip, an elderly doyenne of the business who had been hairdresser on major movies since the thirties, sat me in the chair. She assessed the top of my head, running her shaky fingers through my hair, before announcing, in a twangy quaver, 'Mousse and finger-combing, I think, Mart'n. We need control.' She told me, as she shaped and sprayed and sculpted, that she had done the same for Brando, Gable, Monroe, Jack Lemmon, Bette Davis and a thousand others.

As I left her caravan, I bumped into my fellow guest-star, Rod Taylor who, in the fifties and sixties, had been the Mel Gibson of his day. It took me a moment to relate this jolly balding fellow to the smouldering star of *Young Cassidy*, *Giant*, and *The Birds*. I was resisting the temptation to say how much I had enjoyed all those films – for fear of being thought a toady – when another actor came up to him and thrust out a hand. 'Mr Taylor,' he said, 'this is such an *honour* for me. You are my favourite actor, I *love* your work. You are *awesome*. You are my hero.'

'Oh, good,' said the genial Rod, immediately hugging him. 'I can see we're going to get on great!'

Our director, Anthony Shaw, came bouncing into the caravan

a few minutes later. He told me I wouldn't be meeting Mom till after lunch. Mom? It turned out that he was Miss Lansbury's son. Then executive producer Peter Shaw arrived. He was Angela's husband. The script was written, I had noticed, by Bruce Lansbury. Angela's brother. As Anthony and I walked together to the set, he introduced me to a young actress who was playing an Irish maid. 'This is Felicia,' he said, 'Mom's niece. Oh, and you'll meet David later. Nephew.'

We shot several scenes of the family show that morning, which involved me in various costume changes, from the peculiar tweed to a jazzy green number. I still hadn't met Angela. A few minutes before lunch, Anthony realised he needed to reshoot part of the first scene, in which the camera reveals the time displayed on a clock directly behind me. He felt he hadn't got it right. He apologised, telling me I would have to change back into the tweed one more time. 'We've got to do it now, Martin,' he said, looking anxiously at his watch. 'We shoot Mom straight after lunch. Sorry.'

I employed a favourite LA phrase: 'No problem.'

Tommy from wardrobe, taking it easy in a deck chair, called after me languidly as I scurried from the set, 'Can you manage, Mart'n?'

'No problem,' I repeated as I dashed by, thinking haughtily: 'In England my dresser would already be laying the stuff out in the dressing room.'

As I disappeared, Kelly barked, 'Quick as you can, Mart'n. Only five minutes to get this shot in the can before lunch.'

Inside the hutch, I divested myself of the green suit, plus shirt and tie, grabbed the original pink shirt, pulled it over my head and swiftly buttoned it. As I knotted the tie, Kelly was banging on the door, shouting, 'They're ready as soon as you are Mart'n, let's go.'

'I'm being as quick as I can,' I called, climbing into the trousers, buttoning the waistcoat and throwing on the jacket. Then I raced back to the set, past the relaxing Tommy. I took my place once again with all the practised professionalism of an actor getting the director out of a hole.

There was just time to get the shot. Suddenly, as Anthony was about to call 'Action', Betty, the continuity lady, got up from her stool and came forward anxiously. 'Oh no, Mart'n – it's not right,' she said.

I looked at her worried face. 'What?'

'The suit. It's the wrong one.'

I looked. The director looked. We all looked. I should have changed back into the peculiar tweed. I hadn't. I realised at once what had happened. In my haste, I had thrown off the jazzy green outfit, put on the old shirt and tie and then – yes – put the same damn suit back on again.

I felt myself deflating from the buoyant seen-it-all guest-star to the same dim-wit who had missed his cues in Croydon all those years ago. Muttering 'Sorry, sorry everyone', I tore back to the hutch where, this time with Tommy's amused assistance, I got into the peculiar tweed once again.

Anthony contained his impatience and we just managed to get the shot in before lunch. I still hadn't met Angela.

My hard-working American agent, Gordon King, with the approval of Travis, had arranged for me on this same day to meet the producers of another series also being filmed at Universal. I was to go to their studio bungalow during the lunch break. It would all work out very simply. Since I didn't know where Bungalow 467 was, Costas, a unit driver, would take me up there in one of the small buggies that constantly ferry people around the lot.

Ten minutes later, I entered the bungalow to be greeted by Megan, the casting director. I was still wearing the peculiar All-Bran tweed, pink shirt and tie. My hair was riveted to my head, courtesy of Skip's mousse, and my face glowed with the healthy tan applied by make-up artist, Dale. Megan looked at me oddly as she thanked me for coming. She asked me to wait a moment while she 'warned' them. Returning a minute later, she said, 'I've told them you're dressed somewhat eccentrically and wearing theatrical make-up.'

She showed me in and I shook hands with the producers. They didn't seem too impressed. Not surprisingly. The part was that of a sick and emaciated scientist surviving without food or water, trapped on the bleak landscape of a dying TV planet. Dress code? Gritty leather. Not peculiar tweed. 'Murder, She Wrote' it was not.

After a brief chat, and certainly no offer of the role, I found myself outside the bungalow and no sign of Costas. I had forgotten to ask him to wait. I looked at my watch. There was still plenty of time. I wasn't due back on the set for my first scene with Miss Lansbury until two o'clock. I decided to walk. There was really no other option. So, dressed as a tweedy oddball, with the sun blazing overhead, I set off on the half-mile return journey. It was a scene from *Lawrence of Arabia*. After a hundred yards, I took off my jacket, then, after fifty more, loosened my collar and tie and undid my waistcoat. As I trekked onwards I began to feel pain. It was the back of my right heel. The left heel didn't feel too good either. Another few steps and I realised what it was. My shoes were a size too small. They had seemed tight on the set but now, as I reeled beneath the sun's anvil, the pain was excruciating. I was scraping flesh off both heels every time I took a step. I learnt later from Tommy that a British size 9 (my size) is the same as a size 10 in the States. I had told Don at our initial costume fitting that I was a 9. Result: these shoes were size 8 and were killing me.

Eventually I made it back. I went into the lavatory next to my hutch, took off my socks and examined the backs of my raw heels. I pressed the tap on the basin and washed blood off both feet. I rinsed out the socks. Then I visited the loo. When I emerged from the cubicle I couldn't get the tap to work again. I had used up all the water. It was nearly two o'clock. I slipped the shoes back on, tied them loosely, making sure I stayed on tip-toe to avoid further chafing of the heels. Then, holding the wet, bloody socks in one hand, I teetered out into the sunshine. As I limped the few yards to my hutch, Kelly rounded a corner. She had someone with her, an elegant woman in a mid-blue tailored suit. 'Hey, Mart'n,' said Kelly, 'may I introduce –'

I came to a halt, transferred the bloody socks to my left hand, held out my unwashed right hand and said, 'How do you do, Miss Lansbury.'

Angela turned out to be charming. Later that day, during one of the breaks in filming, she told me that originally she had had to audition for the part of Jessica Fletcher. Now her own company ran the show. The popularity of the series over eleven years certainly owed much to the gentle control she and husband Peter exerted over the family business. It reminded me of a repertory company. Nearly everyone in this particular episode had appeared in the series before. 'You'll be back,' Anthony told me one day. I was surprised. We were just about to shoot the sequence where Cyril is unmasked as the killer; I presumed my character would be incarcerated for many years. But the rules for 'Murder, She Wrote' were different. He was right. Less than six months later I had a call from Anthony asking me to appear in another film in the series, this time a story set amongst the New York art world. I was delighted, but surely I couldn't be the villain a second time? 'Sure, Mart'n,' cried the irrepressible Anthony. 'You're the murderer again. Mom loved you.' Then he said, using a phrase I was hearing more and more often in America, 'This isn't Britain. You can be a different killer every season.'

Between murders, Travis arranged for me to meet an important television writer-producer (Robin someone) so that I could secure the part of Albert the Butler in a brand-new sitcom. 'It's a wonderfully *wry* role, Mart'n,' Travis told me. 'Wry is good. Go get it.' According to Travis this Robin/Mr Big was likely to offer me the job. Although the script was still being written I had already received the first three pages. It seemed rather good. And funny. A laid-back British butler attempting to get his employer's limousine repaired by a dozy mechanic who doesn't seem familiar with its advanced technology. The character of Albert reminded me of Gielgud in *Arthur* or Denholm Elliott in *Trading Places*. Nice little part for the car mechanic too, I noticed. I couldn't wait to read more. Rather exciting, the lead in my first American comedy series.

'Yeah Mart'n, don't be late,' Travis warned. 'I told you, it's not like Britain. They don't know who you are.'

Privately reminding myself that plenty of people in Britain

didn't know who I was either, I said, 'Don't worry, Travis, I'll be there.'

'Got your sides?'

'Sides?'

'Pages. You got 'em?'

'Oh yes. I'll be ready.'

'Yeah Mart'n.'

Whatever small reputation you may have achieved in your own country, if you want to work in Hollywood you have to swallow any remaining pride and shamelessly peddle your wares in front of directors, producers and casting people. It's called 'taking a meeting'.

That afternoon I screeched to a halt in the parking lot beneath one of the tallest buildings in Century City, three miles west of Hollywood. I was, despite my assurances to Travis, late. My previous meeting, an hour ago, for the leading part of a mad British major in a Twentieth Century-Fox military series, had overrun. I raced to the escalator and within seconds was consulting the information board in the vast marble lobby. I saw that Mr Big's office was located on the twenty-eighth floor. I hurled myself into the elevator. Five minutes behind schedule. Not good enough, I knew.

I leant against the wall of the elevator, regaining my breath. Somebody had already pressed a button and up we went towards floor nineteen with a quiet whoosh. I extended a finger to press twenty-eight. There was no such number. Strange. Oh well, press twenty-nine. We stopped first at nineteen and my travelling companions got out. Now I was on my own. I blasted up to twenty-nine and scooted away as soon as the doors slid apart. All I had to do was find the stairs that led down one flight to the twenty-eighth. I looked around. Where were they? I headed along the corridor, turned a corner and followed a sign that said 'Emergency Exit', eventually arriving at a door at the end of a further corridor. I pushed it open and found myself standing on a metallic platform – part of a stairway that ran up and a long, long way down the side of the building. Vertigo.

I stood for a moment, confused, panting, then took two

tentative paces towards the guard rail. My footsteps echoed around the fathomless well. Feeling like a fly on the side of the Cape Canaveral launching gantry, I grasped the rail for a second before, gingerly, beginning my descent to the floor below. Having arrived, I grabbed the handle of the door to the twenty-eighth and jiggled it up and down. It was locked. I knocked. Nothing. Panic. I went cautiously back up the metal stairway to the twenty-ninth and tried the door. I knew already, somehow, that it would be locked too: these doors could only be opened from the inside. I knocked. Waited. No one came. I caught sight of a notice on the wall: 'Attention. There is an emergency button on floor thirty. Press for assistance and details of escape route across roof.' I clanged up to the next floor, found the button set into the wall and pressed it. Waited. Nothing. Pressed again. Suddenly a voice emanated from a small grille and inquired curtly: 'Yep?'

Clearing my throat, I put my mouth to the opening. 'Er, hello.' My voice came bouncing back from the abyss. 'Hello. I'm afraid I'm trapped. On the stairs outside.'

The grille then asked, 'Where are you?'

'I'm on the thirtieth floor,' I replied, 'I want to get into the twenty-eighth.' I concluded, like the white rabbit in similar circumstances, 'I'm late.'

'Uh huh,' said the grille. 'Which floor you say?'

'The thirtieth. Trapped. Definitely trapped.'

The grille now began to assume control. 'OK. Stay where y'are. Don't move. Someone comin' to get you.'

I hung around on the thirtieth. The minutes ticked by. I thought, I've blown it. It's all over. Even if I am rescued I'll never get to be the butler now. Far too feverish. Wry is out of the question.

Finally a voice from above broke into the booming silence: 'Hey you! This way in!'

Looking upwards I saw no one, my vision obscured by the metal latticework of the platforms. I called out, absurdly, 'Where are you?' Even the echo sounded puny with panic and relief.

'Thirty-third,' came the sonorous reply.

Gripping the rail and holding my briefcase up in front of me in a businesslike manner, in case he thought I was a mad bomber, I started to ascend. I could see, as I climbed, that James Earl Jones would have been well cast as my rescuer. He was a security guard, huge and black in a blue and silver uniform. One hand was at the ready above his holster, the other he held out, either to ward me off or to assist me up the last tread. As I came alongside him I started to explain the circumstances. And the urgency. 'I'm an actor and –'

He rolled his eyes. For a moment I thought he was going to give the standard Hollywood reaction: 'Really, which restaurant?' Instead he murmured, with a wryness that would not have disgraced Albert himself, 'Isn't everybody?'

I asked if he could unlock the door to the twenty-eighth floor and let me in. He shook his head, said 'Nope, that's a violation' and ordered me to follow him up to a higher platform. I did so, and just as I was remembering the notice about the rooftop escape route, he produced a large key and unlocked the door to the thirty-third floor. We went through it and along the corridors to the elevator. As we got in I was about to remind him that it doesn't stop at the twenty-eighth when I saw him jab the button marked 'Lobby'. We rode down to the ground. As the doors slid open, James Earl indicated another set of elevators on the other side of the hallway. 'Over there is *even* numbers,' he explained, 'These here are *odd*. You dig?'

I dug. Yelling thanks, I ran across to the even numbers, whooshed up to twenty-eight and, two minutes later, was apologising profusely to Mr Big's hatchet-faced receptionist for being so late.

'No problem,' she intoned, without looking up. 'You know what? They're not back from lunch yet.'

I lay in a chair, gasping and looking over my pages, until finally she told me that Robin, plus director and casting assistant, was finally ready for me. I marched down the corridor into the office, cleared my throat and bade them a Jeevesian 'Good afternoon'.

A stunningly attractive girl of about twenty-six with long honey-blonde hair, cornflower-blue eyes and freckles, ensconced behind a large mahogany desk, flicked me a half-smile. 'Hi, I'm Robin.'

I made a rapid mental adjustment: Ms Big. (Robin is just as much a girl's name in California. I have since made the acquaintance of Michael, Jaimie, Timothy, even Terence. All girls.)

'Good afternoon,' I said and sat down. Fine. The twenty-minute wait had given me time to recover. I recovered a little more and met Robin's cool gaze. She didn't seem anxious to speak again. I nodded and turned to the other two, who sat at each corner of the long desk. They didn't speak either. All three appraised me – in silence. It was obviously up to me to take charge. I opened the meeting with a congratulatory comment or two about the excellence of her first three pages of script and invited discussion as to how the character might develop. What were her thoughts on the subject? What were any of their thoughts? I threw the meeting open. Still none of them spoke. They simply studied me as if I had just landed from the moon. I remembered the words of Travis: 'This isn't Britain, Mart'n.'

As I was about to offer a few ideas of my own, Robin suddenly said, crisply, 'OK, Marvin – you see what it is? A skit on Batman, right?'

For a second I couldn't follow her drift. Then I saw. Of course. It was Batman's butler, asking 'Joe' to repair this extraordinary-looking black-finned vehicle – the Batmobile itself. My breezy assumption that I was in control began to dissipate. 'Ah.'

'So, Marvin. What d'ya reckon?' prodded Robin.

I thought quickly. This may not be Britain – but a great part is a great part. And it's clear from the script that it's going to be a very funny character in the series. So why not? This is America. New adventures and all that. I smiled. 'Great. I'd certainly like to see the rest of the script when it's finished.'

Robin shrugged. 'Sure, if you want.'

'Well, you know,' I pursued, 'to see how the part develops.'

She looked blank. 'Hey, that's it,' she said.

Again I didn't follow. 'What?'

Her lovely eyes took on a steely glint. She seemed sulky now, like a teenager fed up with being cross-examined by her father. She turned to her male colleague, a whey-faced kid with a stud in his left nostril. He had sat silently all this time, slouching in his chair and eyeing me morosely. Now he spoke in a whiny voice: 'She said that's it. That's the part. Get it?'

More light began to dawn. 'You mean just that little scene? That's all there is?' I caught the unflinching gaze of the third member of the team, a sallow, lumpy girl with a short, greasy fringe who might have been in her gap year before going on to art school. I assumed (if the morose boy was the director) that she was the casting person. She had pulled the high neck of her black sweater over her chin so that it hid her mouth. She said nothing. She might have been smiling or puking.

The gorgeous Robin, bored now and impatient, glanced at her watch and said, 'Yup, that's all there is, Marvin. It's a cold opener. To start the show. Wanna do it?'

I learned afterwards, from Travis, that a 'cold opener' is a short scene that usually takes place between the end of the previous programme and the commercial break: a sort of 'teaser' to prevent the viewers changing channel. It's a tiny sketch and doesn't necessarily relate to what follows. Robin's script, I finally understood, was *not* based on the humorous escapades of a wry British butler. The star part was, in fact, Joe the mechanic and the series followed his adventures in the motor trade. The cold opener was just a brief joke in which Joe dreams he is repairing the Batmobile.

In the end I was spared from having to make a pride-ingesting decision. 'Yeah Mart'n,' said Travis on the phone. 'Fox loved your madness. You got the part.' It took me a moment to realise that he was referring to the first of my two meetings that day. I had secured the part of the whacky major .

'Yeah Mart'n,' continued Travis expertly, 'you can forget wry – mad is better.'

Having played my share of shady characters in home-grown television series such as 'Supply and Demand', 'Casualty', 'Lovejoy', 'Frost', 'Morse', 'Boon' and 'Scarlet & Black', I felt more than qualified to inhabit a few Hollywood villains. Traditionally, we Brits have been considered ideal casting in these roles. When I arrived on the set recently to begin shooting for a movie, *The X-Ray Kid*, the assistant director looked straight through me at first. But when I opened my mouth and began, 'Excuse me, I wonder if –', he cut me short and called immediately to the director, 'Bad guy boss is here.'

One day, I received a script for a new American spy series called 'Shadow-Ops'. Its stars were to be four glamorous under-twenty-three-year-old girls. My part, if I got it, would be the leading Russian villain, General Steck, the most vicious, morally bankrupt degenerate ever encountered in a television film. His mission in life was to torture and attempt to put to death the attractive young people as they battled against his evil ambitions for world domination. Nothing new there, but rather fun to act. Travis told me the 'Shadow-Ops' production team were keen to meet me. Apparently, their casting director, Betsy, had seen my recent villainy in 'Murder, She Wrote' and thought the nifty way I smiled, and murdered while I smiled, might suit them very well. I was summoned to Paramount Studios to read for the part.

Before going I decided to have my hair cut, Russian style. I thought this a sensible idea as, the previous week, at a meeting for the role of a mittel-European scientist, the director had remarked tactfully, 'Very good – but I notice you are not entirely Hungarian.' This time, I decided, I will at least *look* convincingly Russian. I went to the famous Hollywood barber, Nick Mitchell. Nick, a tough rollerblading sixty-five-year-old ex-actor (of course), understood at once what was required. Being a disciple of Lee Strasberg, he immediately picked up the scissors and geared himself into the moment: 'Mart'n, were you ever in Korea?' he croaked, taking his first hack at my locks. Before I could reply, he answered the question himself: 'No, you were a kid in England, I guess.'

He then told me he had been a helicopter pilot in that war. He slashed and cut, waxing savagely lyrical, as he relived his time in the thick of battle. He related, as he cut and thrust at the top of my head, how he had tried to get the chopper off the ground while South Koreans, under fire from Communist forces, were grabbing at it from below, trying to climb aboard to safety. 'God, it was hell, Mart'n,' he snarled through gritted teeth as he hewed and sawed, revisiting the horror of that time. Finally, the scissoring ceased, he paused for breath and we surveyed the devastation in the mirror. Sadistic barbarous Steck, to the life, stared back: cruel, crew-cut, frightening.

That afternoon, the ravages of the Korean War having been fought on top of my head, I drove to Paramount. Travis had called me earlier about the meeting. It was, he said, a 'walk-on'. If I had had more hair it would have bristled. 'I don't play walk-ons,' I told him sharply.

He came back, quick as a flash: 'Now, Mart'n, calm down. A walk-on simply means you don't drive onto the studio lot. You park in the street and *walk* on. Got it?'

I parked, and walked on. I was early. I strolled in the sunshine along the flower-edged paths. I felt strangely relaxed as I ambled past the neat bungalow offices, and along the side of buildings named after Gary Cooper, Bob Hope, Dietrich and von Sternberg. I made my way beyond the famous Paramount arch and eventually found the two-storey pavilion that was my destination. The scent of flowers and (surely) the hum of summer bees gave these quiet gardens an almost idyllic quality. The smell of newly cut grass reminded me of cricket fields in Croydon long ago. Strange. I told myself: this Steck business is going to be a shoe-in.

I walked up the steps and, surrounded by about ten glamorous twenty-two-year-olds, all studying 'Shadow-Ops' scripts, I added my name to the list of auditionees. I spotted Betsy, the casting director, as she shepherded the next girl into an inner office. She waved to me, almost deferentially I thought. 'Hi, Mart'n. Thanks for coming. Won't keep you waiting long.'

No problem. I leant on the balustrade and glanced idly at my script. I could see a reflection of my Pork Chop Hill head in the glass door of the veranda. Good, I looked bad. Finally, Betsy emerged and ushered me ahead of her towards the office. Getting meaner by the minute, I moved forward, totally focused. Steck was ready for the 'Shadow-Ops' team. 'Yeah Mart'n, you have to *be* Steck,' Travis had told me. 'You have to solve the problem for them of how to cast the part. Let 'em fall in love with you.'

Not sure that anyone could actually love the monstrous Steck, I strode into the room, all set to greet them with a brutal smile and curt nod. I looked round. There was no one there. No writer, no producer, no director. Just Betsy, entering behind me, who smiled and went to her seat. She saw my surprise and explained that this was a 'pre-read'. 'I'm sure you'll be meeting the producers tomorrow,' she said reassuringly, 'but *I* wanted to hear you first.'

Ah, well. I'd played to small houses before. Never mind. I'll use my anger. I sat down, then stood up again, wholly possessed by the character of Steck. Travis is right, I thought. I'll solve her problems. Here goes. I threw back my cropped head arrogantly and read the first speech in a malignant Russian accent. Betsy looked up suddenly, startled, then read the next cue. She was impressed, I could see. I read on, cool and hard. My pitiless tone rose to a ferocious climax as I outlined to the 'Shadow-Ops' girls what sophisticated forms of torture it would be my pleasure to bestow. My characterisation filled the room. I finished by moving forward, leaning slowly across the desk and gazing deep, deep into her eyes. I gritted my teeth like Nick Mitchell and twisted my mouth into a last malevolent sneer. I sat down.

Silence. Neither of us moved. Then she shifted in her chair, looking slightly pale. She swallowed and said quietly, 'Wow. Well. That was fabulous, Mart'n. I was completely terrified.'

I allowed a brief smile to play across my features. 'Thank you,' I said modestly. In my own voice.

She rose, took my hand in both of hers and said, 'Mart'n, I'm going to tell the producers about your beautiful read. It's a privilege to have your incredible talent in this room. You were *so* scary. I'll be calling your manager later this afternoon.' I felt invincible as I strode back down the scented avenues. I had solved the problem for her of how the part should be played.

Back at home an hour later, the phone rang. It was Travis. I started to tell him that the part was virtually in the bag, when he stopped me: 'Mart'n, you didn't get the job.'

'What?' Suddenly I was under twenty-three myself, disbelieving, resentful, disappointed. 'But why?' I heard myself whining. 'I thought she was impressed.'

'Yeah well Mart'n,' said Travis, 'I asked Betsy why you didn't get it, and –'

'And – ?'

'She says you weren't frightening enough.'

'But – but –'

'No buts Mart'n,' said Travis savagely, 'this is Hollywood. You must learn to love "no".' He hung up.

Occasionally, even in a film and television city where Emmy Award winners audition for supporting roles, a script arrives with 'yes' attached. Or 'yes probably'. A few days after the Steck adventure, Travis phoned, beginning the conversation in his usual manner: 'Yeah Mart'n, how tall are you?'

I told him six foot exactly.

He seemed not to have heard and repeated the question.

'Six foot,' I said again.

He started to sound tetchy: 'Mart'n, do you read me?' He enunciated carefully: 'How tall?'

I began to twig. Was he seeking an *alternative* answer? I checked it out. 'Do you mean, Travis, it might be better if I were taller?'

I heard him sigh impatiently at the other end. I could imagine the chalk face tightening, the lips starting to quiver. 'No Mart'n', he snapped. 'Keep trying.'

'Shorter?' I offered.

'Thank you, Mart'n, you've got it.' I sensed him raising his never-seen eyes to heaven behind the Ray-Bans. He had another go: 'Now Mart'n' (with infinite patience), 'how tall are you?'

'Five ten?' I suggested.

'I'll tell 'em,' he replied crisply and the phone went down.

It soon became clear that I had been offered a role in a special episode of a hugely popular series on CBS television, 'Walker, Texas Ranger'. Its star (and producer) Chuck Norris, former world martial arts champion, is almost an American icon. The series is filmed in Dallas, where it is clearly impracticable for actors to travel for an audition. 'Yeah Mart'n, the only problem –' Travis explained when he rang back ten minutes later, '– Chuck doesn't like his guest-stars being taller than him. They want you for the role though – someone's bringing you a script right now.' He added, as he put down the phone, 'Just don't be tall.'

Half an hour later the bell rang at the garden gate. As I went to answer it, I had a sudden thought: whoever has brought the script may be a spy who'll be reporting my actual height back to Chuck. I slowed my pace and, when I reached the gate, called, 'Are you from "Walker"?'

A voice came from the other side of the hedge. 'Sure. I have a script for Marvin Jarvis.'

'That's – me.'

I knew what to do. I called out to the unseen figure and asked if he could slide the script under the gate.

The answer came back, 'No. I have to hand it over, in person, to Marvin.'

Better be on the safe side. There was nothing for it. I bent my knees and moved the last few paces as Groucho Marx, before opening the gate and taking the script from the young man who stood there. He was under twenty-six and therefore the right age for a Hollywood producer. He looked me up and down. Definitely trying to determine whether I would dwarf the star. I slouched cunningly against the wall and inquired if he was one of the producers. 'Not yet,' he said. 'I'm just the messenger.' I took no chances, waiting until he had driven out of sight, before lengthening upwards again and locking the gate.

The script was intriguing. Commander Colin Draper of Interpol (my part) arrives in Dallas in pursuit of the deadliest assassin in the world, the Viper, who may (or may not) have been the second gunman involved in the assassination of President Kennedy. Whose help does he enlist in his quest? Our hero, Walker, of course. Filming was to take place on the actual locations associated with the shooting: Elm Street, Main Street, the grassy knoll, the Book Depository. I flew to Dallas a few days later.

Director Tony Mordente, lead dancer in the original *West Side*

Story, looked at me closely as we stood on the grassy knoll, but said nothing. I had taken the precaution of standing slightly below him on the lowest part of the slope. Suddenly a murmur from the watching crowd signalled the arrival of the star. Chuck was among us. He stood at the highest point of the slope, dwarfing us all. I looked up at him. He was certainly taller than I had anticipated. This fine figure of a ranger was no midget. He began to bear down towards me from the top of the knoll. What was it about the way he moved? Of course: the Principal Boy in the old pantomimes at the Croydon Grand. Here, suddenly, was Dandini, cantilevered towards me in great high boots and tall black hat. And somewhere in the middle, above the heels, below the hat, behind the beard, stood Chuck himself. He swung out a hand as he neared me. 'Great to have you on the show, Mart'n.'

I stood my ground. My lower ground. The one thing I was not going to do was tower over him and be sent back to LA on the next flight. He moved down the slope a final pace. Now we stood level with each other. I kept my knees a little bent as a precaution. I needn't have worried – he was still head and shoulders above me. Thank god. I made the decision. I flexed my Groucho knees and stood tall. I was ready to pursue the Viper flat out. Chuck had got my measure and the part was still mine.

'Hi Mart'n, hi Rosalind – welcome to my nightmare!' James Cameron, director of the film *Titanic*, climbed from the vast indoor tank of water and took off his goggles. He shook hands cordially, showering water from his blue wetsuit like some great aquatic animal. It was September, 1996. Jim had recently seen us as Mama and Papa in *Emily's Ghost*, a small film set in Edwardian times made by the Children's Film Unit for Channel 4. As a result, he had invited us to play the Duff Gordons, British aristos who famously survived the *Titanic* disaster. We were happy to oblige. Another adventure. The parts were not large ('Yeah Mart'n, they're cameos,' Travis had said) but the whole project sounded fascinating. The money was good, and surely our cameos wouldn't take more than a couple of weeks to complete.

Ros and I had arrived earlier that day in Rosarito, Mexico

where the entire movie was being made. We were driven along the coast road to the set, which was housed in a vast studio complex, specially built for this film, on the edge of the Pacific. Paramount-on-Sea. About a mile from the compound we rounded a bend and there, suddenly, straight ahead, was *Titanic* itself, its four great funnels rising eerily into the sky. It seemed to be afloat on the open sea, though as we approached we perceived the illusion. What we were actually seeing was the top half of a gigantic hydraulic model of the great ship – almost as large as the real thing. It was built on dry land but, from this angle, seemed to be riding at ease against the turquoise backdrop of the ocean. Later – many months later as it turned out – it would be flooded with millions of gallons of water, then rocked and swayed and angled and manoeuvred, in one of the most continuously convincing shipwreck sequences ever filmed. As we drove through the gates on this pleasant Mexican day, we felt rather as those doomed passengers of eighty-four years ago must have done as they embarked at Southampton, unaware of what lay ahead. Our iceberg was going to be a long wait.

We didn't know this, of course, as Jim wrung us by the hand and thanked us for joining his blockbusting dream. He was a tall, crew-cut, blond-bearded man of about forty, with a hook nose and a manic look in his eye. The director as Ahab. That afternoon he was preparing to shoot a scene in which hundreds of passengers and crew struggled for life in the icy Atlantic, grabbing at bits of floating wreckage, deck-chairs, cushions, lifebelts, anything to help keep them afloat. As we stood watching them rehearse this uncanny re-enactment, Josh McLaglen the first assistant director, waist deep in the tank, shouted into his megaphone, 'Who wants a bathroom break?' Forty Mexican extras, all of whom had been immersed for several hours, stood up in the water and put up their hands like children at the swimming baths. Josh allowed them to scramble out.

Jim, after a shouted exchange about the lighting with Russell Carpenter, his director of photography, seemed to have time to chat with us. We talked about the Duff Gordons' behaviour in their near-empty lifeboat and how Sir Cosmo (my role) handed out cigars to the crewmen while hundreds were drowning only a short distance away. Legend has it that his gesture was meant as a reward to the men for not rowing back into the maelstrom, in case the boat should be swamped by desperate people attempting to climb into it. It later emerged that Duff Gordon had also handed five-pound cheques to several of the crew. Ostensibly, this was to help them replace their lost kit. But perhaps, it had been suggested at the inquiry afterwards, it was a retrospective bribe to go along with the cigars. All very intriguing, though hardly dealt with in Cameron's current script.

'Hey, Mart'n,' said Jim, preparing to get back into the tank, 'why don't we put the cigar stuff into your lifeboat scene?' This sounded promising. He said no more and swung his legs over the side, disappearing into the morass of floating debris. Kate Winslet, whitened face and red hair beaded with ice particles from the make-up department, took up her position in the water. She had played my daughter in a television film when she was fourteen and now called out, 'Hello Dad!' At her side a lean young man of about twenty-two grinned and went into a brilliant impression of a drowning Michael Jackson. He would fast become the most popular young actor in America, Leonardo DiCaprio. The Jackson impression was to pall somewhat over the coming, interminable, months.

Cameron had waded out to where Leo and Kate were waiting to do another waterlogged take as doomed lovers, Rose and Jack. Jim's script originally contained fascinating vignettes of a number of characters whose stories are part of the legend of the *Titanic*, including the Duff Gordons'. Although he shot a great deal of this detail, it became clear that, to draw the greatest audience into the cinemas, the movie, finally, had to be something simpler – Romeo and Juliet at sea, instead of the true story of the *Titanic*. Nevertheless, the setting and minutiae of the film were precise and authentic, even down to the cutlery in the first-class dining room, and the Beluga caviare we all ate for a week during the shooting of the dinner scenes. Cameron's knowledge and under-standing of the history of the disaster is immense, but so is his understanding of how to reach the biggest popular audience. If he had merely remade A Night To Remember (the best and most authentic account of the disaster, filmed in the fifties starring Kenneth More) then Titanic would never have found its world-wide 'youth audience'.

Laurence Olivier once said memorably, 'Acting I do for free – they pay me to wait.' This was very much what happened to Ros and me (and various other British actors, most of whom had been flown out from Britain). The only difference between our experience and Olivier's was that it was nearly all waiting and, finally, very little acting. Sometimes we began sequences, to find that, after waiting a month to complete them, they had been cut. Some scenes stayed in the film only to hit the deck in the final edit. The famous cigar scene was one of these. Others remained on the schedule for many months, while actors who had waited, under hotel arrest, from September till the following March, were finally abandoned and 'let go'. Certainly, with a preliminary cut of nearly five hours, audiences surely had reason to be grateful that the film was finally reduced to a mere three and a quarter. Our contracts were watertight even if our parts were not, and our American agents, Badgley Connor King, had even held Jon Landau, co-producer, to a clause that provided us with a self-drive car during the filming. It quickly became apparent how practical this was. The hotel where most of us were staying was about six miles from the nearest town, Rosarito. Without cars, actors had either to call for a taxi or rely on various vans that the company sent from the unit transportation department.

As we waited, day after day, to begin work on scenes that were constantly being delayed, the hotel began to feel more and more like an isolation clinic for lost actors. Jonathan Hyde was waiting, like us, to make his first appearance in the movie. He was playing Bruce Ismay, managing director of the White Star Line. He and I would often meet, like fellow inmates, as we strolled the grounds, and reminisce about our past lives in England, now just a remote memory. Sometimes we played tennis. We hired equipment from the hotel and took a golfing buggy to the tennis court. Jonathan always trounced me. Never mind, it passed the time. We sometimes had a drink in the clubhouse afterwards and chatted about the Royal Shakespeare Company. He had been there for several seasons. I told him I had just been asked (by the brilliant young director Matthew Warchus) to play Claudius in *Hamlet*, at Stratford, starting in January. 'No chance, chum', snickered Jonathan. 'We'll all be here till March.'

Surely not.

Nothing to do. At least we're being paid. Yes, but I want to be in *Hamlet*.

At night some of the actors sit around the bar. Eric Braeden, suave American soap-opera star who is here to play J. J. Astor, comes over to me. 'Martin, I hear you once have played Hamlet,' he says in dark brown tones, with just a trace of his native German. 'It is my life's ambition to play Shakespeare.' He leans close to my ear and murmurs, '*To be or not to be* –'

'Ah ha,' I say, smiling. 'Yes. Very good.'

'*That is the question*,' he continues. '*Whether 'tis nobler in the mind to suffer . . .*'

I nod and smile again but he is not to be deflected. He continues on through the speech. When, finally, he gets to '*and lose the name of action . . .*' I open my mouth to say, 'Well done', but he's in there like lightning with '*Tomorrow and tomorrow and tomorrow*'. I subside into my drink, thinking 'and this is only his first day'.

One night, a new patient, Bernard Hill, comes into the bar. He has just arrived from London. We older inmates, who have already been here for some weeks, eye him askance. He is here to play the captain of the *Titanic*, E. J. Smith. He tells us he's not pleased about having his hair dyed white for the role. It's going to interfere with his next movie. 'Not a happy camper,' mutters Jonathan Hyde from his usual corner.

Bernard orders a glass of Chardonnay, takes one sip and exclaims, 'Bloody 'ell, what do they call this? This is shite!'

He reminds me of Geoff Boycott on foreign assignment who can't wait to get home to Yorkshire. I know how he feels.

Jonathan pronounces quietly, like the oldest inhabitant, 'He'll have to stop grumbling if he's to keep sane in the asylum.'

Time passes. Creeping its petty pace from day to day. Ros and I decide one morning to drive to the film set for lunch. Our contractually provided unit car is a spanking new silver Ford Taurus. We leave the hotel, turn left on to the coast road and bowl along by the small jerry-built shacks that sit uneasily on one side of the Mexican highway. On the opposite side stand grander Spanish-style gated residences, yards from the sea. We pass the curio shops on the edge of the Popotola Road and in ten minutes arrive at the studio. It looks more like an unfinished industrial estate than the location for the most glamorous movie of the decade. We turn right into the compound and, as usual, produce our special laminated *Titanic* identity cards so that at least two armed security guards at the gate can check us in. These cards don't have our names on them, but bear those of our characters – Sir Cosmo and Lady Lucille Duff Gordon. 'OK, Sir Cosmo,' nods one of the guards. He seems oddly reluctant this morning to let us in. Nevertheless, frowning slightly, he waves us through and we drive into the parking lot. As we get out there is a tremendous smell of burning rubber. I look towards the back of the car. Smoke is billowing from above both rear wheels. Ros starts to mention fire extinguishers. Anxious Mexicans run up, shouting and looking concerned. One of them gets down on his back and looks under the car. Another examines the wheels. Finally they get up and say, 'Brakes'. The others join in. 'Brakes,' they chorus. They are all in agreement and I suddenly realise they are sniggering. At me. I see what has happened. I have driven the car eight miles without releasing the handbrake. *Titanic* is getting to us.

At lunch, I asked producer Jon Landau if, as there seemed no likelihood of us filming this week, we could return to Los Angeles and be 'on hold' there, rather than endless weeks of more isolation. He agreed. Jonathan Hyde accompanied us on this and several other occasions. Various actors out from England used our LA base as a place of recreation and refreshment during the long lay-offs. Nobody could quite work out why there were such protracted delays. It seemed that Jim's meticulous approach, combined with the intricacies of much of the hardware and technology, meant that a scene that looked on paper like a one-day shoot could take up to two weeks. Sometimes more. Rumours of the escalating millions of dollars that these set-backs were costing filtered through to the movie trade press. *Titanic* was already being characterised as the disaster movie of all time.

While 'on hold' in LA, I spent time investigating the possibility of producing *A Night To Remember* as an audio book. It seemed a shame to waste all the *Titanic* research we'd been doing, especially if most of our scenes were going to disappear. I had thought that James Cameron and Jon Landau might have tied up the recording rights. I found, to my surprise, that they hadn't. So, having secured them on behalf of the BBC and CSA Telltapes, when I arrived back at the location for another session of waiting I started on the job of adapting Walter Lord's moving account of the disaster. A year later, and not unconnected with the unprecedented success of the movie, our own production swiftly became a bestseller.

On one of my return trips to Mexico, I decided to bring Bernard Hill a beautiful bottle of Chardonnay from the Grgich Hills winery. I flew down on the turbo-prop plane from LA to San Diego where Larry or Bob or Manuel would be waiting to drive me across the border and along the coast to the hotel. I was the last passenger to leave. Edna the stewardess handed me my bag and, as I walked the short way across the front of the plane to the airport building, I heard a crash of glass and a splat on the tarmac. I didn't have to look round to know that it was the Chardonnay, which had been balanced precariously near the top of my bag. It had rolled out and there it was, spread in a thousand shards across that little portion of the airport. What to do? I continued walking – feeling rather like the father in *All My Sons*. Suppose, I imagined, the plane, in taxiing prior to its return journey, burst its tyres on the broken glass. Suppose it wasn't discovered and took off towards Los Angeles. And suppose some of my *Titanic* colleagues were on board and suppose it crashes on landing because of the ripped tyres. Clearly the weird world of *Titanic* disasters was getting to me further. Having checked that none of my fellow actors was waiting to board the flight, I reported the mishap anyway. When I got to the hotel I found that Bernard's grumble factor had subsided considerably, even without benefit of an eminently drinkable Chardonnay from the Napa Valley.

When I drove to the set next morning, security seemed tighter than ever. I wasn't surprised. Some weeks before we had heard that the Mexican mafia had demanded protection money from Paramount and Twentieth Century Fox, joint owners of the studio. This had been refused and apparently four Mexican security guards had been killed. The atmosphere on the set was, understandably, very strange. Nobody seemed to know definitely what had actually taken place. I never found out if the rumour was true or just another myth to join the others that had grown up around the *Titanic* since 1912. Certainly Jim now had a personal bodyguard and, it was said, never stayed in the same place for two nights running. It was rumoured that the Mafia wanted to kidnap him and hold the film to ransom. David Warner, waiting around to play the manservant, Lovejoy, told me that he had attended a script meeting with Cameron. While David discussed the development of his character, Jim's huge African-American bodyguard stood there, poised, eyeing him the whole time. 'When I got up at one point to demonstrate something,' said David, 'the guy moved in sharply as if I might be going to make a frenzied attack on Jim.'

It was interesting to watch our director in extended action on the set when, after many false alarms and 'on holds', we finally gathered to shoot the sequence where third-class Jack attends a dinner, courtesy of Rose, in the first-class dining room. Tension ran high. The set itself was built at the bottom of a specially excavated pit the size of a football field. Later, it would be spectacularly flooded. The heat was intense and the air filled with tiny floating particles of specially woven, totally authentic *Titanic* carpet.

I have plenty of time, nearly a week, sitting at my end of the dining table in my white tie and tails, to watch and listen.

Jim and first assistant Josh are edgy with each other. They are like two prison guards as they constantly shout instructions to the Mexican extras at the thirty tables surrounding the main table, where twelve of us are seated. Jim gives the orders and Josh repeats them, bawling them out across the vast room. To make matters worse, the other assistant, Sebastian, roars out a Spanish translation. This leads inevitably to misunderstandings, culminating in the Mexican sound operator in charge of the music play-back system failing to come in on cue. 'I never want to see that guy again,' yells Jim, eyes popping with fatigue.

But it's not always like that. Over the course of one long afternoon and evening, I observe – from behind the camera – as Jim directs Leonardo in a crucial speech in which Jack tells us all something of his background and ambitions. A director with blockbusting credentials, Jim seems equally at home in the minutiae of text and character. The speech is long, though only a portion of it remains in the movie. Gently, line by line, shot by shot, Jim draws from Leo an interpretation of remarkable finesse and grace. We are all moved by the performance. Jim's sensitivity to his actor is impeccable; his direction an object lesson in tact and discernment.

But today is different. Jim reminds me of a hyperactive boy with a hugely expensive and complicated train-set that he is trying to piece together in his playroom. His friends (the crew and the actors) who have been allowed to come in and help him play, keep messing things up. In any case, he really wants to do the whole thing himself. He knows best, after all. It's his game. And he's the only one who understands how the track fits together. He's tired, often angry, and won't suffer any fool gladly. But suddenly there'll be warm flashes of bonhomie when things go momentarily well. Then he'll drive obsessively on to the next bit of the game, at another part of the train-set, where one of the little chums from next door is allowed, say, to set up the signals at the side of the track. It's not, of course, how our hero wants it, so he grabs the equipment and does it himself. And what he does is undeniably brilliant. Why didn't we think of that? This is an astonishing film *auteur* at work. He has a vision of what he wants and he's only happy when it is achieved. It is gone two o'clock in the morning, the end of a long, long day; there will be four more days before this sequence is completed. He makes a speech to the entire cast and crew, apologising for any loss of temper and thanking everyone for their extreme patience. He does it with such charm and sincerity that we forget that we've been eating the same dinner for twenty hours. Good old Jim. We're glad, after all, that we came round to play. Just Jimmy knows best. Pass the caviare.

Before returning to California for yet another lay-off, Ros and I decided to change our Mexican pesetas for US dollars at the bank. The rate of exchange in America being so low, it was sensible to swap our largely unspent expenses locally. We drove into Rosarito, parked and approached the bank's exchange window – which opened directly on to the sidewalk. I stood guard, looking anxiously up and down the dusty main street, while Ros conducted the business. Transaction completed, we moved swiftly away, still maintaining a sharp lookout for the gangsters who, it was rumoured, lay in wait for tourists (and visiting film actors) ready to grab their money. A substantial sum had now been transferred to Ros' bulging bag. We got into the car and drove off, feeling a bit like gangsters ourselves.

A couple of minutes later we became aware that a truck was following us. I waved it on but it stuck on our tail. I speeded up. So did the truck. It hooted. I paid no attention and gripped the wheel. It hooted again and, glancing in the rear-view mirror, I saw its flashing light. Police. I took my foot off the accelerator and drew in to the kerbside. Immediately a youthful uniformed Mexican swung out of the vehicle and came towards us. I wound down the window. 'What's the problem?' I inquired, placing my *Titanic* pass under his nose. *Titanic* was the watchword here. It had brought temporary prosperity to the area with plenty of work for builders, carpenters, drivers, bricklayers, plumbers. Mafiosi. Everybody was making something out of the movie.

The young man studied my Sir Cosmo identification. He seemed to lose confidence and looked back uncertainly towards the truck. His partner, a big, sweaty, middle-aged cop in shades and stetson, heaved himself out and ambled over. He bent down and peered into the car. I sensed he had recently enjoyed fish burritos. He reviewed both our passes, then growled quietly, 'Why you not respect the law?'

'I do respect the law,' I replied. 'I want to respect it.'

He grunted and demanded my driving licence. I handed it over. After examining it for some seconds, he looked again at the *Titanic* pass. He handed it back to me but pocketed my licence. I was just working out how I could explain that I wasn't, in fact, Sir Cosmo Duff Gordon, merely pretending to be him in the film, when he said sharply, 'No, you don't respect. Follow round to Policia.' Things were looking bad. Both men returned to their truck and we set off in convoy towards the police station.

We had a problem. We had heard a great deal in the past weeks about the Mexican police. Even the guidebooks warned against placing too much confidence in their incorruptibility. Now, as we drove behind them, we were in a movie of our own. 'Do you think the cops spotted us at the bank window?' I asked.

'Of course they did,' said Ros. Then, thinking quickly in true Joan Crawford fashion, 'What are we going to do with the cash? It's enough to pay his salary for six months.' Keeping an eye on the truck, we scrabbled around looking for a hiding place. The glove compartment seemed barely adequate for such a large bundle. And what if they searched the car anyway? We drew up at the police station just as Ros was stuffing the package down the front of her jeans.

The sweaty cop had alighted and was walking towards us. 'Cosmo – out of the car,' he ordered. 'You too, Lucille.' We got out and stood awkwardly in the forecourt.

He gestured for us to follow. I had a vision of Ros being strip-searched, the money discovered, a dank cell and a prison sentence. We were led to a small bare office that contained only a desk and a chair. He closed the door, turned and, putting his mouth close to my ear, said in a low voice, 'You will pay fine.'

Ros and I had the same thought: 'Does he mean a bribe?'

'What for?' I prevaricated.

Breathing through his open mouth, his face still inches from mine, he said, 'You pay. You pay me. You no make stop at Alto sign.'

Trying not to inhale, I said 'What do you mean?'

Ros had already got his gist: 'Oh, I see. You mean we drove straight over a Stop sign?'

'*Si!* Cosmo – he must respect the law.' He smiled for the first time. 'He must pay.'

Moving my face out of the fish dinner and thinking only of the huge wad in Ros's jeans, I asked tentatively, 'How much?' I really didn't know what to expect. Something hefty no doubt. Fifty dollars? Five hundred? More? The tiny room was acrid with sweat and lunch as the cop seated himself behind the desk and folded his arms. He was grinning now. I was desperately wondering if I had enough readies on me, without having to trouble Ros. I doubted it. This could be embarrassing.

He leant forward, humourless again: 'Sir Cosmo, your fine will be – sixty pesos.'

Oh god, how much was that, a thousand pounds? Two? I worked it out, brain spinning. I had the answer – less than ten dollars. We stared in amazement. He laughed at our obvious relief. The tension visibly lessened as I counted out the notes.

'I wonder if I could have a receipt?' I inquired.

Still enjoying himself, he tore a blank sheet from his notebook and presented it to me. Then he heaved himself up, opened the door and propelled us back into the sunshine. He stood at the edge of the forecourt, grinning broadly. 'Hey,' he said, 'you forget your licence.' I took it from his outstretched hand. He guffawed and, as we set off towards the car, he called out, 'Remember, Cosmo – you respect the law!'

And so *Titanic* went on. Christmas came and went. Of course, Jonathan Hyde was right – I never got to Stratford to play Claudius. I managed to slot in various other, smaller, jobs in LA during the long waiting periods. Often we would be flown down to Mexico with sudden urgency to shoot a scene, only to find, when we arrived panting off the plane, that it had just been cut. New scenes, not in the script, would show up on the schedule then mysteriously disappear again, unshot.

Finally, in the late afternoon of 17 March 1997, Ros and I were picked up from the hotel to be driven to the set. Jim was going to complete the scene in which Sir Cosmo and Lady Duff Gordon are lowered down the side of the ship in their lifeboat. As they

drop to the sea, they catch sight of Leonardo, peeping from a
porthole, trapped just below the water-line. This will be our last
scene. We had actually shot part of the sequence six months
before.

At six in the evening we are dressed and ready. Third assistant
Joaquin comes into the dressing room to announce that there will
be a delay. Oh really? Apparently there are high winds blowing
off the Pacific, so, although the crew will continue to set up our
stuff, they will also be preparing an alternative shot, indoors, with
David Warner. Since we have been waiting to shoot this
particular scene since September, we scarcely react, like zombies
who have been too long in the asylum to bother any more.
Beyond surprise.

We slump in Ros's dressing room, half ready, watching
television. The night wears on. A cleaner in the corridor mops
up a mix of mud and water that has blown in from the real world
outside. I can smell disinfectant. It's like being in a great
hospital in the middle of the night. Midnight. There's still no
news as to whose sequence will be shot, ours or David's. It's his
last scene too. Things are getting surreal. We are like patients
poised for a final check-up and discharge. At one in the
morning David wanders in and we chat for an hour. He's ready
in costume too. It's a sort of contest to see whose scene will be
chosen and, consequently, who will be wrapped and finished.
Conversation runs out and he leaves for a meander round the
corridors. We doze in front of the telly. I am dimly aware, in my
semi-comatose state, of sounds, half-heard conversations, the
occasional distant squawk of a walkie-talkie. I get up and pace
the corridors too. No sign of David. What's happening? One of
the stunt-men wanders by. Any news? I inquire. He tells me
David has been taken to the set. The patient has been
summoned by senior surgeon Jim. Oh well. Good news for him.
No going home for us.

At three o'clock we learn more. Someone from the wardrobe
department tells us that David has almost completed his scene
and he'll be going home. Ah, so the operation was successful.
Lucky him.

But at three-twenty a.m. there's a sudden flurry, dressers scuttle about and Spanish voices jabber in the corridors. Joaquin dashes into the room to say that Jim is waiting for us on board. We must hurry. He is going to shoot our scene after all. The winds must have died down. We leap to our feet. Suddenly I am retying my bow-tie, Ros is clamping on her hat and there's a van at the door to ferry us the four hundred yards to the ship. We pile in, trying to remember how we played the other part of the scene all those months ago. We get to the location and, just like our real-life counterparts, hang about on deck while the ropes from the davits that will lower us to the ocean are being sorted out. It's still windy. If we have not entirely understood before, we now get a very clear picture of the chaos of that April night in 1912; nobody quite knowing what is happening – where, when, and how soon.

Josh McLaglen stands upright in our lifeboat as it hangs perilously along the side of the ship. We scramble in to join some of the extras that were with us last year. The boat is lowered. Again, we get a real-life jolt as it rocks on the water. It rocks once more as James Cameron vaults in beside us. He is quiet tonight, his face tense, eyes darting as he checks his watch, the wind, the light, the water. 'Great boots,' he says abruptly to Ros, as he lines up the first shot. But he's not happy. He spends a long time attempting to focus on the porthole below the surface, where the Duff Gordons are supposed to see Leonardo trapped. It's hopeless. The water refracts Leo's image into a tiny elipse. Jim gives up. He films the whole sequence on us, operating the hand-held camera himself. We try several takes, the boat tilting madly. Our acting feels strangely authentic.

Jim, unwilling to be beaten, has one more go at shooting the elliptical porthole. Still no good. Leo looks like a tiny shrunken gremlin. Forget it, says Jim savagely. We haven't completed the scene. Maybe he'll try it on another day. Maybe not. He disappears up a ship's ladder with a terse ''Night', already planning tomorrow's nightmare. Dawn is coming up and the night's work is over.

Two hours later, back at the hotel, we get a call. Jim has

decided the sequence is impossible to complete; he has cut it from the film. Plus the one that should follow it. My best scene. We've finished. We can go. Cut loose. Discharged.

Two hours more and, as we are waiting at reception for our taxi to the airport, one of the remaining inmates strolls by the desk. He doesn't know it yet, but his one line as a sailor will later be cut. Already he seems remote. Part of something fast disappearing in the wake of six months on *Titanic*. He looks at us with dull eyes, enviously; he has another two weeks' treatment in the clinic before he can follow. As the taxi arrives, he can't resist a parting shot. He's just been on the phone to England, he tells me. The production of *Hamlet* at the RSC, he's heard, is *brilliant*.

February 1999

Los Angeles

Taking the curtain call now, though of course there's no curtain in-the-round. It's been a hot evening for me, as usual. Round and round that stage, dishing out David Hare in equal portions. We bow under the lights, acknowledging the applause. Some of the audience have risen to their feet, clapping vigorously. Others, clapping as they go, are already moving towards the exits so as not to miss their restaurant reservations.

Out of the glare, into the dressing room, off with the winter gear. *Skylight* is finished for tonight. David Hare tucked into abeyance until tomorrow, same time same place. A swift good night to Cindy and Lars and I'm through the stage door, across the floodlit forecourt, ducking and weaving through some straggling audience members. One or two of them call after me, 'Great show.'

'Still sweating?' says one guy as I slow down momentarily to avoid knocking him headlong into the fountain. Sorry. He detains me with, 'Where're you acting next?' He sounds as if he needs to know to be certain he's not there.

'Somewhere,' I reply, 'I'm not sure', and I'm off again towards my car. Still sweating.

It's dark on the freeway now, just a few tail lights glowing red in the distance. I'm speeding along. None of the entrapment of a few hours before.

Cool. The lanes are clear and it's an open run all the way ahead. Unless there's an unforeseen hold-up. Who knows? As Ayckbourn says, 'See what happens. Mm.'

Yodel-ar-i-tee!

Index